Chunky

The Best Bits from *Acorn Antiques*
to Kitty and more

Chunky

The Best Bits from *Acorn Antiques*
to Kitty and more

Victoria Wood

Introduced by Celia Imrie
Commentary by Jasper Rees

First published in Great Britain in 1996 by Methuen London,
an imprint of Reed International Books Ltd
Up to You, Porky first published by Methuen London in 1985
Barmy first published by Methuen London in 1987
Right Down the Middle first published in *Chunky* in 1996
Mens Sana in Thingummy Doodah first published by Methuen London in 1991

This edition published in 2023 by Trapeze,
an imprint of The Orion Publishing Group Ltd
Carmelite House, 50 Victoria Embankment
London EC4Y 0DZ

An Hachette UK Company

1 3 5 7 9 10 8 6 4 2

A CIP catalogue record for this book is
available from the British Library.

ISBN (Hardback) 978 1 3987 0750 4
ISBN (eBook) 978 1 3987 0753 5
ISBN (Audio) 978 1 3987 0754 2

Typeset by Input Data Services Ltd, Bridgwater, Somerset

Printed in Great Britain by Great Britain by Clays Ltd, Elcograf S.p.A.

MIX
Paper from
responsible sources
FSC® C104740

www.orionbooks.co.uk

To all those very special people who have assisted in
my personal growth and helped me become the
uniquely flowered human truth unit that is wholly 'me'!
From all the awesome aspects that make up 'myself'
– I thank you.

CONTENTS

INTRODUCTION

I was mightily thrilled the day Victoria asked me to be part of her new show *Victoria Wood As Seen on TV*.

When I opened that first script, I was cast, with Duncan Preston, as a couple of *Play School* presenters 'wiggling our fingers', and also a character called Miss Babs who ran an antique shop, in Episode One of a rather dodgy soap opera . . .

By the way, I only ever had two customers in *Acorn Antiques* (the same two dear supporting artists) – and I never sold a thing . . .

From its very first seven-minute segment of her TV show, the extraordinarily prolific Victoria wrote it up for the West End into *Acorn Antiques: The Musical!*, where I got to play the now-favourite Miss B all over again.

What I found so astonishing was how generous Victoria was, giving away so many of her golden jokes to all of us in her company. Years later, I remember turning around in my front-row seat at her one-woman show in The Royal Albert Hall and hearing Victoria's entire audience crying with laughter. Young/old/mums/dads/boys/girls and especially young men . . . her humour touched and tickled us all.

Only today, I was in a very smart gentleman's outfitters in Jermyn Street and was told *dinnerladies* was the managing director's favourite programme.

I was very proud to be part of her gang.

Victoria Wood was a truly adored and utterly original talent.

Celia Imrie

EDITOR'S NOTE

Many of the scripts Victoria Wood submitted to her publisher were not a precise record of what viewers had seen on television. Where she made improvements, additions or, most commonly, cuts, these discrepancies from the broadcast version are noted.

Much of Victoria's comedy contains cultural references that will have made sense to an audience at the time of broadcast, but to younger fans coming across her work in more recent years they are likely to mean much less. So this edition of *Chunky* includes footnotes which help to clarify who or what she means when she jokes about, for example, Charlie Cairoli or Jackie Trent, slipper baths or silver service.

Where appropriate, the footnotes also draw attention to certain themes that crop up elsewhere in Victoria's work: not just her fondness for Alma Cogan and Estée Lauder Youth Dew, but also for certain types of joke structure and even for specific gags that were too good not to recycle.

In the footnotes, the following abbreviations are used: VW (Victoria Wood), JW (Julie Walters), *W&W* (*Wood and Walters*), *LB* (*Lucky Bag*), *ASOTV* (*Victoria Wood As Seen on TV*), *ADB* (*Victoria Wood's All Day Breakfast*), *DL* (*dinnerladies*), *ATT* (*Victoria Wood With All the Trimmings*).

BODY COPY

My first part was a comedy char in a production of *The Rising Generation* by Ann Jellicoe. This was the summer of 1968 and I was fifteen. It wasn't till about ten years later that I realised she wasn't called Angelico. It was a wonderful summer, spent rolling around on dusty floorboards in baseball boots and jeans from Millets, with the other members of the Rochdale Youth Theatre Workshop, doing improvisations and rehearsing plays. I was a prompting wolf in *Dracula* and spent my offstage moments squinting down a cornflake packet muzzle trying to read the script.

I did all sorts of other exciting things, like fall in love, and drink pints of mild, and eat pudding and chips on a tray with gravy, the only meal I miss now I'm a vegetarian. I spent all my spare time there till I left home to go to university in Birmingham, and I think I learnt more there than anywhere.

University was a culture shock. All the other students on my course seemed to be tall and blonde and beautiful and know about Stanislavski. Everyone was having sex the entire time as well, so there was all the worry of making sure you had left the house in clean underwear as well as fretting about pronouncing Chekhov.

I lived in a bedsitter in a house full of mad people. I shared a Baby Belling cooker on the landing which took half an hour to heat a tin of soup. I could never wait that long and used to drink it cold and then hang my stomach over the gas fire.

The woman on the same landing used to ask me to read her medicine labels. 'Two teaspoons daily,' I told her helpfully one morning. Once I was on the bus I realised it had been a bottle of Baby Bio.

I got an audition for *New Faces* while I was still at university. This was a very high-rated talent show and I saw it as my passport to stardom. While rehearsing for the first heat I signed an exclusive management contract with a certifiably insane ex-band leader from Hove. I never read the contract because I thought it would look as though I didn't trust him, which I didn't, and to this day I have no idea what it said.

After *New Faces* my career didn't so much take off as reverse into the departure lounge, as every offer of work was turned down by the barmy band leader and I sat in my bedsitter eating tins of mince and feeling uneasy.

The next few years were a mixture of television appearances and sticky interviews with the dole office. They couldn't understand why I was singing on *That's Life* one week and signing on for my eleven pounds the next.

ATV did a song and sketch show the summer after I'd been on *New Faces*, starring other winners like Marti Caine and Lenny Henry. It was one hundred and twenty-five pounds a week, a big improvement on eleven. When I met Marti the first thing she said to me was, 'The money's rubbish.' Lenny was sixteen and terribly enthusiastic. He had great long legs and kept knocking chairs over and laughing.

I felt bad because I was too big for most of the costumes. They kept riffling through the racks and sighing, 'If only you'd lose two stone you could wear this of Anna Massey's.' I never did.

The sketch show was watched by less people than tuned into *Some Aspects of Shrimps* on the Open University and it was back to the dole office. They gave Marti her own show and Lenny had a job on tour with the Black and White Minstrels. I was saved from a life of tinned mince by comedian John Dowie who took me on tour with him. It wasn't a big tour, in fact we were home by Wednesday, but he knew more than me, which was handy. We didn't trash any hotel rooms, but I think he fused a hairdryer in Swansea.

But I was out of work mainly. Then I met Geoffrey. Then we were both out of work. Then we moved to Morecambe. Which meant we could be out of work and have a large selection of old people to queue behind in the Post Office. We tried to pretend that living near people called Winnie who hated us was fun.

Geoffrey got a job on the end of the pier, in an Olde Tyme Music-Hall. I have noticed that the more 'E's and 'Y's there are in a show like that, the more likely it is to have an actress from Surrey singing, 'Don't Dilly Dally on the Way'. Geoffrey did a very good magic act but unfortunately it came after the entire audience had left the theatre to get back to their boarding houses for cocoa. If you ever have to write a thesis on what killed the music-hall, the answer is cocoa.

I did a revue at the Bush Theatre in Shepherd's Bush and someone asked me to write a play. I didn't know it was supposed to be difficult so I wrote one, *Talent*. It was done at the Crucible Theatre Studio in 1978 and then at the ICA in London. It was set in a seedy backstage room with a dirty carpet. We had to put a notice up to stop the cleaners hoovering it.

Peter Eckersley, a producer at Granada, bought *Talent*, and we did it on television in 1979. He was a wonderfully clever and funny man. I did two more plays with him, and the pilot show of *Wood and Walters*, and then he died. It got too difficult to work with him after that and we parted company.

I had another play on at the Crucible in 1980, *Good Fun*, about a cystitis rally. Julie Walters played a sort of Avon lady and did an exciting dance number in a shocking pink suit. I was described in one review as 'dominating the stage like a witty tank'. I was thrilled.

I've toured regularly since 1984 and have many happy memories. I think it was Southampton where a woman asked for her money back at the end of the first half. 'That's not Sooty,' she said. And the Beck Theatre, Hayes, where the manager leant against the dressing room door while I was making up, saying, 'I thought you'd have sold more tickets than this, it's very disappointing.'

I had a baby in 1988, which proved my theory that stretch pants alone do not make an effective contraceptive. I was planning to eat my placenta, but wasn't sure how that squared with my vegetarianism, so settled for toast. Motherhood brought many joys, but catching sight of the underneath of my neck in the mirror of the Tommee Tippee Activity Centre wasn't one of them.

I toured with both my children when they were babies, and still now when I go into a hotel room my first thought is to put the pot pourri on top of the wardrobe. Once when my little boy had chicken pox and wouldn't sleep, I took him in the bar with me disguised as a handbag.

I have met many interesting people in my job, and also many celebrities. Dolly Parton was extremely charming and sang live in the studio beautifully. Of course I wasn't really listening, I was trying to see if she'd had any ribs removed. It's not an operation I would fancy, though I would quite like to have some old cardboard boxes taken out of my lobby. I don't suppose this is available on the National Health.

I am forty-three this year, and am waiting to see whether this is the year my bosoms will hit the floor and bounce right up again. This may be the year I go to the make-up counter for skin cream and find I have gone straight from 'Greasy' to 'Ageing'.

And of course for the last twenty years I have been struggling to get to know my husband, the mysterious Geoffrey Durham, the Audrey Hepburn of the conjuring world. I could have done it without him, but it would have been crap.

Up to You, Porky

THE VICTORIA WOOD SKETCH BOOK

To Peter Eckersley, who liked a laugh

INTRODUCTION

When Victoria Wood's first sketch shows were broadcast, no one had a video recorder. She even joked about it in the pilot episode of *Wood and Walters*, broadcast on ITV on New Year's Day 1981. 'Good evening, ladies and gentlemen. Or for those of you with video recorders, where did you get the money?' A full series followed twelve months later. Victoria then kept away from television for a couple of years to develop her career as a stand-up. By the time she returned with *Victoria Wood As Seen on TV*, broadcast in early 1985, still only 14 per cent of British households had a machine on which you could tape a programme in order to watch it later. Imagine: the best sketch show ever and if you weren't in, you missed it.

Back then, sketches that are now part of the national furniture were there for two minutes on your telly, and then they were gone. So Victoria's growing legion of fans had only their memories to fall back on. We've got *what* in the skirting board? What was it again you'd have to do if her bum were a bungalow?

Answers to such questions were eventually to be found in *Up to You, Porky*, which was published in October 1985. It was a slim volume. Victoria whittled nearly six hours of television down to thirty-five scripts, the majority from *As Seen on TV*, plus nine from *Wood and Walters* and two character monologues from her live show *Lucky Bag*. The imbalance reflected Victoria's partiality. New to sketch-writing in *Wood and Walters*, she gave vent to her nerves in 'Toddlers'. Two infants dangle in swings.

Julie: Thought of any jokes for this sketch yet?

Victoria: Nope.

By the time she got to the BBC in 1984, Victoria had grown in confidence. Most obviously, she fell back less on anxiety about her looks as a source of comedy. Compare 'Skin Care' from *Wood and Walters*, where the joke's on Victoria, with 'Cosmetic Surgery', where it proved much funnier to target the beauty industry than its blameless customers.

She submitted her choice of sketches to her publisher Methuen after *As Seen on TV* had been broadcast. It represents what she reckoned would work best in print, though plenty of the material long since thought canonical is not there. Top of that list is 'Swim the Channel', now seen as the apex of her spoof mini-documentaries about ordinary people. She included three others instead, which like many of the longer scripts were heavily cut before they were shown on TV.

Also, it's a curiosity that, rather than publish only sketches that had been broadcast, Victoria chose others that hadn't made it into the final cut of *As Seen on TV*. Among them were unseen scripts for her daytime presenters Margery and Joan, and for Kitty. So you just have to imagine 'Kitty: Two' inimitably delivered by Patricia Routledge.

One of Victoria's greatest creations, Kitty grew out of Dotty, who popped up regularly in *Wood and Walters* to dispense life tips from her armchair. Putting them side by side in print enabled readers to trace a line between them. But there's another thing about Kitty. In her first monologue, the eagle-eyed might notice a change between the published script and what was broadcast. 'Good evening,' she says at the start of 'Kitty: One'. 'My name's Kitty. I've had a boob off and I can't stomach whelks so that's me for you.' That's not what she said on TV: 'I could have married; I've given gallons of blood and I can't stomach whelks . . .' A great believer in the comic rhythm of three, Victoria improved the structure of the gag before it was recorded. Was it an oversight that she handed an earlier version to her publisher? It certainly allows us to see how she tautened scripts.

The biggest deviation from the written script is in 'The Woman with 740 Children'. When Victoria and Julie Walters came to record it for *Wood and Walters*, battling to be heard on a crowded set over the wailing of many babies, accuracy was clearly sacrificed as they raced to the end of the take. What's on the page only vaguely overlaps with what they actually said.

Victoria dedicated her first book of sketches 'to Peter Eckersley, who liked a laugh'. As a producer at Granada, he televised her first play, *Talent*, and would commission two more dramas with songs. His sudden death shortly before *Wood and Walters* was recorded contributed to her ambivalent feelings about her debut show.

Eckersley was the visionary who truly launched her. The terrible manager who in the mid-1970s nearly killed off Victoria's career before it had even started is commemorated in the title. He had a number of fat-shaming nicknames for her, and she cites one of them in 'The Boutique'.

Customer: They look a bit small to me.
Assistant: It's up to you, Porky.

So he made himself useful in the end.

THIGS I LIKE

by Vicky Wood age 32

The thigs I like are dferent ones. One is wen I am wasing pulester trosers in my wahing maschine and I rember not to open the door wen it is in PAUS and full of water and the water do not go on me.

ANothe thig I like is wen I have ben shovling anthercite and I sneze and it coms all black on my sleave then I know my nose hares are woking propaly.

A thiNg I like allso is wen I am cleanig my Hondaccord befor a jurnyllist has to to get in ti it and I Find a very small peice of FrutAnD nut I eat it under the grealever. A thin I do not like is wen I find FuitandNUT under wehre my bottom gos and it is meltied on to the vellor veloo fuzzy stuff.

Anothe thign I like is wen pople come up to me and dig me in the papershop and sey Pleases settle a bet I stand to lose a gin and pep on this? ar you or ar yuo not Jiulie Walters and I say no and they look ded dispointed but I do not care and think ha-ha-ha like MUTTLEY in WACKY RACES

And I like as well wen the man from MEPHTHUN (cant spell it) pone up and say we have some lambnatid covers gong begging do yuo have any old skechs we will pay hansomly but not for xxxx ages. And the last thig I like is wen I haev filled a hwole page and i can stop writing and watsh WACKY RACES.

So that is the end of THIGS I LKE

SKIN CARE

A department store. An over-made-up sales assistant is behind the cosmetics counter. A girl enters.

Assistant	Good morning, madam. May I interest you in our skin-care range, though I have to admit that from here your skin looks flawless?
Girl	Thank you.
Assistant	But then again, I failed my driving test because I couldn't read the number plate. *Do* you have any spots?
Girl	No.
Assistant	Would you like some? I'll just do a quick check on the computer. Colour of eyes?
Girl	Blue.
Assistant	Grey. Hair?
Girl	Blonde.
Assistant	Mousey. Condition of pores: open, closed?
Girl	They're sort of ajar.
Assistant	Let's see. Dear me. To we in the trade, that's not so much of a complexion – more of a doily.
Girl	Don't you sell a product that would close them up a bit?
Assistant	Well, we do an astringent, but really, with pores that big, you'd be better off with a darning needle and some pink wool. You see, it's really your greasy skin that's at fault.
Girl	Is it?

Assistant	We do sell this – I don't know if it's strong enough for what you need, but it brought my chip-pan up lovely.
Girl	I'm starting to feel quite bad about what I look like.
Assistant	Good. Now, about your wrinkles.
Girl	Laughter lines.
Assistant	Nothing's that funny. We can arrange plastic surgery. £15 including bed and breakfast.
Girl	Why is it so cheap?
Assistant	The surgeon's bleeding hopeless.[1]
Girl	Well, it sounds like I'm so ugly, nothing's going to be any use.
Assistant	Oh, I don't know, madam. There's our special formula lipstick.
Girl	What good's that?
Assistant	It's six foot high, you can stand behind it. Can I help you, madam?

---

1 VW would flesh out this idea in 'The Boutique'.

BRONTËBURGERS

Guide Right, I'm your official guide. Now before I show you round, I'll just fill you in on a few details, as we call them. As you can see, we're standing in the hall of the Haworth Parsonage, where Haworth's parson, the Reverend Brontë, lived here with his daughters, the famous Brontë sisters, now, alas, no longer with us — but they have left us their novels, which I've not read, being more of a Dick Francis nut. Now, if you pass by me into the parlour (mind my vaccination) . . . This is what was known in those days as a parlour, somewhat similar to our lounge-type sitting-room affair in modern terminology. I'm afraid the wallpaper isn't the original period to which we're referring to, it is actually Laura Ashley, but I think it does give some idea of what life must have been like in a blustery old Yorkshire community of long ago.

That portrait on the wall is actually of Charlotte Brontë, one of the famous Brontë sisters, and of course to us she may seem a rather gloomy-looking individual; but you must remember these days she'd have a perm, or blusher, or I suppose even drugs would have helped her maintain a more cheerful attitude. In fact, she'd probably not be dead if she was alive today. Now if you'd like to hutch through to the Reverend Brontë's study . . . This is a typical study in which to do studying — as you can see there's a table, chair . . . (oh my poncho, I've been looking for that . . .) and I like to imagine this elderly old gentleman hunched over a sermon, probably thinking, 'Where's my cocoa, I suppose those darn girls are in the middle of another chapter,' or something like that he may have been thinking – we just can't be sure . . . Of course he died eventually, unfortunately. You must remember this is an extremely exposed part of the United Kingdom, I mean, it's May now, and I'm still having to slip that polo-neck under my bolero.

On the table we see the Reverend Brontë's gloves. They tell us such a lot about him. He had two hands, and he wasn't missing any fingers. We think they were knitted by one of the famous Brontë sisters. I don't suppose their brother Branwell could knit and anyway being an alcoholic he'd never have been able to cast on.

Now if you'd just hutch up the stairs . . . We're looking out over the graves to the hills beyond. And, fairly clearly in the distance we can hear the wind 'wuthering'. That's an old York-shire word; some other old Yorkshire words are 'parkin' and 'fettle'[2]. The room in which we're now standing in was origi-nally Charlotte's mother's bedroom. In fact Charlotte's mother died in this room, and Charlotte died in here too, so better not stay too long! (Just my joke!) In that glass case you'll see what we call a day dress – that is a dress worn in the day, not at night – we think belonging to Anne or Emily, presumably not Branwell, unless he had more problems than history's prepared to tell us.

A few dates for the date-minded. The Brontë family moved here some time in the nineteenth century, and lived here for quite a number of years. As I say, Charlotte died in this room

---

2 See also the Associated Fettlers and Warp and Weft Adjusters Silver Band from 'Brassed Up' in *ATT*.

– those are her slippers. And I like to imagine her in this room, with her slippers on, dying.

Now if you go through the far door, yes, do move my moped . . . Now this room was at one time Branwell's room. I think people tend to forget Branwell was fairly artistic himself. Of course, he was lazy, conceited and a dipsomaniac, so these days he'd have probably been in the government.

Now if anybody would like a souvenir to take home as a souvenir, we have Brontë video-games, body-warmers, acrylic mitts, pedestal mats, feminine deodorants and novelty tea-strainers. Snacks and light refreshments are available in the Heathcliff Nosher Bar, so please feel free to sample our very popular Brontëburgers. Or for the fibre-conscious – our Branwell Brontëburgers.

Oh – just a little message for the 'Yorkshire Heritage' coach party. Can they please re-convene at two in the car-park ready for this afternoon's trip which is, I believe, round three dark Satanic mills, Emmerdale Farm, and Nora Batty's front room? Thank you.

THE WOMAN WITH 740 CHILDREN[3]

A battered-looking housewife opens the door to a bright young reporter.

Reporter   *(in doorway)* Mrs Mather? Kate Harnson – *Weekly Woman.*

Woman   Oh yes, come in. *(The reporter takes her coat off in hall.)* You'll have to excuse the mess.

Reporter   Good heavens, it's not surprising. Is it true you had the biggest surviving multiple birth in the world?

Woman   I believe that's correct, yes. Anyway – come through.

They go into a room absolutely packed with little children, toddlers and babies. Also dummy babies lying on floor, on mantelpiece, top of TV etc. The reporter looks round for somewhere to sit down. All the chairs are covered in babies.

Sit down – just put them on the floor.

---

3 A first line was added in the recorded version.

    Woman: Sorry I can't remember your name.

A lot of the lines in this sketch were altered (see introduction) and others were cut, either before the recording or, more likely owing to the pressure of the moment, during.

Reporter   *(opening her notebook)* I'll just get the details first. How many babies did you actually have?

Woman   We think it was seven hundred and forty-two, but a couple got mislaid when we left the hospital – about seven hundred and forty we think now.

Reporter   And this was all as a result of taking a new fertility drug?

Woman   Well not exactly. We'd been married twelve years and I hadn't, you know, conceived. I blamed it on my husband because he'd had an accident leap-frogging over a drinking fountain. But anyway, the doctors said no way could I have babies until we consummated the marriage – well by that time I was desperate – I'd tried everything else. So – I won't dwell on the ins and outs but we had two marvellous doctors and they talked us through the whole thing.

Reporter   What about the fertility drug?

Woman   I took that off my own bat. It came free with a magazine. It wasn't your one it was the other woman's one. I took a double dose because my sister only has it for the serial, and that and the sex – that's the medical term – did the trick.

Reporter   I suppose it was a tremendous shock?

Woman   Well yes, I was hoping to give birth to a seven-year-old girl, but . . .

Reporter   Must have been a tremendously long labour.

Woman   Well, the doctor that delivered the first one, he's retired now. I know by the time it was all over the pound was only worth seventy-five pence.

Reporter   I suppose your day is one long round of feeding and changing?

Woman   Not really. I never eat breakfast and I keep the same clothes on all day.

Reporter   I meant the babies. I should have thought just feeding them was a full-time job?

Woman   Well it would be if I gave in to them. I mean when I first came home from the hospital it was four-hourly bottles and sterilising everything – after two days I'd had

	enough. I dragged them all into the kitchen, I said here's the grill, there's the fish-fingers, get on with it.
Reporter	Didn't they complain?
Woman	Well most of them can't talk yet thank goodness. I got a few dirty looks obviously.
Reporter	You seem to have things pretty well under control now – what problems do you anticipate as they get older?
Woman	Just when they go to school and I have to listen to the same knock-knock joke seven hundred and forty times, having to hide seven hundred and forty selection boxes on top of the wardrobe, that kind of thing . . .
Reporter	Has your husband been helpful?
Woman	Very. He left me.
Reporter	And other people?
Woman	Incredibly kind. They send clothes – they're not baby clothes but the thought's there.
Reporter	Has there been any talk of sponsorship?
Woman	One television company has shown great interest in one of the children,[4] thinks he has great potential.
Reporter	Oh really? Which one?
Woman	Now you're asking. No idea. All look the same to me *(lifting one out from under a cushion)*. They get everywhere.
Reporter	Well thank you very much for taking time off to talk to me.
Woman	Not at all. Here, would you like a couple to take home with you?
Reporter	No, really –
Woman	No bother. We've got loads. I'll just find you a carrier. *(She comes back with two babies in a box.)* OK? Can you see yourself out? *(The reporter leaves.)* All right – I wasn't going to embarrass you in front of company, but which one of you's nicked my fags?

---

4 Although VW won't have known this when she wrote the sketch, one of the 70 young stars was called Victoria Wood.

GIRLS TALKING[5]

Film. A street. Jeanette and Marie in school uniform (ankle socks, track shoes, short skirts, shirts and ties etc) leaning against the wall. A male interviewer is heard in voice over throughout the film.

Interviewer Jeanette is fifteen, Marie is fourteen and a half. Both are from broken homes and living in an area with a high level of unemployment.

Jeanette Not really been to school since I was five. Five or six. I go in, like, if there's something happening, like vaccination, or a nativity play.

Cut to Marie in mid-speech.

Marie Well it's just boring like, isn't it? They don't teach you about anything important – like how to inject yourself, it's all geography and things.

Interviewer Maybe you think it's not worth being qualified as there are so few jobs in Liverpool . . . ?

Jeanette There is lots of jobs. The government wants to keep us unemployed so we won't smoke on the buses.

---

5 In the recording, more questions from the interviewer were added.

Cut to Jeanette.

I could have been in a film but it was boring . . .

Interviewer What film was that?

Jeanette Documentary on child prostitution.

Interviewer You've actually been a prostitute?

Jeanette Yeah but it was boring. The sex was all right but they kept wanting you to talk to them.

Cut to Marie.

Marie Music? Kid's stuff really, isn't it?

Jeanette The government puts things on the record underneath the music.

Interviewer Sorry?

Jeanette Like, you know, messages that you can only hear with your brain.

Interviewer What do they say?

Jeanette Like telling you what to do.

Marie Keep you under.

Jeanette Don't say 'tits' in the reference library.

Marie Don't gob on each other.

Interviewer Is there much sleeping around amongst young people?

Marie No, it's boring.

Jeanette It's like for your Mums and Dads really, isn't it?

Marie Like drinking.

Interviewer Don't you and your, er, mates drink?

Jeanette We used to drink battery acid.

Marie But it burns holes in your tights.

Interviewer Do you sniff glue?[6]

Jeanette That's for snobs really, isn't it?

Marie Grammar school kids sniff glue.

6 Cut from here to 'see your future'. The TV audience was thus deprived of a reference to Estée Lauder Youth Dew, the fragrance whose name VW found seductively amusing.

Jeanette	We sniff burning lino.
Marie	Cot blankets.
Jeanette	Estée Lauder Youth Dew.
Interviewer	What effect does it have?
Marie	Fall over mainly.
Interviewer	Doesn't sniffing heighten your emotions?
Jeanette	Oh yeah, you get a lot more bored.
Marie	Things that were a bit boring get really boring, and that's great.
Interviewer	How do you see your future – do you think you'll get married?
Jeanette	We'd like to, 'cos it's easier to get Valium if you're married.
Marie	But we can't can we?
Interviewer	Why?
Jeanette	The government are bringing out this thing – you can't get married unless you've got a going-away outfit. It's got to be –
Marie	Suit.
Jeanette	Yeah, suit, and it's got to be in two colours that match.
Marie	And you have to have a handbag and slingbacks.
Jeanette	It's just not on.
Marie	My mother's got enough to do paying off my shoplifting fine.
Interviewer	What happened?
Jeanette	A duvet fell into my shopping bag.[7]

Cut.

Interviewer	Have either of you got boyfriends?
Jeanette	We have, like, one between two.
Marie	Just to save time really.
Interviewer	And what does your boyfriend do?
Marie	He gets tattooed a lot.

7 Recycled from 'Sex', a sketch VW wrote for *In at the Death*, a revue at the Bush Theatre in 1978.

Interviewer Yes, what else does he do?

Jeanette   He has them removed a lot.

Cut.

Interviewer Any ambitions?[8]

Jeanette   I'd like some stretch denims.

Interviewer I suppose you can't afford any?

Jeanette   You can apply for a grant.

Marie   For denims.

Jeanette   But not stretch denims.

Interviewer How do you feel about teenage pregnancies?

Marie   We've got used to them now.

> *They sniff a bottle of perfume. Jeanette falls over. Marie looks bored.*

---

8 The rest of the sketch was cut from here.

YOUNG LOVE: ONE[9]

Carl and Gail are a slow-witted Northern pair, sitting on a wall because they can't think of anywhere to go.

Gail	Do you love me, Carl?
Carl	Yeah, you're all right.
Gail	Do you think about me when you're cleaning windows?
Carl	Yeah, some of the time.
Gail	Do you think about me when you're having your dinner?
Carl	Depends what it is.
Gail	What do you mean, Carl?
Carl	I might if I'm having a Scotch egg, but if I'm having crisps, I'm concentrating on opening t' bag, aren't I?
Gail	What about at night?
Carl	What about at night?
Gail	Do you think about me then?
Carl	In bed?
Gail	Yeah, or under it.
Carl	When I'm in bed, Gail, I'm reading *The Puzzler*, aren't I?
Gail	Yeah, but, when your mam's put light out, and you've just closed your eyes, what do you think about then, Carl?
Carl	My shammy leather.

---

9 The first exchanges all the way up to the pause were cut.

Pause.

Gail	When we get married, Carl, where will we live?
Carl	Well, we're living in my mam's sideboard, aren't we?
Gail	Yeah, but after that. Shall we have an 'ouse?[10]
Carl	Nah. Penthouse flat.
Gail	What's that, Carl?
Carl	It's got fur rugs, hasn't it?
Gail	What colour?
Carl	Well, it depends, dunnit? If it's off an animal, it'll be animal-coloured, won't it? Or there's orange.
Gail	Where is it?
Carl	What?
Gail	This flat.
Carl	Well, they're all in London, aren't they? And there's two in the Isle of Man.
Gail	Is that the same as France?
Carl	France is abroad i'n't it? They have different bread and allsorts.
Gail	Different allsorts? You mean not liquorice?
Carl	Eh? Anyway, they're on t'roof.
Gail	What?
Carl	Penthouse flats.
Gail	I'm not living on a roof. My knitting'll roll into t'guttering.
Carl	Who's been telling you about guttering?
Gail	You did. When we were kissing goodnight[11] last night, and we snuggled up, and you said you had something to tell me, and you told me about guttering.
Carl	Yeah, well, I won't always be that romantic.
Gail	OK Carl.

---

10 In the recording VW says 'an house'.
11 Changed to 'saying goodnight'.

THIS WEEK'S FILM

Voice over   This week's film is a wartime classic telling of the exploits of the happy-go-lucky crew of a Lancaster bomber. Made in 1941, we bring you *Dropping Them on Dover.*

Jean stands by the window staring out into the night. She waves as the planes go by. There is a knock on the door. Enter Smithy, an RAF chap nervously gripping his cap.

Jean   Hello Smithy. Where's Bob?

Smithy   He isn't with me, Jean.

Jean   Go on.

Smithy   He's bought it.

Jean   I see. I think I knew, you know. I think he knew. As he left yesterday morning he turned at the gate and called, 'Jean, don't save my bloater'.[12] What happened?

Smithy   Are you sure you want to hear? It's not awfully pleasant.

Jean   War never is. Go on.

Smithy   *(sitting down and lighting his pipe)* As you know, we're a pretty ramshackle bunch. The wireless operator can only get *ITMA*[13] and the rear-gunner won't sit with his back to

---

12 A herring cured by salting and light smoking.

13 *It's That Man Again* was a popular BBC radio comedy which ran for a decade from 1939. *LB*: 'It was quite an old plane. I was sitting next to the rear-gunner.'

	the engine. And I guess the old bomber isn't up to much.
Jean	What do you mean?
Smithy	Well it's not a Lancaster, it's a Silver Cross.[14] There isn't a bay for bombs, just a tray underneath where you put your shopping. Well last night we were over the Moehne Dam.
Jean	But you bombed that last month.
Smithy	Yes, but Bob thought we should go back and see if that's where he'd left his ration book. On the way back the port engine started to misfire.
Mother	But wasn't it checked before you took off?
Smithy	Well yes but – God, the boys are young now. My ground crew do their best but, you know, they've got homework to do . . . Cubs . . .
Jean	What happened, Smithy?
Smithy	The starboard engine went, we lost height, we were over land but didn't know where.
Jean	Go on.
Smithy	Bob gave the order 'Bail out and if you're caught pretend to be German'.
Jean	That's terrible.
Smithy	Yes it was. Bob landed first – said, 'Heil Hitler' in his best accent and was stabbed to death with a pitchfork.
Jean	Why?
Smithy	We'd landed in Margate.
Jean	Poor Bob. He always was a bit of a duffer.
Smithy	Jean?
Jean	Yes Smithy?
Smithy	It may be too soon to ask you this, but I've always admired you and if I don't ask now I never will.
Jean	Go on Smithy.
Smithy	Could I have his bloater?

Music.[15]

---

14 A famous British pram.

15 In the recording, JW has a pipe stuck into her mouth.

IN THE OFFICE

Beattie	You look tired, Connie.
Connie	I couldn't get off last night. I even had Dick throw a brick at my head to stun me but . . .
Beattie	Have you tried jamming your head in the tumble-drier and switching on?
Connie	No?
Beattie	It worked for me. Then of course the body gets accustomed.
Connie	Like deodorants. They work for a certain amount of time and then bang – people are backing away with handbags over their noses.
Beattie	You're not ponging too badly at the minute, Connie.
Connie	I've had my armpits stripped. A peel-off paste. Quite simple to apply though it has marked my cork flooring.
Beattie	Oh, do you have cork? We have tufted shag.
Connie	We have to be able to mop, you see, with Dad's habits . . .
Beattie	Dicky bladder?
Connie	We call him Dad, but . . . he can trot to the bogetory as neat as you please when he's not engrossed, but if it's Mavis Nicholson or the Cooking Canon then he won't budge and there you are with it all over your adjustable seating.
Beattie	Can't you put him in a home?
Connie	Well we could, but I'm using his head for a flower arrangement at the moment.

Beattie	Is that an evening class?
Connie	Yes. I put down for Ju Jitsu but I came out of the wrong lift.
Beattie	What's in your sandwiches?
Connie	Soap powder. I think it's these drugs I'm on. Quite nice though. What's yours?
Beattie	Coconut matting. I'm doing the high-fibre.
Connie	Did you watch the news?
Beattie	The nine o'clock?
Connie	Yes. Nasty blouse.
Beattie	We stayed up for *News at Ten*. Three bangles and a polo-neck, thank you.
Connie	No, her ears are in the wrong place for a polo-neck.
Beattie	You need to be Princess Di, really.
Connie	They've the length of bone, haven't they, royalty?
Beattie	The Queen's not got long bones.
Connie	No, well she's spent all that time stood about – with natives waggling their doodahs at her.
Beattie	My cousin's on Male Surgical and she's very short – must be the same thing – the standing.[16]
Connie	Is that the one who went on *Opportunity Knocks* dressed as a cheese and tomato sandwich?[17]
Beattie	No, that was Madge. She didn't win. She got out of rhythm with the xylophone.
Connie	Our next-door's had sex again last night.
Beattie	Not again!
Connie	I mean, I like a joke, but that's twice this month. I could not think what the noise was. I thought our central heating had come on a month early. And then somebody called out, 'Don't bother Ken, I'll do it myself', and I thought, well it can't be the central heating. Have you got gas?

---

16 Cut from here to 'the xylophone'.

17 Talent show first presented by Hughie Green in 1949. Les Dawson hosted the last series in 1990.

Beattie   No, methane. Well I thought, why not, while I'm on the high-fibre . . .

Connie   Does it work the cooker as well?

Beattie   Oh yes, though a leg of pork takes seven days to cook through.

Connie   I can't keep it down, pork. Not since a Jehovah's witness told me about their mating habits.

Beattie   Pigs? What do they do? *(She glances off.)*

Connie   They enjoy it.

Beattie   They don't.

Connie   They do. Now, are you still having pork and pickle fancies for Shona's wedding?

Beattie   I'm not.

Phone rings.

Family Planning, can I help you?

DOTTY ON WOMEN'S LIB[18]

Dotty   Good evening. Here I am again – in spite of a touch of groin strain. Some of you may be shocked to hear the word, but I believe in getting these things out in the open – I was the first woman in our crescent to say 'boob', and I've never regretted it.

Now, where was I? Oh, yes, my groin. Nothing to worry about – had a heavy day's hoovering yesterday, and I'm afraid I got carried away behind the cistern with my crevice-tool.

Now, the other evening I was snuggled up to Daddy in the lounge alcove, when something came up unexpectedly. Normally, with Jack, this kind of thing wouldn't arise. He turned to me – I was winding the wool for a mauve Guernsey, and Jack was picking his teeth with a library ticket – and he said, 'Chuckles', he said, 'what do you think to Women's Lib?' I was at a loss, which is very unusual for me. (When a burglar alarm went off in our crescent, and was mistaken for the four-minute warning, I was the only one who thought to cancel the milk.)

---

18 Dotty was hard to learn and deliver verbatim. In the recording, there is very minor ad-libbing by JW that deviates from the script.

Well, I've now ruminated on my position. I was unfortunately unable to get hold of a copy of *The Female Eunuch* by Germaine Greer, but I did read *Doctor in Clover* by Richard Gordon, which was the next book back on the left. So I'm not much further on in my research into Women's Lib, but I have found out what a sputum cup's for.

Girls – about this burning of bras we keep hearing about. *(Very loudly:)* A: *(To member of audience:)* No, not you, darling, you carry on. A: Some would say you don't get a decent jelly unless you put it in a mould. And B: There's nothing nastier than the smell of scorched elastic. What it boils down to is this – men and women were put on this earth for different purposes. A man is designed to walk three miles in the rain to phone for help when the car breaks down – and a woman is designed to say 'you took your time' when he comes back dripping wet.

No – that's just my lighthearted way of saying we girls are genetically programmed to rinse those dusters. Let's face it, if God had meant men to have children, he would have given them PVC aprons.

No time for more, unfortunately. Next week I shall be discussing politics, international terrorism, the unemployment figures, and how to make attractive earrings out of kidney stones. Till then, good evening.

COSMETIC SURGERY

Little shop. A dim girl is behind the counter. Enter a female customer.

Girl   Can I help you?

Customer   I saw your advert.

Girl   Oh right. Well, the paraffin heater's nearly new.

Customer   No, the cosmetic surgery advert.

Girl   Oh, in the butcher's window? Sorry. Have a seat. Right.

Gets out bloodstained order book.

Don't worry, that's liver. Now, have you been to us before?

Customer   No.

Girl   Thought not, as you're not limping or visibly mutilated.

Customer   You mean things can go wrong?

Girl   Well, not every time. It's just that Mr Heathbury, the surgeon – do you know him? – he used to be Heathbury's Plumbing and Gasfitting, in the High St, he's got the drinker's disease, delirium, what is it, delirium . . .

Customer   Tremens?

Girl   Yeah, when you shake. But it's all right, we keep everything very blunt, to be on the safe side. And I'm for ever bringing him in a coffee.

Customer	Into the operating theatre? But doesn't everything have to be sterilised?
Girl	The milk's sterilised. I think that's why he does so many breast operations, you know, somewhere to put his doughnut. So, what was you after having? Only I must tell you Mr Heathbury doesn't do the below-the-waist, you know, the married organs. We don't do sex-changes.
Customer	Why not?
Girl	Well, we've had a lot of trouble with a Mr Brearley,[19] who, you know, wanted the full conversion job, pipes re-laid, all on-site rubbish removed. And he's been round here several times since, getting very unpleasant in a pinafore dress, complaining he still can't get the top C on 'Midnight in the Oasis'.[20] So we just do the basics now, facial hair.
Customer	Removal?
Girl	No, we don't do removals.
Customer	Do you remove facial hair?
Girl	Not properly. We can tint it for you. We do breast augmentation, providing we've just done a breast reduction and that we have the right bits left over. We do apronectomy, you know, removing the stomach flesh of overweight people, that's very popular. In fact, we've had to hire a skip.
Customer	Do you do nose jobs?
Girl	Yes we do two. A big blobby one and a sort of little pointy one.
Customer	Why?
Girl	Those are the only ones he can do.
Customer	I was wondering – I've lost a lot of weight, I could do with having all the loose skin removed, here.

---

19 Probably named after VW's friend, the actor Roger Brierley, who would bequeath his name to a GP in *Housewife, 49* and a pair of suburban snobs in *That Day We Sang*.

20 'Midnight at the Oasis', first recorded by Maria Muldaur in 1973, was a pop song with no top Cs.

Girl	Yes, we've done that before. The lady came out with lovely upper arms, very tight skin. It was just if she went out in the sun, she had to prick them with a fork.
Customer	I'll leave it for now.
Girl	OK.

The girl stands up; she's got three legs.

Customer	Good heavens!
Girl	I know, isn't it awful – I can't resist, it's the staff discount.

THE REPORTER

A cheerful young girl reporter rings the front door bell: the door is answered by a weeping widow.

Reporter Widow Smith? I'm from the *Herald and Argus*. I believe your husband's just died and he was quite well known or something.[21]

Widow Yes.

Reporter We thought we'd do a little piece on him, just a few inches.

Widow I'm not sure.

Reporter It's just there haven't been any jumble sales this week – we're a bit strapped.

Widow Come in then, I haven't done much tidying up, since . . .

They go in.

Reporter Good excuse, a death, isn't it, to bunk off the housework? If somebody dropped dead in our house, I'd be quite pleased.

Widow Would you like a drink?

Reporter Depends what he died of. If it's anything catching, I won't bother, ta.

---

21 Changed to 'famous'.

Widow	It was his heart. It was very sudden. Biscuit?
Reporter	No, ta. Tried my bikini on last night, nearly had a heart attack.

She picks up a photo.

This him? He looks quite sick on this actually, doesn't he?

Tears from the widow.

He looks a dead nice bloke, though. So – he did what exactly, drop dead?

Widow	He collapsed in front of the television.
Reporter	What channel?
Widow	ITV, I think. A 'Carry On' film.
Reporter	Oh, I love them. You didn't tape it, did you? Did he topple grotesquely out of the chair or anything?
Widow	Just slumped sideways. He spilt his coffee.
Reporter	It's left a nasty stain – I bet you could have killed him when you saw that. And he wrote, what, books, was it?
Widow	Thrillers. The 'Captain Black' stories.
Reporter	They're full of glamorous women, aren't they?
Widow	That's right.
Reporter	Who did he draw them from, then? Did he do a lot of sleeping around, because if he did it's no wonder he dropped dead, really.
Butch	*(off)* Hello?

Butch enters, a large insensitive man.

Reporter	In here, Butch! This is our photographer. This is the grieving widow, Butch. Husband popped off while watching a 'Carry On' film.
Butch	Great, love. Is he here? Can we prop him up somewhere, love?
Widow	No, he's . . .

Butch   Not to worry. Have you got a bikini, love? Thigh boots, hot pants?

Widow   No.

Butch   Does this wall come down?

Butch kicks it.

Reporter   He did spill his coffee in the throes of death, apparently.

Butch   Yeah, that might do. Hang on.

He chucks some tea on the rug.

That should show up better. Now, if you hold this up with one hand, love, and sort of point to the stain, do me a face love, a bit disgusted, a bit sort of rueful, like 'how the heck am I going to get this stain out', kind of thing. Can you just hop up on the telly for me?

She climbs up; he sweeps all of the ornaments off the top.

Just move these a sec – you'll have to crouch down a bit for me, just cup your chin, sort of 'me husband's popped his clogs but life goes on' kind of thing. Can you stop crying – I'm getting a bounce-off.

Reporter   We could call it 'Carry On Crying', Butch.

Butch   Great, fabulous. Thanks very much love, if you want any prints, just pop in to the office.

The reporter and Butch leave. The widow begins to take an overdose. The reporter comes back in.

Reporter   Did I leave my . . . stop, don't take any more. Butch! Quickly!

Butch comes back in.

Butch   Oh that's smashing, love. Just turn the bottle round to me, love, then I can see the label, that's fabulous. Now hold me a pill up, and can you look sort of [22] 'I'm topping myself but I can still have a laugh about it', kind of thing. Now take another and hitch your skirt up . . .

---

22 The rest of the script was cut from here.

YOUNG LOVE: TWO

Gail	Carl?
Carl	What?
Gail	Do you know the facts of life?
Carl	Some of them.
Gail	Which ones do you know?
Carl	Gravy. I know how that's made. I know where my mam's apron is.
Gail	Do you know where babies come from?
Carl	'Course I do. They come from women.
Gail	Yeah, but how come?
Carl	Don't ask me. You want to send off for a pamphlet.
Gail	What's that?
Carl	They tell you what's what. We've got one at home about lagging.
Gail	Well, can I not just read yours then, and not send off?
Carl	No, you want a, er, wotsit pamphlet.
Gail	What?
Carl	You know – 'at it'. What is it you want to know anyway?
Gail	Well it were something me mam said about my honeymoon.
Carl	What?
Gail	She said I've not to wear my pixie-hood in bed. She said men don't like it.
Carl	Won't bother me.

Gail	Will it not, Carl? And you know I always sleep in a pac-a-mac.[23]
Carl	So what?
Gail	Do you really not mind, Carl?
Carl	Why should I? I'm not going to be there, am I?
Gail	In the honeymoon?
Carl	Well, it's the money, in't it, Gail? We can't both go. You go this year, I'll go next.
Gail	All right, Carl.

Pause.

Gail	Carl?
Carl	What?
Gail	What's your favourite sandwich?
Carl	Treacle.
Gail	Just treacle?
Carl	And bread.
Gail	Mine's not.
Carl	What?
Gail	Treacle.

Pause.

	Carl?
Carl	What?
Gail	Don't you want to know what my favourite sandwich is?
Carl	Nope. That's your feminine mystiquery, that.
Gail	What?
Carl	Not knowing.
Gail	What else do you not want to know?
Carl	I don't want to know where to catch a bus for Haslingden.
Gail	OK, Carl.

---

23 This line and the following two were cut.

ON CAMPUS

Film. A modern university campus. Selina walks uncertainly round holding a piece of paper and a musical instrument in a case. She goes inside the Music Department.

Selina   *(Voice Over)* I'm partly wanting to go to university for the education, and also for the social life. Just the words, 'on campus', they just have such an exciting sound.

TITLE 'ON CAMPUS'
Selina waits outside a door marked 'Music Auditions', the door opens, she grimaces at the camera and goes in. We hear the beginning of what is possibly a violin solo.

The audition room. Selina is playing for a panel of three elderly and middle-aged judges. She is playing 'Ebb Tide' on a Casio electronic miniature keyboard, very solemnly, with the sheet music on a music stand.

Selina comes out of the room, shaking.

Male Interviewer   *(Voice Over)* How did you get on?

Selina   It was very hard, much tougher than I imagined. Loads of questions about people I've never heard of. Johann

Sebastian somebody . . . I just don't know . . . I think I played 'Ebb Tide' as well as I've ever played it. Fingers crossed.

The halls of residence. Cars pulling up. Parents and girl students carrying gear in. Camera follows Selina and her parents as they carry in a chest freezer.

Selina's room.

Selina Just stick it down here for now, Daddy. I don't know where it should go till I get my Simon Rattle posters up.[24]

Mummy Lovely view of the tower, darling.

Selina That's where everybody commits suicide apparently. It was in the prospectus. Look, I'll sort all this lot out, you go.

Mummy All right, lambkin. Oh, Daddy's bought you a little present.

Daddy It's just some marijuana, something to hand round. The girl in the shop seemed to think it was the right sort.

Selina I don't know if people smoke it any more, Daddy, it's not like when you were at college.

Daddy Well, I don't know, just chuck it in the bin if you don't want it. Have you got a bin?

Selina Yes! Honestly, look, I'll be fine, do go, honestly.[25]

Ad-lib farewells and kisses. Parents leave. Selina stands by the window, a tear in her eye.

---

24 The sketch all too accurately reflects VW's years as a drama student at the University of Birmingham. Rattle became the principal conductor of the City of Birmingham Symphony Orchestra in 1980, so this was a local reference.

25 Added:

Mummy: We'll come and see you often. And bring food. Bye.

Interviewer *(Voice Over)* Homesick?

Selina   Well, it's all a bit strange, that's all. Room seems quite small now we've got the freezer in. I've never lived away from home before. Well, I've been grape-picking, but that was in our conservatory – didn't have to go abroad or anything . . .

Noise of girls outside.

Suppose I'd better go and introduce myself, meet my mates. Sorry – can I just squeeze . . . ?[26]

Hilary's room. Hilary and Selina sitting on the bed rather self-consciously, drinking coffee. Hilary has acne, wide thighs and speaks in funny voices.

Hilary   I've brought my guitar, so any peculiar wailing noises you hear through the wall, it'll be me! Little me! Not so little, unfortunately.

Selina   I play 'Ebb Tide' actually, on an electronic keyboard. So if you fancy the odd duet . . .

Hilary   The odd duet! Very odd, if we're playing!

Selina   Wonder how much coffee we're going to drink before the end of term.

Hilary   Gallons. Gallons and galloons. In fact, I have to go to the loo, the lavatree. Excuse me a mo!

Selina   I think she and I will be pretty good mates. That's Hilary – she's doing religious studies and her second subject is netball, I think. She got here a day early so she's going to show me the spin drier and the milk machine.

Hilary comes back in.

---

26 This line and Selina's reply were cut.

Hilary	There's a place to dry tights across the way – if drying tights turns you on!
Selina	Er – your zip's undone.
Hilary	Whoops! That settles it. Back on the old diet. Can't have the boyfriend going off me.
Selina	What does he do?
Hilary	He's at school. Head boy, but we don't talk about that.
Selina	You're not really fat anyway.
Hilary	My hero!

Hilary's room.

Interviewer	*(Voice Over)* So where are you off to tonight?
Selina	Well, tonight's the last night of Freshers' week, so everyone in Blakers, that's Blakethorpe Hall, we're all going to Peewee, that's Peabody Tower next door. And we're all having a sort of 'do' in the television room – so if anyone wants to watch television that's jolly hard cheese. And we all have to dress a little bit crazily – not difficult for me. So I've borrowed this rugby shirt from a rather nice mech. eng. student called Nick, and I'm wearing my school hat, just bash it up a bit[27] – so I'll probably miss my first tutorial. I think this part of the film'd better be X certificate.

TV room seen through window. A few wimpish students with tinsel in their hair are doing folk dancing. Hilary is on one side having a miserable time.

The Music Department. Selina is walking along the corridor.

---

27 Cut from 'And we all have to . . .' and replaced with 'I'll probably have the most horrendous hangover tomorrow morning.'

Selina I think I thought everyone in the Music Department would be more stuffy – really sort of classically orientated. But everyone's really loony like me. We've got a wind ensemble, and there's a really crazy string quintet with would you believe, two cellos! And I've started a – well it's a pop group. We'll probably start doing gigs quite soon, I should think.

A practice room. Selina on the keyboard, girl on the recorder, and two weedy boys on the oboe and the viola, are nearing the end of 'Copacabana', which they are playing very slowly and rigidly.

Selina I think we really got somewhere with it that time. I liked the little *legato* bit you did before the double *forte*, Robin – very effective, wasn't it, Tanya? Phew, I'm whacked. Where's the Party Four?

Music. Tracking shot past all the lit-up windows of the hall of residence. There is a girl at each window studying by the light of an Anglepoise. At Hilary's window we see her squeezing her spots and eating the last but one of a box of Mr Kipling's Bakewell Fingers.[28]

Hall of Residence. Corridor. Selina and other girls are giggling and closing the lift doors.

Selina We've just put all Hilary's furniture into the lift; and then we're going to jam the doors. Get lost, she's coming.

They scatter as Hilary approaches, in netball skirt and hockey boots.

---

28 Cut from 'The Music Department' to here.

Communal kitchen. Food lockers and Baby Bellings. Selina and friend Maggie are heating tomato soup.[29] *Maggie unwraps crumby packet of Anchor.*

Maggie   Some twerp's been at my butter. Bet it was Hilary.

Selina   Maggie!

Maggie   Well, I bet it would have been if she hadn't . . . God knows how they ever got her on the stretcher, legs that size.

Selina   Shut up, Maggie.

Interviewer *(Voice Over)* Do you think you had anything to do with Hilary's suicide attempt?

Both   No, not really, did we?

Selina   I think going away to university for the first time, it's a strain on anybody, the lectures, making your own coffee, buying soap-powder, there's a lot of pressure. And if you're fat and ugly with a hopeless personality, you're probably better off taking an overdose or something.

Interviewer So you're not badly affected by this business with Hilary?

Selina   I might have been when I first came, but not now. I've been here ten days and I can cope. Actually, it's great that her room's empty, because I've got somewhere to put my freezer.

---

29 VW had just such a mini cooker in her digs. In stand-up, she'd joke about how it took half an hour to heat a tin of soup on one. She also mentions it in her introduction to this book. *DL*: 'How do you do placenta on a Baby Belling?'

SHOE SHOP

The assistant is a smiling, mad, middle-aged woman. A customer enters.

Customer Hello, there's a pair of shoes in the window.
Assistant That's right. We do that because it's a shoe shop.
Customer They're black lace-ups, fifteen ninety-nine.
Assistant Are they?
Customer Yeah, can I try them on?
Assistant On your feet?
Customer Yes.
Assistant All right, why not?

She blunders into the window and comes back with any old pair.

Customer No, sorry, the black ones, they're a flat lace-up.
Assistant Beg pardon?
Customer Those aren't flat.

She breaks the heels off.

Assistant Flatter now.
Customer But they're red.
Assistant They are quite red, aren't they?

Customer   I want a black pair.
Assistant I know. I can never get what I want when I go shopping.
Customer   They're in the window.
Assistant Are they?

She runs into the window.

Get out! Get out! We think we've got hens in the skirting-board. We found droppings by the pop-sox. I think they're droppings. Mrs Brinsley says they're Janine's liquorice allsorts – she won't eat the black ones. Now what was it you wanted?

Customer   Not these, I want the black ones.
Assistant They've been swept up. You don't think someone might come in asking for hen-droppings in a shoe-shop.
Customer   Hen droppings are white – sheep droppings are black.
Assistant I don't think we've got sheep in the skirting-board, unless they're breeding them very small. They may be, with Lady Helen Windsor[30] setting a trend for fingerless gloves.[31]
Customer   Can I try on the black lace-ups in the window?
Assistant Well you can, but everyone in the street will be able to see you.
Customer   Can you get them in my size and I'll try them on here?
Assistant All right, we're not busy.
Customer   I'm five and a half.
Assistant You're very tall, do you take vitamins?
Customer   My shoe size is five and a half. Do you have the black lace-ups in that size?
Assistant We might have.
Customer   Can you go in the stockroom?

---

30 The daughter of the Duke of Kent, born 1964. This was quite an obscure royal reference even in 1985.

31 This and the preceding line were cut.

Assistant Yeah, I can go anywhere here, toilets, backyard, they're
          very free and easy . . .

          *She goes off, singing 'Look at me, I'm as helpless as a kitten
          up a tree'. Comes back with the shoes.*

          Are these the ones?
Customer Yes.
Assistant I don't like them.
Customer What?
Assistant Because I know this woman, and she has a pair and she
          got knocked down by an industrial tribunal, and the
          doctor says she's to wear ponchos.
Customer I haven't got a poncho.
Assistant Neither had she. We did a sponsored crochet but she
          moved to Norwich.
Customer They're a bit tight.[32]
Assistant Janine? Can I have your shoe horn please?

          *Janine chucks it over. The assistant scratches her back with
          it and chucks it back.*

          Ta. What were you saying?
Customer No, they're too small.
Assistant You're like me, broadfooted – and are you a Taurus and
          can't stick cabbage?
Customer No.
Assistant You're not like me, then. Look, you better go. They don't
          like me sitting down and talking in shop hours.
Customer Couldn't I try a bigger size?
Assistant No, I'm in enough trouble as it is. You come in here
          asking for hen droppings, you want to get changed in
          the window – this is a shoe shop not a soft porn video
          merchant's, and I should know because my husband

---

32 Cut from 'and the doctor says . . .' to here.

runs one. Well, he's not my husband, but he rubbed up against me in a sports jacket so he's as good as. And it's no good offering me used notes and trips to Bermuda because I've got a rare skin disease and can't go in the sun without a *Woman's Realm* on my head. So you can stuff it because I know my rights; I voted Conservative but the chappy didn't get in because lots of people round here had to stay in and watch television that night, and I never wanted free milk anyway, I'm allergic – sores run in our family.

Girl goes. Janine wanders over.

Janine   Wrong size?
Assistant   Yes, she was like me, broadfooted.

DANDRUFF COMMERCIAL

Actress   All through the winter, right, I didn't seem to have dandruff at all, then I went on holiday, because I know this married man, and his wife thought he was away working, blah, blah . . . usual thing.

So there we were, lots of sex and everything, sun – and I got really brown, and we're lying on the beach one day, and John said, that's not his real name, because he's quite well known . . . and John said, 'Hey, what are those white specks on your leg?', and I look down, and I had all this terrible dandruff, all round the tops of my legs. Like really obvious with my tan – and it was like, you know, bikini dandruff. Like really a turn-off for him, and it was a problem for me, because if I don't sleep with him I don't get my rent paid, anyway, so then a friend said, why not paint your legs white . . . and I said like, why don't you mind your own business, 'cos I was, you know, fairly narked by this time.

Anyway – then another friend said why not try – dadah! – the new shampoo, your shampoo, and it was great, really fabulous – dandruff went by about third day, it left a few scars and it rotted my pants but on the whole, I'm really pleased, yes . . .

TODDLERS

Victoria and Julie dressed as toddlers – woolly hats, etc – in two swings. The kind with bars at the front. Front blank, they swing gently for some time.

Julie   Thought of any jokes for this sketch yet?
Victoria   Nope.

They carry on swinging.

THE PRACTICE ROOM

A stuffy music student is practising something fiddly and classical on the piano. Enter a beaming chain-smoking cleaner; she stands listening to the pianist making mistakes.

Cleaner   Having trouble, are you?

Pianist   Yes, a little.

Cleaner   Music like that – it's all the same whether you play it wrong or not, isn't it? Do you not know any proper tunes?

Pianist   I'm sorry?

Cleaner   Do you know 'Dream of Olwen'? Lovely that. That were on in Women's Surgical the night I had my cervix cauterised. Tell you what – do us the 'Harry Lime Theme' *(hums a bit)*. Great that. Now, that's dead easy – my Uncle Albert could play it and he had a metal plate in his head.

Pianist   I'm sorry.

Cleaner   No, you're all right. Quite a blessing, really. If he sat with his back to the aerial we could get Welsh television. Back inside now, poor old thing. Shoplifting. Caught outside Tesco's with half a pound of skinless links stuffed down his trousers. That caused a certain amount of confusion as well – he was nearly had up on two charges. *(Picking up concert programme off the piano:)* Go to concerts a lot, do you?

Pianist	When I can, yes.
Cleaner	Yeah, smashing. Ever see Renato do 'Moonlight Sonata'?
Pianist	No, I don't think . . .
Cleaner	On roller skates with the xylophone strapped round his neck. Finished up in a wicker basket whistling 'Colonel Bogey' while a woman in a sequined bra thrust spears through all parts of his body.
Pianist	Gosh. I suppose he escaped unscathed?
Cleaner	No, he bled to death, actually. There was some kind of a mix-up over who was working the trap-door. *(Drops ash inside piano.)*
Pianist	Er, I don't think the principal would think that was terribly good for the Steinway.
Cleaner	Tough titty. He's lucky Mrs Harris is off sick. She always says what's the point dragging round to the toilet when there's timps handy. No, I'm only kidding. It were only an old French horn.
Pianist	I must get on, actually.
Cleaner	I see that Janet Baker were here last week.
Pianist	Yes, it was marvellous. We could hear her practising in number seven.
Cleaner	Ooh, so could we. There's me trying to listen to 'Mystery Voice' on the wireless. In the end I knocked on the door, I said for God's sake put a sock in it or give us something a bit more cheerful. I told her, I said you'd get booed off down the British Legion, you would. I said call yourself a music lover? She didn't know nothing – 'Tie a Yellow Ribbon', 'Bright Eyes' . . .
Pianist	Well, I must persevere . . .
Cleaner	Don't mind me, you carry on.[33] Having lessons, are you?
Pianist	Yes. Professor Hartley. *(Bum note.)*
Cleaner	Ask him for a refund. *(Laughs.)* No, I'm only kidding. I tell you a lovely pianist could learn you a few things

---

33 This and the preceding speech were cut.

	– Bobby Crush. He can cross his hands over and everything. Lovely smile. Going to turn pro?
Pianist	I like to think so, one day.
Cleaner	Hey – I know. They're looking for someone down the snug at the Winston. Good job – £5 a night and any ploughman's they've left over from dinnertime. It wouldn't have fell vacant, but some of the lads got a bit tanked up and tried to jam pianist's head in the lid. It were a scream. Anyway shall I put a word in for you?
Pianist	Quite honestly, I do aspire a little higher than the snug.
Cleaner	What, the lounge? *(Doubtful.)*[34] Well, maybe. They do more your classical stuff – 'Lara's Theme', 'Edelweiss' . . .
Pianist	I won't be able to get a job anywhere if I don't get this right.
Cleaner	You know what you're doing wrong?
Pianist	What?
Cleaner	Well, that dotted semi-quaver is tied over the bar, and the middle note of the triplet isn't accidental.[35] *(Leaving.)* And another thing – your nails need cutting.

---

34 The rest of the speech was cut.

35 This could have been a mistake by a copy editor. In the recording, JW correctly says 'an accidental'.

SUPERMARKET CHECKOUT

An impatient woman customer is having her groceries checked out by a slow girl on the till. She looks at a packet of bacon.

Till girl It's got no price on. Did you notice how much they were?
Customer No, I didn't.

She looks round and holds up the bacon.

Till girl Won't be long.
Customer Good.

Long pause.

Till girl We're a bit short-handed today. Us that works here gets the old food cheap, and if it's something like a pork pie, you can actually die, apparently. So the girl that checks the prices, she's probably, you know, passed on.
Customer Honestly, I thought you girls on the tills knew all the prices.
Till girl I've only come on the till today. I was in meat packing before, then an overall came free so I come here.
Customer But surely you wear an overall when you're packing meat?
Till girl No, you must bring something from home. I had our dog's blanket.

Customer	You can't have dogs in a place where food is prepared.
Till girl	I didn't. It's dead. It were called Whiskey. It ate one of the pork pies from here.
Customer	But you do wear gloves, don't you, when you're wrapping meat?
Till girl	I did, woolly ones. I get a lot of colds, I like to have something to wipe my nose on. I liked it in the meat-packing department, it were dead near the toilet.
Customer	Well it sounds disgusting. Who's in charge of that department?
Till girl	Mr Waterhouse. He's not here. He goes to some sort of a special clinic on Thursdays. I'll do your veg, anyway.

She coughs and splutters all over it.

Sorry. I've caught this cold off Susan on smoked meats. They're not smoked when they come, but she's on sixty a day.

Customer	It's all over the cauliflower.
Till girl	Sorry.

She wipes it on her overall.

Corned beef, ninety-eight. It's funny how much tins can actually blow out without bursting, isn't it?

Customer	You can't sell a blown tin.
Till girl	We can, they're dead popular.[36]
Customer	Oh look, how much longer is this going to take?
Till girl	Do you want me to ask the supervisor?
Customer	Yes, thank you.

The till girl speaks into intercom.

Till girl	Hello?

---

36 Cut from 'Corned beef . . .'.

Intercom	Hello?
Till girl	Hello, Mrs Brinsley, it's Gemma here.
Intercom	Hello, Gemma, nice to talk to you.
Till girl	Nice to talk to you, Mrs Brinsley. How's your boils?
Intercom	Worse.
Till girl	So putting you on the cheese counter hasn't helped? Well, what I'm calling about, I've a lady here, and she's brought me a packet of bacon with no price.
Intercom	Is it streaky?
Till girl	Well, it is a bit but it'll probably wash off.

She wipes it with filthy dishcloth.

The sell-by-date is 5 August 1984. No, hang on.

She scrapes something off.

1964.

Intercom	Three and nine.
Till girl	Three and nine, thank you.
Customer	You mean that bacon's twenty years old?
Till girl	I don't know. I was away when we did addings. *(She finishes checking out the rest of the stuff.)*
Customer	This place is a disgrace – filthy, unhygienic, the food's not safe to eat, the staff are all positively diseased.
Till girl	That's two pounds seventy-one pence, please.
Customer	On the other hand, it's very cheap and easy to park. Bye.

KITTY: ONE[37]

Kitty is about fifty-three, from Manchester and proud of it.
She speaks as she finds and knows what's what. She is sitting
in a small bare studio, on a hard chair. She isn't nervous.

Kitty   Good evening. My name's Kitty. I've had a boob off
and I can't stomach whelks so that's me for you. I don't
know why I've been asked to interrupt your viewing like
this, but I'm apparently something of a celebrity since I
walked the Pennine Way in slingbacks in an attempt to
publicise Mental Health. They've asked me to talk about
aspects of life in general, nuclear war, peg-bags . . .

I wasn't going to come today, actually. I'm not a fan of
the modern railway system. I strongly object to paying
twenty-seven pounds fifty to walk the length and breadth
of the train with a sausage in a plastic box. But they offered me a chopper from Cheadle so here I am.

I'm going to start with the body – you see I don't mince

---

37 In the first Kitty monologue, VW made subtle improvements to help establish her very particular character: 'your viewing' was changed to the more specific 'your telly viewing', 'I strongly
object' to 'Wouldn't you object . . .', 'female gibbons' to 'the female gibbon', and 'as it happens' to
'as a matter of fact'.

words. Time and again I'm poked in the street by complete acquaintances – Kitty, they say to me, how do you keep so young, do you perhaps inject yourself with a solution deriving from the placenta of female gibbons? Well, no, I say, I don't, as it happens. I'm blessed with a robust constitution, my father's mother ran her own abbatoir, and I've only had the need of hospitalisation once – that's when I was concussed by an electric potato peeler at the Ideal Home Exhibition.

No, the secret of my youthful appearance is simply – mashed swede. As a face-mask, as a night cap, and in an emergency, as a draught-excluder. I do have to be careful about my health, because I have a grumbling ovary which once flared up in the middle of *The Gondoliers*.[38] My three rules for a long life are regular exercise, hobbies and complete avoidance of midget gems.

I'm not one for dance classes, feeling if God had wanted us to wear leotards he would have painted us purple. I have a system of elastic loops dangling from the knob of my cistern cupboard. It's just a little thing I knocked up from some old knicker waistbands. I string up before breakfast and I can exert myself to Victor Sylvester[39] till the cows come home.

There's also a rumour going round our block that I play golf. Let me scotch it. I do have what seems to be a golf-bag on my telephone table but it's actually a pyjama-case made by a friend who has trouble with her nerves in Buckinghamshire.[40]

38 Operetta by Gilbert and Sullivan, first performed in 1889.
39 Popular band leader.
40 Cut from 'I have a system of elastic loops' to here.

Well, I can't stop chatting, much as I'd like to – my maisonette backs onto a cake factory, so I'm dusting my knick-knacks all the day long.

And I shall wait to see myself before I do any more. Fortunately, I've just had my TV mended. I say mended – a shifty young man in plimsolls waggled my aerial and wolfed my Gipsy Creams, but that's the comprehensive system for you.

I must go, I'm having tea with the boys in flat five. They're a lovely couple of young men, and what they don't know about Mikhail Barishnikov is nobody's business. So I'd better wrap up this little gift I've got them. It's a gravy boat in the shape of Tony Hancock – they'll be thrilled.

She peers round the studio.

Now, who had hold of my showerproof? It's irreplaceable, you know, being in tangerine poplin, which apparently there's no call for . . .[41]

She gets up and walks past the camera.

There's a mauve pedestal mat of mine, too.

---

41 Replaced with 'I shall be cross if it's missing. It's a lovely tangerine poplin and I doubt I shall find another.'

YOUNG LOVE: THREE

Gail	Carl?
Carl	What?
Gail	Would you rather have a red washing-up bowl and a red washing-up bowl, brush I mean, or a brown washing-up brush, I mean bowl, and a brown washing-up brush, or a yellow washing-up bowl and a brown washing-up brush?
Carl	Why?
Gail	Just wondered.
Carl	We want to be investing in paintings, us.
Gail	Picture paintings?
Carl	Yeah. Something with elephants.
Gail	I don't really like elephants, Carl.
Carl	Well, you say what's to be on t'painting, then.
Gail	I know, let's have a painting of digestive biscuits, 'cos we both like them don't we, Carl?
Carl	No, it's got to be something like some scenery.
Gail	All right, then, some digestive biscuits and a Alp.
Carl	All right, but they better be chocolate.
Gail	Why are they called Alps, Carl?
Carl	Well, people go ski-ing on them, and fall off, don't they? And they go 'Help Help' but it sounds like 'Alp' 'cos they all have ear-muffs on.
Gail	You're dead clever, you. You should have gone to – where is it, they have scarves?

Carl	Oxford and Cambridge.
Gail	Yeah, you should have gone there.
Carl	For three years?
Gail	Yeah.
Carl	And lose all t'good-will on the window-cleaning?
Gail	Never thought of that, Carl.

THIS HOUSE BELIEVES

Schoolgirl Mr Chairman, Lords, Ladies and Gentlemen, I am speaking to oppose the motion 'This house believes that school uniform should be abolished'. Oh, so this house believes that school uniform should be abolished, does it? Does it really think it's a good idea for everybody to come to school wearing exactly what they please? I think we should see some pretty funny sights, don't you?

But to be serious for a moment or two, let us first examine the history of school uniform in some detail. If you care to look at the Bayeux tapestry, which I think everyone would agree is pretty old, you will see that nearly everyone on that tapestry is wearing uniform – and of course there are many other examples of this.

But to bring us right up to date, I think we can do no better than look at the finest schools in our country today, – Eton, Winchester, Harrow, St John's School Leatherhead, where my brother goes – and see whether they wear uniform or not. They do. Lots of it. And I do not pick those schools out for snob reasons: plenty of ordinary people go to them, such as architects' children, and many leave and go into the music business, so you cannot say uniform has made them fuddy-duddy, as

Derek Bainbridge would have had you believe previous-
ly.

All right then, let us picture a typical school day without uniform. Just suppose one catches two fourth years
hanging round the Lower Corridor pegs at five to nine
and one requests them to sign the Punishment Book.
How are they to know I am a Punishment Monitor if
I am not wearing my red Punishment Tie? In fact how
can they tell I am a monitor at all if they can't see my
monitor's cardigan as opposed to everyone else's pullover
who's not a monitor? If this kind of thing were repeated
all over the school I don't think we'd get much work
done, do you?

But there is yet another side to this vexed question. Were
we not to wear uniform, do you really want to have to
get up earlier in order to choose what to wear? I, for one,
don't want to stand dithering in front of eleven pairs of
trousers keeping my mother waiting in the Range Rover,
do you? But to take my analogy a stage further, Derek
Bainbridge claims that the official uniform is expensive
and a great strain on the parents of the poorer children.
Well it seems to me if people's fathers took the trouble
to pass exams in accountancy and business management
like some people's fathers, they would have plenty of
money for new blazers and other things such as holiday
flatlets in Fuengirola. But I digress. And furthermore – if
some people cannot be trusted to sign the Punishment
Book without drawing private parts on it, I don't really
think they can be trusted to dress suitably for school *do
you*? I think we can all imagine what would happen if
certain people arrived in backless sweaters only to find
the heating was off due to education cuts. I think certain
people would find they were crawling to other certain
people to borrow their monitor's cardigans, don't you? A

hypothesis which, as Hamlet said, is devoutly not to be wished.

Finally, to sum up, let me just give you three reasons why I think you should vote for me, against the motion.

One: I think school uniform promotes a sense of identity and team spirit.

Two: it prevents discrimination on the grounds of class and economic differences.

Three: my father is now the sole supplier of uniform to this school, and anyone who votes for me will get a discount.

Thank you.

GROUPIES[42]

The dressing-room. Bella and Enid, two dim but beaming typists, with woolly hats, speech impediments and thick glasses, approach. The star, a thirty-nine-ish male singer, is relaxed but sweaty after the show.

Knock on door.

Star	Come in. *(The girls stick their heads round the door.)*
Bella	We just come round to say it were a really great show tonight. Really smashing, wasn't it?
Enid	Yeah.
Bella	Yeah. *(They beam at him.)*
Star	Come in, girls.
Bella	Are you not busy?
Star	Never too busy to see the fans who've put me where I am today. *(They come in.)* So – you enjoyed the show? That's good.
Bella	Oh it were great, wasn't it?
Enid	Yeah.
Bella	Yeah. Mind you, we're right easily pleased.

---

42 The star was played by Alan Lake, third husband of Diana Dors. VW and JW were reunited with him a year later in Russell Harty's 1982 Christmas show. Five months after Dors's death in 1984, he committed suicide aged 43.

Star	Would you like a signed photo *(indicating a pile on dressing-table)*?
Bella	Do we?
Enid	No.
Bella	No. We don't, thanks.
Star	Oh – OK. Well, look girls . . .
Bella	And I can't think of anybody else that would want one, can you?
Enid	No.
Bella	No, I can't. Everyone at the office thinks you're really dated.
Enid	'As-been. *(Laughs inanely.)*
Bella	Except Mrs Singh.
Enid	She's Indian.
Bella	She'd never heard of you. Who is it she likes?
Enid	Max Jaffa.[43]
Bella	That's right. *(They beam.)*
Star	Well look girls – I must be fair – I like to spend an equal amount of time with all my fans – I'm sure there must be quite a few waiting outside.
Bella	No there aren't, are there?
Enid	No.
Bella	No. In fact some people didn't even stop till the end. *(They laugh.)*
Star	There's nobody waiting?
Bella	No. Is there not?
Enid	No.
Bella	No.
Star	Most towns I play, to be frank – they're bursting the door down to get at me. Not just ordinary fans – you know, er, groupies.
Bella	That's us.
Star	Sorry?
Bella	We're the groupies. Aren't we?

---

43 Popular bandleader.

Enid	Yeah.
Bella	Yeah, we are.
Star	I'm sorry, I'm not –
Bella	We do everyone that comes here. It's like our 'obby, isn't it?
Enid	Like rugs. Making rugs. 'Obby.
Star	And you're sure there's nobody else here?
Bella	No. Just us. What do you want doing?
Star	What kind of things do you normally do?
Bella	Whatever they ask for. Versatile, aren't we?
Enid	Whatever is asked for we will do.
Bella	They all have different things they want doing, don't they?
Enid	John Hanson.[44]
Star	What did he want?
Bella	What were it?
Enid	Haddock.
Bella	And scallops.
Enid	On a tray. And a can of Vimto.
Bella	We've posted letters for Ivor Emmanuel.[45]
Enid	Played Monopoly with Larry Grayson.[46]
Star	But, girls – most groupies . . . I don't know how to put this.
Bella	What?
Enid	What?
Star	Most groupies just want to sleep with – whoever it is.[47]
Bella	Do they? Larry Grayson never said nothing about that . . .
Enid	What? Sex?
Star	Well, yes . . .

---

44 Tenor and actor. As a student, VW saw him at the Alexandra Theatre in Birmingham. In *Acorn Antiques: The Musical!*, Bo Beaumont remembers having worked with him in *Café Continental*: 'And John Hanson, what was his solo?'

45 Welsh actor, best known for singing 'Men of Harlech' in *Zulu*.

46 Comedian. Much of his humour derived from his flamboyant campness.

47 Changed to 'make love with'.

Bella and **Enid**   Oh . . .

Bella   *(as they tear off their hats and coats)* Ooh I like the sound of that much better, don't you?

Enid   Yeah.

Bella   Yeah. I were bored stiff with Monopoly, weren't you?

Enid   Yeah.

Bella   Yeah. *(They have both stripped down to their liberty bodices, heavy duty bras etc.)* Right – which of us you want first?

The star resignedly begins to unbutton his shirt.

MARGERY AND JOAN: ONE

Margery is cooking. Joan is standing too close, watching.

Joan	And that's just ordinary clear honey is it, Margery?
Margery	Just ordinary clear honey, Joan – whoops, it does tend to go everywhere if you're not too careful.
Joan	So the best thing is to *be* careful, Margery, or it will get everywhere – would that be right?
Margery	Absolutely. Now, I'm taking my four ounces of flaked almonds from my nice little pottery bowl I bought in Malaga.
Joan	What we'd call a Spanish bowl, then Margery?
Margery	That's right, Joan, but of course if the viewers have never been to Spain – some of them are perhaps disabled or agoraphobic – an ordinary vinyl or plastic bowl will do just as well. Just scrape up those last few crumbs . . .

The bowl smashes on floor.

Joan	My goodness, quite a noisy little bowl, Margery. Looks like you'll have to be flying back to Spain, Margery, to get another one, perhaps?
Margery	Well, I'm unfortunately not able to fly, Joan, since the plane crash that killed my whole family, and in which I injured my pelvis.

Joan   I'm glad you brought that up, Margery, because we'll be talking about fatal plane crashes and whether it's worth taking sandwiches next week. So see you then.

Fade in music, fade out dialogue.

      And this is just plain evaporated milk, is it Margery?

Margery   No, it's condensed.

Joan   Condensed, I beg your pardon. Easy to muddle up, I should think, especially if you have tunnel vision or are thinking of getting it . . .

FILM CLASSIC

Black-and-white film. Freda and Barry[48] *in belted rain-coats are under a viaduct in the rain. They are snogging. She breaks away.*

Freda   Barry, no!

Barry   By 'eck, I've never thought of myself as romantic, Freda, but you've got a cracking bust.

Freda   I've got to go, Barry, I'm on first shift down pit.

Barry   Snog a bit longer and then catch last bus.

Freda   I can't.

Barry   I'll give you t'threepence.

Freda   It's not the money. My mam's being buried tomorrow, and I've got to mek t'sandwiches.

Barry   Just a bit longer – I haven't finished unbuttoning your cardigan yet.

Freda   I'm not in the mood.

Barry   What's up, love?

Pause.

Freda   What do you think?

---

48 No comment.

Pause.

Barry	Oh no. How did it happen?
Freda	You know flicking well how it happened.
Barry	But we were dead careful.
Freda	Not careful enough, Barry.
Barry	Did you try gin?
Freda	Yes.
Barry	And hot baths?
Freda	Yes! Shut up – it's no good.
Barry	What am I going to tell me mam?
Freda	You'll just have to tell her t'truth. The whippet got wet, caught cold and died.

SERVICE WASH

An old bag is folding clothes.

Old Bag   I can remember when pants were pants. You wore them for twenty years, then you cut them down for pan scrubs. Or quilts. We used to make lovely quilts out of Celanese[49] bloomers. Every gusset a memory. Not bras. They won't lie flat. We didn't wear bras till after the war, round here. We stayed in and polished the lino.

I didn't see an Oxo cube till I was twenty-five. That's when I got my glasses.[50] And we weren't having hysterectomies every two minutes either, like the girls these days. If something went wrong down below, you kept your gob shut and turned up the wireless.

We never got woken with a teasmade. We were knocked up every morning by a man with a six-foot pole. It wasn't all fun. We'd no showers. We used to club together and send the dirtiest one to the Slipper Baths.[51] We might have been mucky but we had clean slippers.

---

49 Cheap material used in the production of clothing. In the recording, it got a smaller laugh, suggesting that even then it wasn't a reference all the audience understood.

50 These two sentences were cut.

51 Public baths introduced to promote hygiene, so-called because users would drape a towel over them to protect their modesty. The covered baths were thought to look like slippers.

And it was all clogs. Clogs on cobbles – you could hardly hear yourself coughing up blood. Clogs – when times were hard we had them for every meal, with condensed milk, if we were lucky.

And no one had cars. If you wanted to get run over, you'd to catch a bus to the main road. And of course, corner shop was the only one with gas, so you'd to go cap in hand if you wanted to gas yourself.[52]

For years we had to make our own rugs. We used to stitch mice on to pieces of sacking. We weren't always making jokes either. I once passed a remark about parsnips and couldn't sit down for a week.[53]

Oh, but I shall never forget the Coronation. 1953. We all crammed into the one front room and stared at this tiny grey picture. Somebody had cut it out of the paper – nobody got television till the year after.

I think we were more neighbourly. If anyone was ill in bed, the whole street would let themselves in and ransack the parlour.

And we didn't do all this keep-fit. We got our exercise lowering coffins out of upstairs windows. In fact, if people were very heavy we used to ask them to die downstairs.

It wasn't all gloom. My brother went to Spain, which was very unusual in those days. Mind you, that was the Civil War, and he got shot for trying to paddle.

---

52 Cut from 'Clogs – when times were hard'.

53 These two sentences were cut.

We couldn't afford holidays. Sometimes us kids would take some dry bread and a bottle of water and sit in the TB clinic, but that was about it.[54]

We had community spirit round here, right to the end. The day they demolished our street it was like the war all over again – dead bodies, hands sticking out of the rubble. The council should have let us know.

That's me done, best be off. Got a bit of cellular blanket for my supper, don't want it to spoil. Ta-ra . . .

54 These two sentences were cut.

THE BOUTIQUE

A tiny dark boutique. A customer is by a rail of jeans. The assistant is up a ladder with a machine-gun and a walkie-talkie.

Customer Excuse me, are you serving?

Assistant I don't think we're actually supposed to serve people – just shoot them if they do something suspicious.

Customer I just wondered if you had these in a different size?

Assistant Hang on. *(Into her walkie-talkie:)* I'm going out on the floor, Eileen. There's no landmines in separates, are there? OK. If you have any trouble with people wanting to buy things, let the dogs out. *(Climbing down.)* Can I help you?

Customer I wondered if you have these in a fourteen?

Assistant You what? This is a boutique, not the Elephant House. *(Laughing up to a two-way mirror:)* Hey, Eileen, got another Fatso in – they never learn, do they? We don't do much above a size eight – I mean, it's so depressing for us, dealing with great wobbling lumps of flesh all day long.

Customer So you haven't got anything in a size fourteen?

Assistant They might have sent something by mistake. *(Riffles along rail.)* There's these.

Customer   I don't really suit green.

Assistant   I shouldn't think you suit much do you, body like that. I say 'body' . . . The day I go over six and a half stone, it's razor blades in the bath, d'you know what I mean? Do you want them, or not?

Customer   Could I try them on?

Assistant   Yeah, well don't break anything. We don't usually let obese people in the cubicles, in case they sweat on the wallpaper.

Customer   They look a bit small to me.

Assistant   It's up to you, Porky. *(Customer goes into cubicle.)* If they don't fit you, the only other thing in this shop that will is the cubicle curtains. They're supposed to be tight-fitting these days, you know. I don't suppose you go out much, do you, being so ugly? I have them that tight, I need surgery to get things out of my pockets. *(She whips back the curtain as the customer has them at the half-way-up stage.)* Hey, Eileen, get the Polaroid. Another one for the toilet wall. *(Customer closes curtain.)* Hey Eileen, Martin went out with someone fat once – eight stone or something she was – he said she was like a waterbed with legs.

The customer comes out in own clothes, puts the jeans in the assistant's hands and leaves.

I don't know why we bother being so pleasant.

MARGERY AND JOAN: TWO[55]

Joan   And, leaving Mr Dixon to get on with his model of
            Sheena Easton in dog food, we'll stroll over to Con-
            sumer Corner, to see what Margery's been buying today.
            Hello, Margery, you've been looking at what, this week,
            Margery?

            *Margery is at a table covered in sex aids, sprays, rubber
            balaclavas, etc.*

Margery Hello Joan. Many people these days are finding their
            private lives have gone a little bit flat, little bit uninter-
            esting, so I've been looking at devices, attachments, in
            fact private sex gadgets in general.

Joan   Lovely. This looks rather nice, Margery – what's this
            for?

Margery Yes it is rather nice, isn't it? It's just come on the market,
            Joan – it's an updating of the old hand-held partner
            stimulator. It's electronic, and the two vibrating pads
            here are covered in wipeable Dralon-effect, and what I
            like very much is the extra socket on the side if there
            should happen to be a group of you, and you need just
            that little bit more power.

---

55 Not broadcast.

Joan	So it's practical as well as being a nice thing to have around the house?
Margery	Absolutely. Now, I was very interested in this –
Joan	That looks like an ordinary personal massager, Margery, what's so special about it?
Margery	What's special about it, Joan, is that not only is it half the price of a conventional rubbing unit, it folds up, and can be slipped into a spectacle case or luncheon-voucher holder.
Joan	So it can go virtually anywhere, Margery?
Margery	Virtually anywhere, Joan.
Joan	So if it's high summer, I'm crossing the River Avon by ferry, I'm in a sleeveless dress, I haven't a shopping bag with me . . . ?
Margery	You can slip it into the pocket of your cardi, or even into the top of your sock.
Joan	Well I don't wear socks myself, but from our large post-bag, I know lots of our viewers do, and next week we'll be delving into that all-important question, What do we do with socks that have got dirty? Bye.

Margery begins to demonstrate a drop-down rubber bra that lights up . . .

GIVING NOTES[56]

Alma, a middle-aged sprightly woman, addresses her amateur company after a rehearsal of Hamlet. *She claps her hands.*

Alma   Right. Bit of hush please. Connie! Thank you. Now that was quite a good rehearsal; I was quite pleased. There were a few raised eyebrows when we let it slip the Pie-crust Players were having a bash at Shakespeare but I think we're getting there. But I can't say this too often: it may be *Hamlet* but it's got to be Fun Fun Fun!

She consults her notes.

Now we're still very loose on lines. Where's Gertrude? I'm not so worried about you – if you 'dry' just give us a bit of business with the shower cap. But Barbara – you will have to buckle down. I mean, Ophelia's mad scene,[57] 'There's rosemary, that's for remembrance' – it's no good just bunging a few herbs about and saying, 'Don't mind

---

56 These seven paragraphs were cut before the recording: Right, Act One, Scene One . . . Where's my ghost of Hamlet's father? . . . The Players' scene . . . Gravediggers? . . . Oh yes, Hamlet, Act Three, Scene One . . . Act Five, Gertrude, late again . . .

57 Added: 'that lovely line.'

me, I'm a loony'. Yes? You see, this is our marvellous bard, Barbara, you cannot paraphrase. It's not like Pinter where you can more or less say what you like as long as you leave enough gaps.

Right, Act One, Scene One, on the ramparts. Now I know the whist table is a bit wobbly, but until Stan works out how to adapt the Beanstalk it'll have to do. What's this? Atmosphere? Yes – now what did we work on, Philip? Yes, it's midnight, it's jolly cold. What do we do when it's cold? We go 'Brrr', and we do this *(slaps hands on arms)*. Right, well don't forget again, please. And cut the hot-water bottle, it's not working.

Where's my ghost of Hamlet's father? Oh yes, what went wrong tonight, Betty? He's on nights still, is he? OK. Well, it's not really on for you to play that particular part, Betty – you're already doing the Player Queen and the back legs of Hamlet's donkey. Well, we don't know he didn't have one, do we? Why waste a good cossy?

Hamlet – drop the Geordie, David, it's not coming over. Your characterisation's reasonably good, David, but it's just far too gloomy. Fair enough, make him a little bit depressed at the beginning, but start lightening it from Scene Two, from the hokey-cokey onwards, I'd say. And perhaps the, er, 'Get thee to a nunnery' with Ophelia – perhaps give a little wink to the audience, or something, because he's really just having her on, isn't he, we decided . . .

Polonius, try and show the age of the man in your voice and in your bearing, rather than waving the bus-pass. I think you'll find it easier when we get the walking frame. Is that coming, Connie? OK.

The Players' scene: did any of you feel it had stretched a bit too . . . ? Yes. I think we'll go back to the tumbling on the entrance, rather than the extract from *Barnum*.[58] You see, we're running at six hours twenty now, and if we're going to put those soliloquies back in . . .

Gravediggers? Oh yes, gravediggers. The problem here is that Shakespeare hasn't given us a lot to play with – I feel we're a little short on laughs, so Harold, you do your dribbling, and Arthur, just put in anything you can remember from the Ayckbourn, yes?

The mad scene: apart from lines, much better, Barbara – I can tell you're getting more used to the straitjacket. Oh – any news on the skull, Connie? I'm just thinking, if your little dog pulls through, we'll have to fall back on papier mâché. All right, Connie, as long as it's dead by the dress . . .

Oh yes, Hamlet, Act Three, Scene One, I think that cut works very well, 'To be or not to be', then Ophelia comes straight in, it moves it on, it's more pacey . . .

Act Five, Gertrude, late again. What? Well, is there no service wash? I'm sure Dame Edith wasn't forever nipping out to feed the dryer.

That's about it – oh yes, Rosencrantz and Guildenstern, you're not on long, make your mark. I don't think it's too gimmicky, the tandem. And a most important general note – make up! Half of you looked as if you hadn't got any on! And Claudius – no moles again? *(Sighs.)*

---

58 Hit musical which had recently been on in the West End, based on the life of the nineteenth-century American showman P. T. Barnum.

I bet Margaret Lockwood never left hers in the glove compartment.

That's it for tonight then; thank you. I shall expect you to be word-perfect by the next rehearsal. Have any of you realised what date we're up to? Yes, April the twenty-seventh! And when do we open? August! It's not long![59]

---

59 Added: 'Right, Connie, I want a word.'

CLEANING[60]

A large, messy, stripped-pine kitchen. Ursula, a large messy lady novelist in a smock sits drinking tea with Kent, a disdainful Northern man.

Ursula   You know, it's amazing: you're the only person who's answered the advert. I just cannot get a cleaner. I'm afraid it's all rather neglected in here.

Kent   Well, yes, I was just admiring that blue mink hat, but I see now it's a mouldy pizza.

Ursula   I'm a novelist, and it's so hard to do everything. Is the tea all right?

Kent   Not really.

Ursula   Oh sorry, is it too strong?

Kent   I'm just a bit perturbed by the way it's taken the tarnish off this teaspoon.

Ursula   Biscuit?

Kent   Have they got chemicals in?

Ursula   Preservatives?

Kent   I was hoping for disinfectant.

Ursula   No, I baked them myself.

Kent   I bet Mr Kipling's worried.

Ursula   Aren't you going to finish it?

---

60 Not broadcast.

Kent	I'll keep it by me – you never know, I may need to force a lock.

Pause.

	Anyone ever told you you've got a look of Molly Weir?[61]
Ursula	No.
Kent	I'm not surprised.
Ursula	Have you been a cleaner for long?
Kent	Well, I was abroad for some years.
Ursula	Really?
Kent	Lived with Picasso, actually.
Ursula	The painter?
Kent	Yes. I had a put-u-up in the back bedroom. I had to come away. It was nice, but, you know, everything tasted of turps. Henry Moore was the same – a stranger to Harpic.
Ursula	You obviously know a lot about cleaning.
Kent	I was approached by 'Mastermind' to set the questions for the specialised subject 'The history of the J-cloth from 1963 to the present time'.
Ursula	Goodness, so you're a sort of academic are you?
Kent	Oh yes. I was all set to be an Oxford don a few months back – it was just a question of me scraping up the bus-fare – but I couldn't see eye to eye with them over the gown. I said Joan Crawford had it right – a padded shoulder demands a platform shoe.
Ursula	I don't really notice clothes – I've had this for years.
Kent	My mother had something similar.
Ursula	Really?
Kent	She used to throw it over her bubble car in the cold weather.

---

61 Scottish actress. VW was such a fan she read all three of her memoirs and cast her as an old woman delivering a fireside tale in the second series of *ASOTV*. VW must have remembered this joke structure when she was writing 'Self-Service' (see note on p 272).

Ursula	This is a lovely old farm table, isn't it? Do you like stripped pine?
Kent	No, I don't. I was brought up in a dresser drawer, so all this brings back the stench of unbearable poverty.
Ursula	Oh goodness! Will you be able to clean it, then, do you think?
Kent	Oh yes. In fact I shall probably get a better finish if I'm shuddering.
Ursula	You see, being a novelist, I get rather engrossed, rather tend to let the housework go . . .
Kent	Mm, it's the first time I've seen windows so dirty they were soundproof.
Ursula	I've been working so hard, I must sort myself out, change this dress . . .
Kent	You know that soup down your front?
Ursula	Whoops.
Kent	Well, they don't make it any more. And I wouldn't go swimming till you've washed your hair; it could be another Torrey Canyon.[62]
Ursula	It's just my deadline – my novel . . .
Kent	There's only one woman novelist struck home with me: Shirley Conran, *Superwoman* – I could not put it down.
Ursula	The new one, *Lace,* have you read that?
Kent	How they could call it explicit! I read right through and I was still no wiser over getting felt-tip off formica.
Ursula	Do you think you'll be able to take this little job?
Kent	Not really, no. I couldn't clean for a woman, I find them a very unnecessary sex.
Ursula	But my name was on the card, it was a woman's name.
Kent	That's no real indication of gender; it could have been an auxiliary fireman dropping a heavy hint.[63]
Ursula	So I can't twist your arm?

---

62 Oil spill off Land's End in 1967.

63 There are plenty of such jokes about gender in VW's work that she doubtless wouldn't have attempted today.

Kent	I'd rather you didn't touch anything of mine. I'm very squeamish, skin-wise. In fact my social life took a real up-turn when I found they did Marigold gloves in large sizes.
Ursula	You're a novelist's dream, I could listen to you all after-noon – do stay.
Kent	No, I can't settle. I keep fretting about dysentery.
Ursula	Oh, just a few secs. I mean, where are you from, for instance?
Kent	Well, I was born under a pile of anthracite on the East Lancs Road. My father was a steeple-jack; he got drunk one day and never came down. I left home at fifteen when my mother caught me in bed with a Bleachmatic.[64] I toured the working-men's clubs with a magic act; I used to close with a song.[65] When I got better at it I used to saw myself in half and finish with a duet. Then I went to Monte, modelling . . .
Ursula	I'd forgotten all about him.
Kent	Who?
Ursula	Monty Modlyn.[66]
Kent	Monte Carlo, as a model. Got into drugs, marijuana, then cocaine, then Shake 'n' Vac. Then I became a monk, but we had words over my safari jacket.
Ursula	Do you have a close relationship with anyone?
Kent	Well, I've hung round a few lavatories, but I usually only stay long enough to buff up the taps. I'm a loner. There'll never be more than one slice in my toaster.
Ursula	Do you still see your mother?
Kent	Oh yes, I go round once a week, take her some Duraglit or a packet of firelighters. I do have four brothers.
Ursula	What do they do?

64 Automatic bleach dispenser.
65 In his professional guise of The Great Soprendo, VW's magician husband Geoffrey Durham had had just such a tough baptism a couple of years earlier.
66 TV and radio reporter.

Kent	They're a string quartet.
Ursula	So is cleaning your main source of income?
Kent	Well, I won quite a bit of Northumberland in a raffle, so I don't go short.
Ursula	So, you don't really need this job?
Kent	No.
Ursula	What pity! You know, I'd love to put you in a novel.
Kent	Oh, you can put me in a novel.
Ursula	Really?
Kent	Piece of pastry – two pounds an hour, four hours a week, I can squeeze you in between Beryl Bainbridge's seventh, and Melvyn Bragg's twenty-fourth.[67] Just change my name and call me broad-shouldered, all right?

---

67 This gag about Bragg's productivity was recycled from *W&W*: 'Next week I'll be talking to Melvyn Bragg about his twenty-ninth Cumbrian novel.'

KITTY: TWO[68]

Kitty   Well, I've come back, as you can see. Kitty. I wasn't struck either way but it was too wet to prick out my seedlings so here I am. Excuse me.

She fiddles with her tongue at a back molar.

The boys in flat five gave me a lattice jam puff to take with and the pips are playing me up. I say pips – I happen to know the jam factory's not quarter of a mile from a firm dealing in balsa wood novelties, so draw your own conclusions.

She gets the pips out.

That's it. They're all my own. In our block, it's always my gnashers they call on if they can't unscrew their dandelion and burdock. One of these fillings is French actually. I went on the hover to Boulogne with the Rummy Club, and we were having a grand time with some pop and a tray of bonfire toffee, when, crack, there I am with bits of molar all down my wind-cheater. I should never have crunched because it was Helen Murchison's toffee, and

---

68 Not broadcast.

she doesn't know a soft ball from a dust-pan and brush.

Anyway, consternation all round. In fact Margery Hunt
went green, teeth are her *bête noire*, but I think that's
because a Swiss dental mechanic once fumbled with her
pedal pushers. Now that, for me, would have turned me
off Toblerone, but then if we all thought the same, we'd
have smaller shopping centres.

So – we land at Boulogne, and I said from the look of
those lavatories there won't be a British Consul here, we
shall have to ask round. Well, I guessed that the French
for dentist would be *donteeste*, knowing how they love to
drag a word out, and so it proved.

Helen Murchison reckons to know a bit of the lingo,
and she popped me a few words on the back of a *Family
Circle* – just the bare essentials: my name's Kitty, could
you bung up my hole till I get back to Blighty type thing.
I found a lovely man who spoke quite good English,
went a bit blank when I mentioned Shepherd's Pie . . .
he patched me up and said something about money, but
I just laughed. That was seven years ago, and I can still
crack a Brazil without wincing.

Kitty checks her watch.

It's never twenty to? This has never been the same since
it went in the Bournvita. I had my friend Win with me
from Kidderminster, and I think we'd had a couple of
liqueur chocolates too many.

I don't drink as a rule, not wishing to have a liver the
size of a hot-water bottle. If I need a 'buzz', as I call it,
I have a piccalilli sandwich with Worcester sauce; that
takes your mind off your bunions, believe you me.

I mean, alcohol in excess can cause untold misery, not to mention the bother of humping the empties. A previous lady below me – I shan't name names (do they get this in Cardiff?) – she would come in at a quarter to six, with her carrier bulging, and it wasn't with Arctic Roll, and by eight fifteen she'd be out by the bins, shouting about coloureds. It's never bothered me, race. I don't care if people are navy blue so long as they don't spit up. There was a lot of that in Boulogne, I remember. I said to Marge, they can stick their bread, I couldn't live here.

Well, I can't stop anyway. There's a play on the radio tonight, set in a maisonette, so I shall have my lobes pricked for *faux pas*.

Kitty gets up as before.

Who took charge of my butty-box? Butty! Tuh.

JUST AN ORDINARY SCHOOL

Film. The school hall: assembly. Girls are singing hymns. One girl, Anthea, is singled out.

Anthea *(Voice Over)* There are all sorts of girls here, even coloured girls, though they tend to be princesses mainly, but really, on the whole, it's just an ordinary school.

The common room. Babs, Anthea and Ceal[69] are lounging about, chatting. It is all very posh.

Male Interviewer *(Voice Over)* And do you ever feel guilty about your fathers spending five thousand pounds a term on you?

Anthea Not really, do you? I don't really.

Babs My father would only spend it on booze or something.

Ceal New taps for his yacht or something.

Interviewer *(Voice Over)* But I mean some parents can't spend that amount of money on their daughters' education.

Anthea Oh, can't they? No, I suppose no . . .

Babs But you make an effort, don't you?

Ceal Yes, you find the money, because my cousin's father's

---

69 How VW and other friends addressed Celia Imrie.

a duke, and he's awfully poor actually, and they sold a
Gainsborough, quite a hideous one actually, and that sort
of brought in enough loot to cover quite a few terms . . .

Babs   Anyway, you don't have to have all the extras.

Anthea   Scuba diving – quite a lot of the girls don't do that now,
do they?

Ceal   Or ballooning, hot-air ballooning. There's only about
ten girls here with their own balloons now.

Interviewer *(Voice Over)* What I mean is: does it make you work
harder, knowing the amount that's been invested in you?

Anthea   No.

Ceal   I mean, a lot of things one learns here, they're not really
going to be very much use when one leaves.

Babs   I mean, we're not going to talk Latin, are we?

Laughter.

Anthea   Or French![70]

Laughter.

Ceal   I mean tying my own shoe-laces, I just won't ever have to
do that . . . so why should I spend hours learning it?

Babs   Or cordon bleu.

Anthea   No, I think cordon bleu's quite good, because, if you're
in for the evening, right, and you're not being taken out
to dinner, and, say, cook's given notice or something,
you might need to know how to cook, or you might
really get quite hungry . . . Actually, I cooked chips once.

Babs and **Ceal**   Oh you didn't, what a fib!

Anthea   Well, I stood jolly near while somebody else did, so shut
up.

---

70 Fear of learning languages was, for VW, a classless foible of Englishness. Anthea won't learn
French, and Kitty can't speak it either (see 'Kitty: Two').

They collapse laughing.

The common room. The girls are as before.

Interviewer *(Voice Over)* The feeling in the town seems to be that the pupils here are rather snobbish and stand-offish.

Ceal People just get the wrong idea.

Babs Just because one's father's Lord of the Admiralty or something, doesn't mean you're posh, particularly.

Anthea My father hasn't even got a title. He sent it back, so . . .

Ceal People seem to think we sit around eating caviar all day long.

Anthea When actually we've only had it three times this term.

Babs And it's jolly cheap caviar anyway.[71]

The dining hall. The girls are queuing up for dinner, holding out thin, white gilt-edged plates.

Anthea Oh, yuk! *Dauphinoise*, no thanks. What's that?

Dinner Lady *Brochet aux champignons de rosée.*

Anthea OK, but not too much.

Babs What is it, Anth?

Anthea Boring old *brochet aux champignons.*

Babs Oh, tediosity.

The common room, as before.

Interviewer *(Voice Over)* What do you think about working-class girls?

Anthea Well, I think there have to be some, otherwise it would be so hard to get served in shops and things.

Ceal And for factories, I think factories would close down, actually, if it wasn't for working-class people.

---

71 Cut from 'I mean tying my own shoe-laces' to here.

Interviewer *(Voice Over)* Couldn't you and your friends work in
              them?

Anthea   We'd be hopeless, honestly. We'd just get sacked, I think.

Interviewer *(Voice Over)* Babs?

Babs   I can barely fit my bassoon together.[72]

Ceal   Actually, my aunt worked in a factory during the war; it
              was her factory, and she said a lot of the girls there were
              really quite decent.

Anthea   On the whole, I think it's better off if we just don't mix,
              that's why it's so nice here, having the electronic gates,
              and the moat . . .

---

*School hall: prize-giving. The orchestra is playing as a girl
leaves the stage.*

Headmistress And now the Oswald Mosley[73] prize for public speak-
              ing. And the nominations are Elizabeth Finsbury, Nella
              Parsley-Donne, Chung Lee Suk, and Anthea Fern Witty.
              Whoops, having trouble with the envelope, and the
              winner is – Anthea Fern Witty.

*Cheers from the audience. Anthea runs to the front as the
orchestra plays a jolly showbiz tune very badly. Anthea and
the headmistress kiss, as she takes her prize.*

Anthea   Oh gosh, I just want to say I'm thrilled to get this . . . I'd
              really like to accept it on behalf of Miss Hewitt and Mrs
              Winchester. I'd like to thank Babs and Ceal for all the
              marvellous help they've been to me – and to everybody
              in the Upper Fifth, I love you – this is for you.

---

72 This and the preceding line were cut.

73 Powerful orator, leader of the British Union of Fascists. Married Diana Mitford in the home of
Joseph Goebbels in 1936. Hitler was a guest. He and his wife were interned from 1940 to 1943.

TURKISH BATH

Two female attendants, both in bikinis over their everyday clothes, with corporation towels round their heads, are chain-smoking and viewing the proceedings.

Thelm	My God, if her bum was a bungalow she'd never get a mortgage on it.[74]
Pat	She's let it drop.
Thelm	I'll say. Never mind knickers, she needs a safety net.
Pat	She wants to do that Jane Fonda.
Thelm	That what?
Pat	That exercise thing – nemobics.
Thelm	What's that?
Pat	Our next-door does it. We can hear her through the grate. You have to clench those buttocks.
Thelm	Do you? She'll never get hers clenched – take two big lads and a wheelbarrow. Who's she clenching them for, anyway?
Pat	Who, next-door? She's remarried again. He's black with an Austin Maestro.
Thelm	Well, she's got someone to notice then, hasn't she? Our Jack wouldn't. Liberace could come in with a long-line

---

74 Changed to 'were a bungalow'. JW made Thelma's speech patterns more northern.

	bra but our Jack wouldn't twig on. First night of our honeymoon, I was in bed, he was making a hutch.
Pat	What for?
Thelm	Bugger only knows. Only bloody animal we've got's him. Filthy. I'm taking his vest[75] to the Antiques Road Show. You're separated, aren't you?
Pat	He's living in the loft. He's got the lilo and the slow cooker; we don't speak.
Thelm	That's the blue of our Margaret's shower curtain.
Pat	Where.
Thelm	Them varicose veins, there.
Pat	Nice.
Thelm	Our Margaret's coming off the cap. Says it's dangerous.
Pat	That's the pill.
Thelm	Is it? I better pop her a note through.
Pat	Can you not phone?
Thelm	The doctor says I haven't to dial.
Pat	What's that scar on Mrs Critchley? Appendix?
Thelm	No, it's just where she's nodded off on her Dick Francis.[76] It's very levelling, a Turkish bath, isn't it? Take Lady Templeton, fur coat, Justice of the Peace – to me she's just jodhpur thighs and an inverted nipple.
Pat	Is Miss Hardy all right? – she's very still.
Thelm	She's either passed out or passed on. Either way *(she drags on her fag)* I'm finishing this.[77]
Pat	That's her from the flower shop, isn't it? Her with yellow flip-flops on.
Thelm	Them's her feet, you traycloth.
Pat	Isn't she bony?
Thelm	Well, I'm not rubbing her down. Like trying to massage a xylophone.

---

75 Changed to 'truss'.

76 Former jockey whose crime novels were set in the racing world.

77 Cut from 'It's very levelling' to here.

There is the sound of a splash, a shriek, a gurgle.

	That's another dropped dead in the cold plunge. Water's too cold. It's getting embarrassing – men coming round to collect their wives and you're saying, sorry she's dead and here's her teeth in a jiffy bag.
Voice	We're ready for a rub down!
Thelm	Hang on! Where's loofah?
Pat	Dog's had it.

Thelm picks up a foul scrubbing brush.

Thelm   This'll do. You bring the Vim.

They amble off.

KITTY: THREE

Kitty is caught unawares, sipping her fifth cream sherry, and chatting affably to Morag.

Kitty No, honestly Morag, I do think that Brillo has helped your freckles. What? Oh, hello. We've been having a running buffet for the last programme. We all mucked in on the nosh; I did my butter-bean whip – it's over there in a bucket. And the director did us a quiche. I suppose it's his acne but I definitely detected a tang of Clearasil.

The producer didn't cook, thank goodness. She's a nice girl, but when someone chain-smokes Capstan Full Strength and wears a coalman's jerkin, you're hardly tempted to sample their dumplings.

Her empty sherry glass is replaced with a full one.

The first day I met her she said, 'I'm a radical feminist lesbian'; I thought, what would the Queen Mum do? So I just smiled and said, 'We shall have fog by tea-time.' She said, 'Are you intimidated by my sexual preferences?' I said, 'No, but I'm not too struck on your donkey-jacket.' Then it was, 'What do you think of Marx?' I said, 'I think their pants have dropped off but you can't fault their broccoli.'[78] She said, 'I'm referring to Karl Marx, who as you know is buried in Highgate Cemetery.' I said, 'Yes I did know, but were you aware that Cheadle Crematorium holds the ashes of Stanley Kershaw, patentor of the Kershaw double gusset, to my mind a bigger boon[79] than communism.' I said, 'Don't tell me the Russian women are happy, down the mines all day without so much as a choice of support hose?'

Her glass is topped up.

It's all right, leave the bottle. In Russia, show the least athletic aptitude and they've got you dangling off the parallel bars with a leotard full of hormones. And what has China ever given the world? Can you really respect a nation that's never taken to cutlery? We bring them over here and what do they do? They litter the High Street with beansprouts. I know what you're going to say – what about the Chinese acrobats?

Kitty is a little inebriated by this stage.

Over-rated. I could hop up on a uni-cycle and balance a wheelbarrow on my eyebrows but I'm far ... too ... busy. If I was to turn to juggling I should never get any rummy played.

Not that I think Britain's perfect. I see life each week from the train window of my Cheadle Saver, and I think I can safely say, people today aren't pegging enough out.[80]

---

78 In the recording, this line is inaudible thanks to studio laughter.
79 Changed to 'a far bigger boon'.
80 Added: 'Well you should see what I see.'

If I was Prime Minister, and thank goodness I'm not, because I've been the length and breadth of Downing Street and never spotted a decent wool shop. But if I were, I would put a hot drinks machine into the Houses of Parliament and turn it into a leisure centre. The income from that would pay off the National Debt, and meanwhile we could all meet in Madge's[81] extension. I would also put three pence on the price of a flip-top bin, because I don't like them, and use the spare cash to nationalise the lavatory industry, resulting in a standard flush.

I would confer knighthoods on various figures in the entertainment and sporting world, namely David Jacobs[82], Pat Smythe[83] and Dolly from Emmerdale Farm.

Before I leave you, I must say I've much loved coming here every week to put you right, and I'd just like to pass on a piece of advice given to me by a plumbing acquaintance of my father's. It's an old Didsbury saying, and I've never forgotten it.

Kitty has forgotten it. She sits blankly. No, she can't remember it.

---

81 Changed to 'Helen Murchison'.
82 Broadcaster, best known for presenting *Juke Box Jury*.
83 Showjumper.

WHITHER THE ARTS?[84]

TV studio, arts programme.

Presenter Later on in 'Whither the Arts?' we'll be visiting the Arnolfini Gallery in Bristol, and taking a look at their Sculpture 84 exhibition, the centre-piece of which is the controversial twenty-foot ironing board made entirely from Driving Test rejection certificates. But first, the much publicised musical *Bessie!*, which opens at last in the West End this week, and Deb Kershaw has been in on the rehearsals, and has sent us this report.

Film. Rehearsal room. People are hanging about. Deb is interviewing the director, the exceedingly pompous fifty-year-old Sir Dave Dixon.

Deb Could you just tell us a little bit about *Bessie!*, Sir Dave? It's a biographical musical.

Dave Yes, it tells the story of Bessie, Bessie Bunter, who was an amazing lady . . .

Deb Sorry, I thought Bessie Bunter was a fictional character.

---

84 In the script, there are no stage directions for gags that were evidently devised on the spot. At the end of 'One Day', Carla breaks the spell by coughing. As the company dances in 'Bessie', they rip away Bessie's school uniform to reveal a sexy basque.

Dave	No, Bessie was a real person, very much so, a real person, and she led an incredible life, actually . . .
Deb	What about Billy Bunter, was he real?
Dave	But oh yes. Though it seems unlikely that he wore those check trousers we – er – see – er – in the illustrations.[85]
Deb	Did you commission the musical, or . . . ?
Dave	I was sent a play about Bessie Bunter, whom I've always been fascinated by, and the very same day I bumped into the American composer, Hamley Marvisch,[86] who said he had a few tunes left over from his last flop, and did I have a show he could dump them in? So two days and a bottle of Scotch later, we'd finished *Bessie!* A day to write the show and a day to think of the exclamation mark.
Deb	Has it altered much from the original play?
Dave	We've opened it up a little. The play was very much Bessie Bunter's schooldays, the fat girl with the little round glasses. We've played around with it, we've brought in the Spanish Civil War, the McCarthy witch hunts, that's a nice duet, great dance routine in Sainsbury's with the whole company on shopping trolleys . . .
Deb	But Bessie's still fat, presumably?
Dave	Well, it's mentioned. We've made it a mental fatness rather than a physical thing. We can't really have a great fat lump walloping across the stage for two hours.
Deb	Is the writer amenable to all these changes?
Dave	Yes, he was fine, most happy . . .
Deb	Is he here today?
Dave	No, he's had some sort of an accident. I think he fell off Chelsea Bridge with some bricks in his pocket, but we're coping . . .[87]

---

85 This and the preceding line were cut.

86 Marvin Hamlisch, a prolific composer of musicals and soundtracks, best known for *A Chorus Line*, 'The Entertainer' from *The Sting* and 'Nobody Does It Better' from *The Spy Who Loved Me*.

87 Cut from 'Is the writer'.

Rehearsal room. Thirty-five-year-old serious actress, Carla, stands by pianist in rehearsal clothes. She is very serious, constantly coughing or clearing her throat.

Carla No, I shan't sing out today, Dennis. I really am going to have to be awfully careful.

Deb Sorry to interrupt, Carla.

Carla No, don't worry, Deb.

Deb Now, you're playing the main rôle, Bessie?

Carla Bessie, yes – great challenge.

Deb Is it a difficult rôle?

Carla Bessie Bunter was actually an incredibly complex person, I've been steeping myself in the literature, and Bessie is so like me, so many similarities, it's quite spooky.

Deb What have you been reading?

Carla *Bessie Bunter Goes to the Circus:* now, I went to the circus – that's rather a remarkable coincidence. I've just read *Bessie Bunter Goes Caravanning:* now, I have an aunt who has a caravan, so I've been down and had a look at it. *(Coughs.)* Excuse me, I've got pneumonia.

Deb Beryl Reid always says she starts with the shoes; if the shoes are right, the character's right. Is that your method?

Carla I start with the bra. If the bra fits, everything falls into place.

Deb What's the song you're rehearsing?

Carla This comes after Bessie has had a secret romance with Anthony Eden, played marvellously by Derek Griffiths[88], and she knows it's only a matter of time before he goes back to the – was it the Conservative government?[89] Anyway, it should be very effective, I'm wearing beige, and she knows she isn't going to see him again, and musn't see him for his sake – it's called 'One Day'.

She sings.

88 Best known in 1985 as a presenter of *Play School*.
89 Changed to 'Conservative party'.

One day,
a feeling-sorry-that-you've-gone day
I will maybe write a note
send it to float
right to your door.
I won't sign it.
I'll just deliver it and go
and no-one but you will know
who I wrote it for.

One day,
a feeling-slightly-put-upon day.
I will maybe send a rose
that no-one knows
from whom it came.
I won't sign it,
I'll just leave it in the hall,
Maybe blow a kiss that's all,
I won't leave my name.

One day,
a wishing-I'd-become-a-don day
I will maybe try and grab
a London cab
to your bungalow
I won't see you,
I won't even ring the bell,
I will simply wish you well,
then I'll turn and go.

The stage is covered in exhausted dancers. Rows and banging are going on, the piano is covered in eighty-seven coffee cups, Carla is sobbing in the stalls, with pals trying to comfort her. Sir Dave sits in the front stalls, affable and relaxed as before, with Deb.

Deb *(Voice Over)* The show opens tonight, there have been many changes, the original cast has been fired, and the show drastically rewritten.

Deb You've gone back to the original concept, Sir Dave?

Dave This was vital, I feel. I mean, Bessie Bunter is a fat schoolgirl – that's the show in a nutshell. It's about being fat, being at school – it's very exciting.

Deb So you've cast a fat actress?

Dave The fatness is crucial. I've been researching into this pretty thoroughly, over breakfast. Do you know that over 89 per cent of people in this country are overweight? Now, that's a lot of tickets. The number we're about to see, if they ever get their *(bleep)* fingers out, is the Act One finale. *(Shouts.)* When you're ready, for Christ's sake, thank you!

The company prepare for the song.

And it's really all about finding yourself, saying take it or leave it, this is me. Because I believe all humans have a value and a right to be respected. *(He turns round to Carla.)* Get the *(bleep)* out of here, Carla, will you? I don't really want snot all over the plush, love. OK Dennis!

'Bessie' walks on-stage dressed as per the Frank Richards books. During the number she rips off her wig, glasses, and gymslip to reveal blonde hair and skin-tight dress. She is backed by a chorus line.

Bessie *(sings)* One day I was Bessie Bunter.
Who was she?
She was just a punter
She was nobody.

Then suddenly
one hot night

had a brainwave
like a spotlight.
Wave goodbye to Bessie,
say hello to me!

Me!
I'm going to be free
I'm gonna to do all those things I've never done before
open the door!
Let's even the score.
I'm looking for life to go and kick it in the crutch
just a touch
to make it clear
that Bess is here
with her one-woman junta
please watch out for Bessie Bunter.

Me!
who else could it be?
I'm gonna go bleach my hair,
wear clothes that show my tits
at the Ritz
I'm Bessie the Blitz
I'm gonna make Dolly Parton look like Meryl Streep
I mean cheap
I mean bad
drive men mad
to make this girl surrender
will they get to my pudenda?
Don't answer that; dance!

The company dances.

Yes!
Here's looking at Bess!
Here's looking at thirteen stone of sex

who can it be?
well it's me!
come and see
look at me!
you'll agree
it's all me!

At the end of the number she completely drops out of character.

They're going to have to change this floor, I'm sorry . . .

MARGERY AND JOAN: THREE

Joan	And we'll have more needlework hints next week, when Philippa will be showing us how to stitch up the mouth of a talkative friend or relative. And now, as usual on Fridays, we're going over to Margery to see what sort of week she's been having. Hello, Margery, what sort of week have you been having?
Margery	Hello Joan. Well, I've been having a very hectic time. On Monday, my husband and I tiled our bathroom – more on that later – and on Tuesday we filed for divorce.
Joan	And so do you think you might follow the trend, Margery, of the rather worn-out middle-aged woman shacking up with a much younger man?
Margery	Well, it's definitely worth looking into, Joan. One nice thing I do like about younger men is that they tend not to wear pyjamas.
Joan	By pyjamas you mean nightwear generally?
Margery	Yes, and striped garments in particular.
Joan	Yes, because, I know from our postbag, Margery, that many of our viewers find folding pyjamas quite an arduous task.
Margery	That's right, Joan, often leading to lower back pain, depression, dependence on tranquillising drugs, and sadly, alas, to suicide.

Joan	Gosh. But you've also been looking at double glazing, haven't you?
Margery	Cheap double glazing, Joan.
Joan	With the emphasis on the cheap rather than the glazing, Margery?
Margery	Absolutely. So –
Joan	So, in effect, we don't have to spend four or five thousand pounds keeping our homes draught-free.[90]
Margery	No. So –
Joan	So how do we go about it?
Margery	Sorry, could you just move away; your breath smells – thanks. Right – a new report just out reports that most of the heat-loss lost from rooms is actually escaping through the glass. That's the see-through part of the window. Now double-glazing can cover up the glass, but it can't take it away. Now a new firm has come up with a revolutionary and much cheaper idea of taking the glass away, and bricking up the spaces where the windows used to be. And hey presto, no glass, no draughts, no heat-loss.
Joan	No light.
Margery	No, I suppose not, Joan.

Fade in music, fade out dialogue.

Joan	I suppose you'll prefer to be in the dark, Margery, if you're planning to sleep with lots of younger men?
Margery	Or I may just blindfold them in the lobby, Joan; I'm fairly loose either way.

---

90 Changed to 'three or four or five thousand pounds'.

MADWOMAN[91]

An oldish, crazy-looking tramp/alcoholic woman is on a bench in the middle of some open concrete area, like a shopping precinct. She's mad and keeps shouting.

Woman   Oi! Who you looking at? Eh? Eh? You wanna get back on your spacecraft you do. Beam me up, beam me up, ha! I can tell spacemen a mile off – oh yes, I've had messages about this.

You look at me here, you think I know nothing – well they seen my brains at Paddington, and they were well pleased, well pleased. Shopping trolley! Tartan, tartan, what sort of pattern's that, eh? Are you Scotch? You don't look bloody Scotch. I been there – Scotch House – I seen their sweaters, very nice wool. They threw me out – I'll be back. Bloody Scotch people, I seen the Loch Ness Monster, and it wasn't talking to Eamonn Andrews,[92] neither.

Oi, trackshoes, trackshoes! Go on, get jogging, fat-arse! Ever had sex? Don't bother. Oh yeah, married twice, oh

91 Not broadcast.

92 Irish broadcaster who hosted *This Is Your Life* for over thirty years.

yeah, telly on, meatballs . . . Oi! Where's your meatballs, Mister? Ha! We don't need the lot of you, magotty old men, you wanna crawl back under your manholes – just leave us girls the sherry and du-vet. I bet she's got a duvet, old jiggle-tits there. They're coming off, bosoms – it's the Council. *(posh)* Bosoms are off this spring, I hear. Lucky for you, pleated skirt!

Oi! Shirley! Shirley Bassey! You're a bit of a blackie, ain't you? Sorry you saved up now, eh? Ten pounds for a pair of shoes! Huh! I'm off to China, outskirts of China, going down the Left Luggage, little plastic shoulder bag, and I won't write no post-cards.

Don't think I can't, khazi-features! I've had letters from right round the latitudes and I can lay hands on them, oh yeah, I can lay any amount of hands on them – no flicking danger.

What you been buying? Little panties? So's you can go jigging about your lounge? You won't be laughing when the Russians put paid to the hot weather. You're laughing now with your nice little strap shoes and your carrier bags, but they're on their way – the Russians are coming – they'll freeze your balalaika for you. Ha! Call yourself a man, Kim Novak? Filthy habits, the lot of you! Shopping about. Too much shopping going on. I'm on to the government about this; oh yeah, I can have this place sealed off – I'm on to it, I'm not joking, piss-belly! I know a lot of people in that line – Dave and Bob, heard of them?

And I'll be here tomorrow; I've had messages about this – this isn't the only planet in the world, jam-lips. *(Points to the bench.)* Nobody touch that!

She walks away, waving her arms about.

Voice Over That was a party political broadcast on behalf of the Conservative Party.

Barmy

THE SECOND VICTORIA WOOD SKETCH BOOK FEATURING 'ACORN ANTIQUES'

To Susie, Ceal, Duncan, and Julie – for the acting

BARMY

Barmy was published in the autumn of 1987, in time for Christmas. Most of its scripts came from the second series of *Victoria Wood As Seen on TV*, which had been broadcast nearly a year earlier. Kitty was back, as were Margery and Joan, while Kelly-Marie Tunstall made her print debut with tall tales from the bus stop. At the heart of the collection was the complete 'Acorn Antiques', Victoria's blissful and brilliant homage to all that was cheap and crass in British soaps.

But any fans who went straight out and bought the book for themselves were in for a surprise, because there was also something called 'The Making of Acorn Antiques'. This latest addition to Victoria's set of mockumentaries would not be broadcast until a week before Christmas when the *As Seen on TV Special* went out. So it may easily have looked like another of those discarded extras, that had been sprinkled through *Up to You, Porky*. The collection contained other as yet unseen sketches from the special: a loving spoof of *Doctor Who* and the zinger-rich showcase for Julie Walters that was 'Self Service'.

In *Barmy*, Victoria was even more loyal to the uncherished runts in her litter which for one reason or another had been cast aside. Nearly a quarter of the forty-one scripts would never make it onto TV. Opening the whole collection with one of them was a statement. Indeed, 'Nora' has a line that pretty much sums up Victoria's entire world view: 'Because life's not fair, is it? Some of us drink champagne in the fast lane, and some of us eat our sandwiches by the loose chippings on the A597.' The gag was quoted in countless tributes after Victoria's death in 2016 and surely belongs in any self-respecting dictionary of quotations. On the other hand, there was no room for 'Waitress!', better known as 'Two Soups'. Victoria may have considered it primarily visual rather than verbal, concluding that the sketch would not translate well to the page.

What else was there? This time, the continuity announcer made the cut, if only once. In the contents page, her entry is referred to as 'Susie (Continuity)' in honour of the actress who brought her to life. (Along with her co-stars, Susie Blake was a dedicatee of *Barmy*, 'for the acting'.) There was much Margery and Joan – perhaps even too much? – who, including the introduction, cropped up five times. 'Lady Police Serial', a parody of the TV drama *Juliet Bravo*, was originally written for the second series, then held back for the special and eventually squeezed out. Victoria would go on to write many more spoofs of police and detective dramas and, for some reason, none was ever broadcast.

As with *Up to You, Porky*, scripts which had been edited down during rehearsal and recording were now restored to their full length, above all 'Today in Hospital' and 'Mr Right'. Other discrepancies could be spotted by the more scholarly fan, especially in 'Acorn Antiques'. Many of the sight gags that Victoria scripted are there in print – Mr Clifford banging his head on the boom mic, for example. But a lot more – Mrs O loitering in view, or the camera having too direct a view of Miss Berta's gusset – would be found in rehearsal.

Across the series, the actors playing these characters gradually drew back the veil to reveal themselves. 'Why, why, why,' snapped the actress playing Mrs O, off camera in episode nine, 'do I always get those darn sunbeds, anybody know?' This was the germ of Bo Beaumont, of 'The Making of Acorn Antiques' and, many years later, *Acorn Antiques: The Musical!* The discovery that Mrs Overall had a name also gave Victoria the title of her collection.

Mrs Overall: When Mr Overall (no relation) was dying, he said,
    'Well, Boadicea, I shall never have to play another game of Travel
    Scrabble.'
Babs: Why did he call you Boadicea?
Mrs Overall: He was barmy, Miss Babs.

PREFACE

Joan	And now it's over to Margery, who's been looking at what's out on the bookstalls this week for those of us who enjoy a jolly good read. *(Strolls over.)* Hello Margery, what's out on the bookstalls this week for those of us who enjoy a jolly good read?
Margery	Hello Joan. Well there's a bumper crop of goodies available, and a varied assortment they are too.
Joan	Golly. For instance.
Margery	*Glamour*, a powerful family saga of a Salford mill girl's rise from the depression-hit thirties to the heights of Hollywood. There's *Saga*, a family story of height-hitting Hollywood glamour and power in the depression, and *Salford*, that's just very depressing.
Joan	And are they full of liberated thirty-five-year-old women doing unspeakably erotic things to bronzed muscly tycoons?
Margery	Yes they are, Joan, so to save a lot of tedious explanations I've brought you a book on tapestry.
Joan	Of course not everything in the publishing world is fiction, is it, Margery? There's non-fiction for instance.
Margery	That's right, Joan. Investigative journalist Campbell Wemyss has brought out *Crippen – Was It Pre-Menstrual Tension?*, and *Country Diary of an Edwardian Lady* lovers will be delighted to hear that there will be a new cake tin out next month.

Joan   And finally and very quickly, Margery, comedy.

Margery   Finally and very quickly, Joan, the funniest book for
                  years fell into my lap this morning. Devastatingly out-
                  spoken, a real rib-tickler but with plenty of pathos as
                  well, it really deserves a much wider audience.

Joan   And that's Victoria Wood's second book of sketches, is it,
                  Margery?

Margery   No, it's your diary, Joan, you left it on the incinerator in
                  the second floor Ladies. Bye!

Joan   Bye!

NORA[93]

Nora   Hello. Have you ever planted your bulbs out in the Autumn and watched them come up in the Spring? Have you? Lovely, aren't they?

Have you ever been out in the garden just after an April shower, and mmm, breathed in that wonderful fresh smell? It's the grass and the leaves saying thank you, really, isn't it?

And have you ever been up on a step-ladder and lost your balance, and grabbed at a frayed light fitting with your bare hand, and been electrocuted? I have. Ooh, it didn't half sting.

And have you ever tried to lose weight by having your jaws wired together, and found you were up half the night trying to liquidize peanut brittle? My neighbour has.

---

93 Not broadcast.

Because life's not fair, is it? Some of us drink champagne
in the fast lane, and some of us eat our sandwiches by the
loose chippings on the A597.[94]

Ooh – and it makes me mad when people complain – I
mean if it starts to rain what do you do? Stick a brolly
up.

And do you know what I'd like to do to these moaners
and miserable complainers – stick a brolly up! I would.

---

94 In VW's live show of the same year, the A597 turned up in Margaret the Usherette's monologue: 'She used to run a restaurant. Well it was a caravan in a lay-by on the A597, but she was
quite noted for her boiled onions.'

NO GOSSIP

Tea shop. Two nice ladies

First lady Did you go to see 'Macbeth'?

Second lady Mmmm. Wasn't a patch on 'Brigadoon'.[95] There was some terrible woman who kept washing her hands, saying she'd never get them clean. I felt like shouting out 'Try Swarfega'. We walked out in the end.

First lady Why?

Second lady Someone said 'womb'.

First lady No.

Second lady Is said to Col – get your duffle – two pounds on a box of Quality Street and someone says womb.

First lady It's happening all over.

Second lady Oh I know. In my magazine story last week, an unmarried couple slept together.

First lady Tuh.

Second lady I mean, in my day, in a magazine, you didn't have sex, you had a row of dots.

First lady That's right, three dots.

Second lady In fact, still if Colin turns to me in the night, I just tap him three times on the shoulder and he goes to sleep quite happily.

---

95 American musical by Lerner and Loewe set in a mysterious Scottish village.

First lady   Dot, dot, dot, yes.

Second lady   Except of course the children grew up thinking anything in Braille[96] was pornographic.

First lady   How are the children?

Second lady   Well, Susan's still Assistant Catering Manager at
Wilkinsons, and she says, in a couple of years, if she
plays her cards right – she could become er, a catering
manager's girlfriend.

First lady   Oh, that's good.

Second lady   And of course she's saving up for her bottom drawer.

First lady   Oh, what's she got?

Second lady   Just the knobs so far, but – oh, and she failed her test
again.

First lady   Oh, what on?

Second lady   Something and nothing. Not looking in the mirror,
and failing to report a couple of accidents.

First lady   And is Tony still in the SAS?

Second lady   No, he left.

First lady   I think you do have to be incredibly tough to stick it;
the violence . . .

Second lady   And then you see, the balaclava was so itchy. And now
he's a lighthouse keeper.

First lady   Goodness, that must be a lonely life – doesn't it affect
him mentally?

Second lady   No, he keeps busy, grows a lot of vegetables. And he's
fallen in love with a tomato.

First lady   An English tomato?

Second lady   Oh yes. He's sent us polaroids, she looks quite nice, still
a bit green – but –

First lady   Has he got over his divorce?

Second lady   I think so. His wife got custody of the stereo and they
sold the children.

First lady   And do you ever see your daughter-in-law?

Second lady   I do, funnily enough – she's our window cleaner.

---

96 Changed to 'Morse code'.

First lady   That's women's lib for you.

Second lady No, she's under a man. He's the skilled half, she just dunks the chammy. Anyway what about you?

First lady   Oh me? Same as ever.

Second lady Still on that diet?

First lady   Still on my diet, still married to Ken, and still General Secretary of the United Nations.

Second lady No gossip then.

First lady   No . . .

MARGERY AND JOAN: ONE[97]

Joan	*(standing by a locked tank of water with a padlocked milk churn inside)* Well, your two minutes is up, Mr Jefferson, and I think we're going to have to leave it there for the time being. We'll possibly pop back a little later and see if Mr Jefferson did in fact manage to extricate himself from that milk churn. Now it's over to Margery to see what she's been getting up to this week. Hello, Margery – how's tricks?
Margery	Tricks? What do you mean?
Joan	I meant how are things going generally, Margery.
Margery	Oh, I thought Trix must be another of your god-awful friends in the Hush Puppies. *(Switching on the studio charm)* Hello, Joan. Now we all know about the frightening side-effects of barbiturate abuse, alcohol dependency and nicotine intake – but have you ever stopped to wonder about the dangers associated with these?

Shakes her closed fist à la Nescafé, and opens her palm to the camera.

Joan	Now correct me if I'm wrong, Margery, but you've got a handful of ordinary industrial ball bearings.

---

97 Not broadcast.

Margery	Well you are wrong, Joan, and I will correct you. Because what I'm holding is the contents of a standard fifty-gram packet of edible cake decorations.
Joan	Well I know that being hit over the head with an adjustable piano stool can give you a jolly nasty headache – but what's so dangerous about these little things, Margery?
Margery	The danger lies in the shiny metallic coating, Joan – the very sparkle that makes these little bimbos an indispensable part of every festivity and celebration from Christmas Day to Boxing Day.
Joan	And is the coating harmful, Margery?
Margery	No it's not, Joan. *(Picking up one ball)* But were a ball to come into contact with a filling *(pointing one out)*, which can easily happen in a party situation . . .
Joan	Someone showing off . . .
Margery	Taking big bites to impress a girl; chewing with their mouth open –
Joan	I must admit I've done that.
Margery	Yes. The ball *(demonstrating)* makes contact with the filling and yaroo, an electric shock. Now one mild low-grade tingler every so often won't do too much damage – but if you've got a mouth full of fillings *and* a heavy cake eating habit – the sort of person who finds it difficult to refuse cake, or who needs cake to feel relaxed in a social situation – even the kind of compulsive chomper who doesn't eat it in public but takes a piece home wrapped in a serviette – then you could be at risk.
Joan	And how can we minimize that risk, Margery?
Margery	Just by taking a few simple precautions, Joan. *(Camera pulls back to show her feet encased in huge Wellingtons.)* Rubber footwear *(puts gloves on)*, insulated gloves, keep a fire blanket and portable resuscitator by the cake tin, have the phone number of your next of kin tattooed on an accessible part of your body – and – *(picking up cake and taking huge bite)* Happy Eating.

Music. Fade lights.

Joan   I never went back to the man in the milk churn.

Faint sound of ambulance siren.

Margery   *(mouth full of cake)* Too late now.

They look round vaguely.

MEN TALKING[98]

Men in close-up, talking in their own homes.

First man   *(sixties)* It was when I was at Freemans, I'd just started on the shop floor, and I was in the washroom, because you couldn't smoke on the floor, that's right – and my pal Eric said, 'Hey, Monkey' – this is before I was bald – 'Monkey – do you know anything about sex?' I said, 'No, I don't, do you?' And Eric said he didn't, but his brother knew. And his brother was on HMS Hastings[99], went down in forty-four, no survivors, so we never found out anything about it. Mind you – I suppose if I had got going with sex, I'd never have had this terrific involvement with miniature dynamos . . .

Second man   *(forties)* And the children were in bed, and June and I were watching the television – it was a nature thing, something about dangerous butterflies – and June turned the volume down and said, 'I'm having an affair.' Silence. Then I said, 'Who with?' She said, 'You don't know him, he's a carpet salesman.' I said, 'Oh.' She said, 'I've told him he can move in on Tuesday, and can we move the hatstand so he's got somewhere to stack his

---

98 Not broadcast.
99 VW must have just liked the name. The real HMS *Hastings* saw out the war.

underlay? Oh, and his name's Rory.' Which it was . . .

Third man *(thirties)* And she got more and more depressed. So I said, 'Look Sheila, if you're that desperate, go back to work and I'll stay at home and look after the baby.' So off she went. And I changed nappies, made the breakfast, did the hoovering, cleaned the cooker, made the beds, went shopping, fed the baby – and by lunchtime I'd had enough. I phoned Sheila at work – I said, 'You'll have to pack your job in, I can't stand it.' It's true.

TODAY IN HOSPITAL

Film. Morning. The front steps of a small hospital. A man is mopping the steps.

Corin   *(Voice Over)* It's seven-thirty in the morning. For some people this will just be an ordinary day, but for others accident or illness will mean they end up spending today in hospital.

TITLE 'TODAY IN HOSPITAL'

Corin hurries up the steps to the cleaner.

Corin   Good morning.
Cleaner   I don't mop steps as a hobby, you know.
Corin   How long have you worked at the hospital?
Cleaner   *(turning away)* They want to bring back National Service, in my opinion.

Corin goes into the hospital.

Casualty. Small and empty except for a young couple, Elaine and Conrad.[100] Corin goes over to the receptionist.

---

100 Though they have different names, anyone who'd seen the first series of *ASOTV* would have taken this dim couple as a reincarnation of Carl and Gail from 'Young Love'.

Corin	Is Casualty usually this quiet at this time in the morning?
Receptionist	It's as busy as can be expected, thank you.
Corin	Did you have a busy night?
Receptionist	We had a comfortable night and we're now resting.
Corin	Have you been put under a lot of pressure by the cuts in the National Health Service?
Receptionist	You'll have to talk to the doctor about that, but I'm sure there's nothing to worry about.
Corin	Thank you.

He goes over to Elaine and Conrad.

	May I ask what you're doing here?
Elaine	We've come about the test-tube babies and that.
Conrad	We want a test-tube baby.
Corin	Why, are there problems . . . ?
Elaine	Yes, we've only got a maisonette, so a little tiny test-tube one would be . . .
Corin	No, they grow to a normal size – they're conceived in the test-tube.
Elaine	Well, we'll never both fit in.

Small ward. Consultant sweeps up to woman's bed with group of students.

Corin	*(Voice Over)* It's ten-thirty and time for the consultant's ward round.
Doctor	Good morning, Mrs Jones.
Mrs Jones	Good morning, Doctor.
Doctor	How are we feeling?
Mrs Jones	Not too bad, apart from the agonizing pain.
Doctor	Good, good. You – let's see how much you've picked up. What can you tell me about Mrs Jones?
First student	She's wearing a nightie, Sir.
Doctor	And?

First student	And a bedjacket.
Doctor	You?
Second student	I rather think it's a cardigan.
Doctor	And how would you propose to find out?
Second student	I'd have it X-rayed, Sir.
Doctor	Allinson?
Third student	In view of the danger inherent in repeated X-rays, Sir, I'd prefer to have a period of observation.
Doctor	X-rays, observation – there's a very simple solution to all this. Winstanley?
Fourth student	Ask the patient.
Doctor	Ask the patient! If you want to know something about the patient, ask the patient! Mrs Jones – is that a bedjacket or is it a cardigan?
Mrs Jones	It's a bedjacket, doctor.
Doctor	Gentlemen – it is a bedjacket. Thank you Mrs Jones, and a very good morning to you.

Another ward. Two nurses, Della and Noreen, making a bed.

Corin	What made you want to be a nurse, Della?
Della	It was that telly programme, 'Angels'.[101] Seemed a nice job.
Corin	What particularly attracted you?
Della	The short hours.
Corin	Sorry?
Della	Half an hour, twice a week, seemed too good to be true. Which it was.
Corin	Noreen – what do you like about nursing?
Noreen	The challenge, the teamwork, the sense of responsibility, erm, the feeling that you're helping people, the satisfaction, the nurse – patient relationship and the drugs. Oh – and I quite like the apron.

---

101 BBC drama about student nurses broadcast from 1975 to 1983.

They smooth the sheets, pleased with the job. An old man's voice comes from under the bed.

Old man   Can I get back in now?
Della   *(shouting down)* No, you stay there Mr Dixon – then the bed stays nice and tidy, all right?
Old man   All right, nurse.

Office of Whizz Kid administrator, very high-tech. He is talking on the phone and checking details on a VDU.

Corin   *(Voice Over)* It's lunchtime, but hospital administrator Kevin Foley wouldn't dream of stopping to eat when there's deals to be done.
Kevin   Mrs Smith? Yes, I'm looking at the figures now – the waiting-list situation – fifteen months for a tonsillectomy, three years for a hip replacement, and five years for two seats in the Upper Circle for 'Cats'. Hip replacement – private? No problem – straight away. In fact there's a special offer this month – buy two hips, get one free. Yes, you can bring your own anaesthetic, though we have to charge corkage. Not at all, nice to do business with you Mrs Smith, *ciaou.*

Puts phone down.

Corin   I hear you've introduced some revolutionary schemes to help the hospital pay for itself?
Kevin   Oh, you heard about that? Yes, I'm glad to say, half of our morgue is now an extremely successful freezer centre.
Corin   Really.
Kevin   Tremendous. You can pop down there, pay your last respects and pick up a very competitive shoulder of lamb at the same time.

Phone rings.

Excuse me.[102]

Recovery room. Noreen shouting at an unconscious man on a trolley.

Corin   *(Voice Over)* It's five-thirty, and here is one of those private patients Kevin Foley is so keen to attract to the hospital. Adam McCalpine is just coming round from the anaesthetic after his operation.

Noreen   Mr McCalpine! Wake up, Mr McCalpine! The operation's over, it's all over, we're taking you back to the ward. Can you hear me?

Man   Mmmm . . .

Noreen   Can you open your eyes for me?

Man   Mmmm . . .

Noreen   And can you give me the number of your Access card?[103]

A corridor. Elaine and Conrad sit outside a door.

Corin   How are you getting on?

Elaine   We've been having tests.

Corin   Fertility?

Elaine   For something, I don't know if it was tility.

Conrad   I had to go in a bathroom with a sexy sort of magazine.

Corin   And how did you get on?

Conrad   I could read most of it.

Hospital entrance. Sirens wailing. Corin stands lit by the blue light of an ambulance. Ambulancemen/women rush by him with a stretcher.

---

102 Scene cut.
103 Scene moved to after the scene with Elaine and Conrad.

Corin	Eleven-thirty, the pubs are shut, in casualty things are hotting up.

Casualty. Corin goes into a curtained-off cubicle where a drunken man is sprawled on the bed.

Corin	Good evening.
Drunken man	That's very nice, very nice, I say good evening, you say good evening, that's all very nice.
Corin	What's wrong with you exactly?
Drunken man	God knows.
Corin	Are you ill?
Drunken man	I'm as fit as a pig – sorry, talking rubbish . . .
Corin	Why have you come to the hospital?
Drunken man	It's a nice little hospital, isn't it? Don't you agree? I think so, nice little marvellous little . . . nurse!

Nurse enters in a rush with a white coat, which she hands to the drunken man who gets off the bed and puts it on.

Nurse	Sorry – took me ages to find it.

He follows her out.

Now, suspected fractured skull, cubicle nine . . .

Outside the Hospital. Dawn. Same man mopping steps as before.

Corin	(*Voice Over*) Another night is over, and so a new day begins for Kevin and Della and Mrs Jones and Mr McCalpine . . .

Elaine and Conrad come down the steps.

Corin	So what happened, in the end?
Elaine	We didn't get one.
Corin	Didn't get what?
Elaine	A baby! They said you've to wait nine months or some-thing – and the things they wanted us to do!
Conrad	Sections of intercost, or something.
Elaine	It was horrible.
Corin	Well, everybody does it, you know.
Elaine	They don't! Come on, Conrad.

They walk away. Corin stands looking at the hospital. Man waves his mop.

Man	Go on, get out of it! You woolly article!

KITTY: ONE

Kitty   This wasn't my idea. *(Looks at watch.)* In fact, had it been
up to me, I'd have been on my second cream sherry in
Kidderminster by now. This lot *(gesturing vaguely and
disdainfully around)* – they phoned me up last Thursday.
I'd just settled down with a Claire Rayner[104] and a quarter of radishes, so I wasn't best pleased. I said, 'Who is it
and keep it brief, because I've a howling draught through
my architrave'; and if I'd wanted to freeze to death I'd
have gone with Scott to the Antarctic and made a day of
it.[105] She said, 'Its Morag from the television programme,
do you remember me?' I said, 'Yes, I do; I lent you two
cotton buds which I never saw back.' She said, 'I've got
the producer for you', so I said, 'I hope you've sealed
the envelope properly', which is an old golfing retort of
mine. On she comes – the producer – I could hear her
boiler-suit creaking even long-distance – 'Is that Kitty?'
I said, 'If it's not, this cardigan's a remarkably good fit.'
She said, 'Kitty – do you like fun?' I said, 'No, I don't. I
had enough of that in 1958 when I got trapped in a lift
with a hula-hoop salesman.' She said, 'Would you like to

---

104 Agony aunt. She was a celebrity guest in the second series of *ASOTV* (see note on 'Madeline',
p 283).
105 Cut from 'Who is it' to here.

come on our new programme? One of our regulars has a skin complaint and has to spend three months eating peanuts with the light off.'

I said, 'Well, I'm quite pushed busy-wise – I'm doing the costumes for the Rummy Club production of "The Sound of Music", and Helen Murchison's Second Act dirndl is a week's work in itself.' (She claims to be dieting but every time we have 'Doh a Deer a Female Deer' there's a terrible whiff of pear-drops.) But that's by the by-pass.

She said, 'Come to the studios, and we'll thrash it out woman to woman.' Well, she's as much like a woman as Charlie Cairoli,[106] but I just said 'Suit yourself' and rang off.

So I fixed up a lift with Mr Culverhouse in flat nine. Well, he owed me a favour and he has got a very roomy Vauxhall. It was no bother to drop me off because he has an artificial arm from the Western Desert and he was coming through to Roehampton anyway to have his webbing adjusted.

So I turn up – I popped into Marks on my way to return a – well, let's call it an item. I'm ushered into the producer – she hadn't changed – new haircut – if it hadn't been bright blue she'd have been a dead ringer for Stanley Matthews.[107] And she won't wear anything approaching a brassiere – when she plays ping-pong it puts you in mind of something thought up by Barnes Wallis.[108]

---

106 Clown.
107 Celebrated 1950s footballer who wore his hair swept back.
108 Inventor of the bouncing bomb, played by Michael Redgrave in *The Dam Busters*.

Well – she stubs out her Senior Service[109] and she says, 'Kitty, how can we tempt you?' and starts boasting about her big budget. I thought if it's that big, why don't you splash out on some foundation garments but I kept well buttoned. So I stated my terms. One – proper remuneration – I'd seen in the papers about Terry so-called Wogan and his astronomical figure – it wasn't my paper – it was wrapped round a small Savoy at my neighbour's. Two – I want to be chauffeur-driven each way; British Rail having gone completely mad in my opinion, all vertical blinds and chilli con carne[110] – and the driver must be blemish-free – because I'm not coming all the way from Cheadle glued to somebody's carbuncles. Three – I must have a decent dressing-room, and not that cubby-hole next to the chocolate machine. How you're expected to gather your thoughts up to the thud of a falling Bounty[111] I do not know. There's a bit of a dubious silence, and the producer says she'll have to ask upstairs – I thought that's leadership for you – where were you when they bombed Plymouth?

Anyway – we reached a compromise – I got what I wanted and they didn't. I've quite a nice dressing room, I have it Box and Cox with the late-night Vicar. And the chauffeur's called Kent. Kent! I said to him, 'That's not a name, it's a cricket team.'

Anyway – I must go. If we beat the traffic, Mr Culverhouse is taking me for a prawn salad at The Happy Rickshaw. Chinese, but we ask for the other menu. *(Getting up)* Morag! Tuh, there's no laying hands on her now she's engaged . . .

---

109 Filterless cigarette which took its name from the nickname for the Royal Navy. Also smoked by James Bond in Ian Fleming's novels.

110 Pronounced 'carn'.

111 Changed to 'in the face of a falling Bounty'.

MARGERY AND JOAN: TWO[112]

Joan	Fascinating as ever, Philippa, and I for one had never really realised how enjoyable and, I may say, hilarious welding could be. Now it's over to Margery for this week's topic of national importance.
	Strolls over.
	Hello, Margery, what's this week's topic of national importance?
Margery	Hello, Joan. Well, we like to pride ourselves on this programme that we cover areas of concern ignored or even overlooked by the media.
Joan	So what scandal or hitherto unrecognized social problem are we tackling today, Margery?
Margery	Unemployment, Joan.
Joan	Go on Margery, this is fascinating.
Margery	Now I'm not a statistician, Joan.
Joan	And you don't look like one, Margery, quite a bonus.
Margery	But I researched into this pretty thoroughly on my way to the studios this morning, in the mini-cab.
Joan	Because you don't drive, do you, Margery?
Margery	No, and so I'm very interested in something we'll be

---

112 Not broadcast.

looking at later, which is a specially adapted diesel-powered waterproof armchair.

Joan   But back to the dreary side of life for a moment, Margery. Unemployment – I've never heard of it. What is it?

Margery I'll deal with that in a moment Joan, but let me tell you this – it affects an awful lot of people.

Joan   How many people, Margery?

Margery Quite a few, Joan.

Joan   Are we talking about fifty-five-year-old-men in flat caps and bicycle clips, Margery?

Margery No, we're talking about unemployment. *(Looking round)* Has something been changed? Marion?

Joan   So if people are unemployed, and basically that means – what?

Margery It means they haven't got a job – Joan.

Joan   Really? As bad as that? Phew. So – I'm unemployed, I haven't got a job, what can I do?

Margery Well of course, there are always lots of jobs advertised in your local paper, and on display at the Job Centre, that's the nice place in the High Street with the orange paint, or if you prefer to work from home – perhaps you have a valuable Afghan hound who can't be left, or cleaning staff you don't trust, then it's worth considering setting yourself up as an investment broker, or writing a best-selling novel.

Joan   So basically there's plenty of work about if we're prepared to scout around for it?

Margery Absolutely, Joan.

They stroll over to another part of the set.

Joan   And what will you be looking at next week, Margery?

Margery Well, you won't be seeing me next week, because I'll be covered in an operating gown – but you will be seeing my gall bladder which Joan will be removing live in the studio by means of a revolutionary new process so simple it can be performed by a nursing sister, or in an emergency, a qualified librarian.

Joan   And I'm particularly looking forward to that, because not only have I never seen a gall bladder, I'm absolutely clueless as to its whereabouts, so I could be getting in quite a pickle.

Lights dim, music in. Joan sits in the armchair and whizzes about. Margery walks off the set.

Margery   I'm sorry, I'm going to talk to Marion about this, I'm not happy . . .

SALESMAN[113]

Living room. Salesman with large samples case, a few encyclopaedias scattered about, a reluctant woman leafing through one.

Man   So all in all, these encyclopaedias are a marvellous investment.

Woman   But I don't think we'd ever –

Man   I'm not saying you're going to read them every day of the week – but whenever you wanted to refer to them – they'd be there.

Woman   That's what bothers me – it's that basically they'd be lying about gathering dust – it's hard enough to keep the house clean as it is.

Man   *(whipping out 'Dustbuster'-type thing from the case)* In that case, may I show you this marvellous little gadget? Runs on re-chargeable batteries, you can do stairs, corners, soft furnishings, cleavages ha ha *(lunges at her – she fends him off)*.

Woman   No, I'm very happy with my own vacuum cleaner, thank you.

Man   *(whizzing it about)* Dog hairs, nails, it's a remarkable little machine, it really is.

---

113 Not broadcast.

Woman	No, stop please. No, the house is only difficult to clean because we're so near the main road, and we get a lot of dust in through the windows.
Man	*(putting away 'Dustbuster' and getting out double-glazing samples)* So you're not double-glazed? It's a marvellous investment, I'm not saying it's cheap, but with what you save in fuel bills, you'll have made it back in eighty or ninety years, no danger.
Woman	Yes, but how much money are we –
Man	What are you – four bed two recep? At a rough guess and using our own trained installation engineers, five thousand eight hundred and seventy-two pounds fifty pence, give or take.
Woman	That's awfully expensive.
Man	They bring their own tea-bags.
Woman	We can't really –
Man	Or you could install it yourself – I say 'you' – obviously one wouldn't envisage a woman hopping around on scaffolding – don't want someone looking up and catching sight of your panty-bits. But your husband could do it –
Woman	He couldn't really, he has a heart condition.
Man	Has he? That must be a worry to you.
Woman	Well, yes.
Man	*(putting away double-glazing and bringing out insurance leaflets and tables of figures)* Is he insured? If he's, what, forty-five, let's see, if he pays seven, ten, say twelve-pound premium, that's not a lot if you consider the price of fags, if he staggers on till two thousand and thirty-eight, make him ninety-seven-ish, he could pick up somewhere in the region of fifty-eight thousand pounds. And if he kicks the bucket prior to that you get the mortgage paid off, a nice lump sum, a mock crocodile handbag and a slo-cooker.
Woman	He is fully insured, thank you.
Man	Well, how about yourself, women's lib and all that?
Woman	No, I haven't got any –

Man   We've a nice ladies' package going, if you don't smoke
                 and come within the recommended doctor's whatsits.
                 Height?

Woman   Five foot four.

Man   Weight?

Woman   Well, I don't really see that – er –

Man   You ladies! Tut tut tut. A bid of a sweetie gobbler, say no
                 more. It is very easy to let those pounds pile on.

Woman   It certainly is.

Man   But getting them off? Another story. *(He whips out can
                 of diet formula from case.)* You would not believe the fab-
                 ulous success we're having with this unique liquid diet.
                 You can't get it in the shops – 300 calories a day, all the
                 essential vitamins and minerals you need, plus natural
                 vegetable fibre so no lavatory hang-ups. And you never
                 get bored because it's in a flavour. *(He shows her the can.)*
                 See? Flavour.

Woman   Well, to be honest – I find this modern-day emphasis on
                 physical appearance rather trivial and pointless – I feel
                 there must be more to life than the everyday here and
                 now . . .

Man   I agree *(putting diet away, bringing out illuminated model
                 of temple and prayer book)*. That's why I'm so thrilled to
                 be associated with the Holy Temple of the Inner Light
                 plc.

Woman   What is it?

Man   You've heard of the Mormons.

Woman   Oh, yes.

Man   It's a little bit like that, not so many wives, not so many
                 Osmonds.

Woman   It's a religion?

Man   It's whatever it means to you, Mrs King. It's a faith, it's a
                 discipline, it's a way of being. It brings together elements
                 from all the great religions of the world, Buddhism,
                 Judaism, Hindu, the teachings of the Dalai Lama,
                 Mohammed, transubstantiation, reincarnation, druids,

naiads, lay-lines – we fuse all these strands into a kind of global mysticism – do you follow me?

Woman I'm not very well up on comparative religion, I'm appallingly ignorant generally, I just don't know what you're talking about.

Man In that case, why don't you buy the bloody encyclopaedias!

REPORTS LOCAL[114]

Serious man at news desk.

Man　　And here in our area rioting and unrest continues in the town centre. Earlier today we had reports of windows being smashed and cars overturned. Our report Sally Hardcastle is down there now with a film crew to bring us this report.

Pause – He listens to his earpiece.

I'm sorry – the film crew are still having their lunch – there's been some delay with the moussaka at The Grill and Griddle. Sally Hardcastle is phoning in this report from the scene of the troubles.

Flash up old school photo with Sally's face circled. He picks up his phone.

What's the situation now, Sally?

Sound of pips.

Hello? What's the situation now?

---

114 Not broadcast.

Sally	*(Voice Over)* Hello? Is that the television studios?
Man	Yes, go ahead, Sally.
Sally	Could you put me through to Studio Three, please, I've got a report for Desmond Hambley.
Man	This is Desmond, you're on the air – go ahead.
Sally	Oh hello, Desmond, I didn't recognize your voice – I didn't think we've spoken on the phone before.
Man	What's the news on the riot, Sally?
Sally	I've spoken to your wife, haven't I, about that buggy? *(Pips)* Hang on.
Man	Are you in the middle of the danger area? It sounds pretty noisy.
Sally	No, I'm in Lewis's. I'm in a booth on the second floor, near the Travel Agents'. The noise you can hear is coming from the cafeteria.

A picture comes up of Sally on the phone, a couple of people waiting behind her.

Man	Ah, we have your picture now.
Sally	Yes, John's turned up, but Dennis is still waiting for his pudding. No, we came away from the rioting because it was so noisy.
Man	Is the situation deteriorating?
Sally	Well, as I said, we came away because it was looking a bit nasty. I was worried about my Renault . . .
Man	Are the police planning to move in?
Sally	Well, I haven't really seen any police – lunch took ages, I had to send my chicken back, it was practically pink, then I looked round the sales, so . . .
Man	Have there been any casualties?
Sally	Look, I don't know, I can't really talk now – there's a lady been waiting for ages, and I haven't got any more change – look, I'll pop back to the studios later, shall I? We'll probably have to make a detour because of this awful riot, have you heard about it? Anyway, look, Sally

Hardcastle, for Local News, Lewis's, second floor, near the Travel Agents'. Bye!

End on Man's face.

DR WHO

A typical episode; in colour but from no particular period. The Doctor and his leggy blonde assistant Fiona (who is wearing a kilt) are running down the usual baco-foil tunnel. Music.

Doctor   Hurry, Fiona!

Fiona   I can't, Doctor, my stockings are rubbing together.

Doctor   In here!

He presses a button on his lapel, which activates the silver-painted up-and-under garage door. They go through the door and stop as they come face-to-face with Crayola at his nerve centre.

Crayola   Well, well!

Fiona   Who is it, Doctor? I'm not very bright and I haven't got my glasses on.

Doctor   It is my old enemy Crayola. Hulloa, Crayola.

Crayola, who has had his back turned to them facing his lousy control panel of blinking lights, turns round. He is the wrinkly sort with the crinkly voice, lots of wires attached everywhere. Hands coming out of some ridiculous part of his body, which is on a caterpillar wheeled trolley. Ears on his chest, mouth on his knee etc.

Crayola	Doctor. It's been a long time.
Doctor	Aeons.
Crayola	As long as that? You don't look a day over five million; how do you do it?
Doctor	Table tennis. *(Crayola laughs.)* We don't have much time. I'll keep him talking, you creep round behind him – disconnect his bladdermite tubing and neutralise his thermalobes.
Fiona	But Doctor, we haven't got the ming-mongs!
Doctor	In that case, I'll creep round behind him and you show him your operation scar.
Crayola	*(suddenly ceasing to laugh)* I think not, Doctor.
Fiona	Doctor, look out!

Through the up-and-under door come the regulation three guards, two men (one black) and one woman – clingfilm wrapped round their heads, huge ears, bin-liner boiler suits, pointing hairdryers at the doctor.

Crayola	Game, set and match I think, Doctor.
Doctor	Run for it, Fiona!

They do so; the guards point their hairdryers at him, he freezes and goes negative.

Fiona	You've killed him!
Crayola	Not at all, my dear. We've merely converted his megaplumfinity into negative kreetathones.
Fiona	But what does that mean?

The guards look at each other and shrug.

Guard	Search me, dear.

MARGERY AND JOAN: THREE

Joan   And we'll be having more childcare hints from Philippa next week, when she'll be telling us why raw steak and angostura bitters don't make a good meal for your newborn baby. Now it's over to Margery, who's been looking into the ancient and fascinating Japanese art of Bonsai. Hello, Margery, you've been looking into the ancient and fascinating Japanese art of Bonsai, haven't you?

Margery   Hello, Joan. That's right. With summer fast approaching, we all need to know how to tan our bodies quickly, and more importantly, safely.[115]

Joan is stunned. Silence.

Well, I'm glad you asked me that, Joan – because as you can see, there is a bewildering array of tanning products on the market. I'll just show a few . . .

She holds up products to the wrong camera, so we see them

---

115 In the recording, Margery looks puzzled, not just because Joan has ignored her segue about bonsai trees but also, perhaps, because this refers to her orange complexion, which VW based on the perma-tanned presenter Judith Chalmers. *Over to Pam*: 'I worked with Judith Chalmers before she was brown.'

*sideways on in long shot. By the time the cameras cut she is
holding them out to a different camera so we get a close-up
of her sleeves.*

Joan	*(blankly)* What happened to Bonsai?
Margery	Scrapped.
Joan	Oh. *(Recovering)* So if I want to get a nice brown tan without burning, how do I go about it, Margery?
Margery	The golden rule, Joan – is – build up gradually. The first two weeks of your holiday, stay in your room with a hat and a pullover. And if you've got an old maxi-coat left over from the early seventies – wear that too.
Joan	And if I'm sixteen or seventeen, and have never seen a maxi-coat?
Margery	If you're sixteen or seventeen, my advice is stay at home and get those qualifications. So to sum up – first two weeks in your room, followed by three or four weeks in a full-length dressing-gown – opening the lapels for a minute or two every other day. Never forget, you can still get a nasty sunburn even at night.
Joan	And what about diarrhoea, Margery?
Margery	I'm still having it every twenty minutes, Joan.
Joan	But you've also been looking at the very latest in household gadgets, haven't you, Margery?

Suntan table replaced by another with gadgets on.

	Or perhaps you haven't, what do I know.
Margery	Yes I have, Joan, and a jolly interesting crop they are too. Now I don't use public transport myself, Joan, but a survey out this month shows that a surprisingly awful lot of people do.
Joan	And that can lead to problems, can't it, Margery?
Margery	That's right, Joan. And one of the worst problems is that at peak periods it's not always possible for a husband and wife to sit together.

Joan	So if hubby's down at one end of the bus, with a hair or fluff on the back of his jacket, wifey can't always get near enough to do anything about it.
Margery	Or she couldn't. Until this little gizmo came out. *(Picks up telescopic pincer thing:)* She can quietly get this out of her tote-bag, disengage the safety popper, and hey bingo, that offending hair is safely in the ashtray.
Joan	Of course one thing about being in a crowd of people is that we can't always be sure of personal daintiness.
Margery	That's right, Joan. Now I don't mind jamming a hand into my armpit and sniffing it in public, but some people do; and for them, these musical dress-shields are going to be a real boon. *(Produces ordinary dress-shield with tiny battery and wiring.)*
Joan	How do they work, Margery?
Margery	Well, I'm pretty whiffy today, so this should show you. Just pop it under my arm here, wait a moment – and if there's any pong at all, this happens. *(It plays a computerized version of 'Edelweiss'.)* And a lovely melody to boot.
Joan	And finally and very quickly, Margery?
Margery	Finally and very quickly, Joan – redundancy.
Joan	What about it, Margery?
Margery	It's upsetting, it's traumatic,[116] but above all, it's embarrassing.
Joan	So how do we keep it a secret, and stop people recognizing us in the queue at the social security?
Margery	Not easy, Joan – at least it wasn't – until this little hoo-hah popped up on general release.

She stands up and picks up a kind of shortened Punch and Judy booth.

---

116 Changed to 'frustrating'.

Light, portable, you can wear this in the dole queue and
friends and neighbours will pass you by, none the wiser.[117]

She puts it on over her head, it comes down to waist level.

And when your number's called and you reach the
window – *(rolls up a little blind in front of her face)* hey
poncho – you can be seen and heard in perfect privacy.

Lights and music.

You'd probably need a bigger size, Joan.

Joan   Thanks a buffalo. At least I'm not sniffing my fingers all
the day long.

---

117 Spoken by Joan in the recording.

CRAFT SHOP[118]

Arty, hand-woven global village-type gift shop. Arty, hand-woven lady owner watches browsing girl.

Owner   Can I help, or are you just browsing?

Girl   I'm just looking for a present for somebody.

Owner   I see you're looking at the jerseys – they're hand-knitted from the unravelled climbing socks of Lakeland fell walkers.

Girl   Really.

Owner   Yes, if you look closely at the yarn you'll spot the occasional toenail or blister.

Girl   What are these?

Owner   Ukrainian prayer shawls, woven by the mothers of Russian dissidents while in a state of euphoria, which doesn't happen very often, which is why we've only got three.

Girl   How much is the chess set?

Owner   Well, I'm afraid it's nine hundred and fifty pounds, but you see it is intricately carved from Lancashire cotton bobbins by disadvantaged Aborigines so –

Girl   Bit expensive.

Owner   We have lots of cheap items – our silk scarves there, two

---

	pounds each, all individually dyed using a mixture of beetroot juice, wild grasses and native saliva.
Girl	I can pay a bit more than that . . .
Owner	Perfume? *(Girl takes a whiff of a tester and backs off, blinking.)* That's an aphrodisiac scent, containing rare herbal essences and secretions from the sex glands of the Tibetan mountain rabbit – and we also do that in a drawer-liner.
Girl	It's a house-warming present.
Owner	Oh – how about these Bangladeshi washing stones – I believe you spread the clothes on one, and bang them with the other. I understand it gets them marvellously clean, though it's probably not tremendously good for the buttons.
Girl	Mmmm.
Owner	Stationery? Cards, paper, envelopes – all hand-printed by goats.
Girl	These are nice – what are they?
Owner	Ah – now they're a set of primitive patterning cogs – they're actually for decorating the breasts of Malaysian sacrificial virgins, but I've found them very handy for pastry.
Girl	No, it's all right, thanks – I'll leave it. I really wanted something a bit out of the ordinary.

KITTY: TWO

She rushes on with bags and parcels, with her coat on.

Kitty   Now I'm keeping this on because I've got a mad dash to get back to Cheadle. The Rummy Club Sound of Music opens tonight. I'm prompter – and our Mother Superior's on tablets so every other rehearsal it's been 'Climb Every What is it?'

Anyway – reincarnation! The producer set me off on it. She had one of those sessions where you lie back and turn into Florence Nightingale. She reckons she's had three previous incarnations: I think one was a Roman soldier, I forget the other two. Looking at her now, I'd plump for a Sumo wrestler and a bull mastiff. But I'm quite interested in the supernatural. My mother and I once paid out for a seance in Widnes. We wanted to contact my father because we were going camping and we couldn't lay hands on the mallet. This medium – she couldn't have made contact with the other side of a bedside table. She just kept saying she could tell we'd suffered a grievous loss. I said, 'Yes, two pounds each to come in, and our bus fares to Widnes.' But I quite fancied regressing to my

earlier lives[119], so I got Mr Culverhouse to hypnotize me.
So I'm lying down – he hasn't got the right sort of watch
so he's dangling a rubberized plug – and he counts me
back to 1901. 'Who are you,' he says. Well everything's
dark, but I sense I'm wearing a corset, so that rules out
Edward the Seventh. Then suddenly, bang, bang, bang,
there's Helen Murchison at the front door assaulting my
knocker as per; so it's away with the hypnosis and out
with the mixed biscuits.

She'd come round on her way back from giving blood,
and why they want it beats me, because the way she eats,
it must be 'A' rhesus nougat. She'd come to tell me her
daughter was finally getting married after four years of
living in sin just outside Nantwich. I said 'What's his
name?' She said, 'He's called Nick, and he's very high
up in sewage.' I thought, that's lucky. She said, 'It is a
church wedding, but under the circumstances the bride's
opted for knee-length shrimp.' She tried to impress Mr
Culverhouse with her elaborate finger buffet, but he sees
the world for what it is after fifty years in cocoa. She
said if I wanted to give a present, they'd made out a little
list. Little! It made the Domesday Book look like a raffle
ticket. Videos, washing machines – the only thing under
a fiver was a wall-mounted Brillo grip. So they're getting
this. *(She produces an awful catering-size coffee tin covered
in wallpaper and ric-rac braid to make a bin.)* I made it!
You can't get them in the shops. I think what makes it
is the ric-rac braiding. I was going to patent it, but I believe there's a lot of hanging around.[120] Oh, and then she
drops another bombshell. She chomps down the last of
the Bourbons and says, 'Kitty – I'm leaving Bill – we're
not compatible.' They never were – he loves opera, and

119 Changed to 'my previous lives'.
120 This and the preceding sentence were cut.

she can't follow the plot of the Teddy Bears' Picnic. She only married him because he was pally with a man who made chocolate misshapes.

Now I must dash – it's curtain-up at seven and these motorways – they're forever coning you off – I blame the engineers. You can see them on the hard shoulder, larking about with their theodolites. *(Gathers her bits together.)* If anybody's been sitting on my wimples I'll play merry Hamlet . . .

WINE BAR[121]

Very 'feminine' and 'nice' girl and slightly older man drink-
ing after work in a wine bar.

Man   Cheers.

Girl   Cheers *(drinks)*. Mmm, quite nice and fruity.

Man   They know me here.

Girl   Really? Because some white wines – they can sort of make you scrunch your bottom up, can't they? But this is quite cordial, isn't it?

Man   Do you think you're going to enjoy working for the company?

Girl   Oh, yes. It's a very choice powder-room, ever such un-usual washbasins, quite opaque.

Man   That's a very attractive dress, if I may say so.

Girl   Oh, do you like it? I think it makes me look a bit extinct, do you know what I mean? I like the fabric, though, it's quite commercialized.

Man   Do you have a boyfriend, or . . . ?

Girl   No, I don't really like steady relationships – they make me feel a bit Rice Krispie-ish, do you know what I mean?

---

121 Not broadcast. VW would revisit the idea in a slightly different form in a sketch for *ADB*, in which an undercover policewoman tries to entrap an innocent man into behaving chauvinistically.

Man	Because I'd very much like to take you out one evening, if I may.
Girl	I don't think so.
Man	Because I'm married?
Girl	I don't really like going out with people from work – it all gets sort of conjugated.
Man	Nobody has to know.
Girl	It always does get out, though. Offices are really ostentatious for gossip, aren't they?
Man	Well, it wouldn't matter, would it?
Girl	Well, it's against company policy, isn't it? People going out with their secretaries. There might be a big sort of moussaka about it.
Man	Yes, but what would be the worst that could happen?
Girl	Well, the worst that could happen would be that Head Office found out and I had to fire you, Colin. Cheers.

MARGERY AND JOAN: FOUR

Joan	*(in neck brace and knee-length plaster)* And as Philippa climbs out of that piranha tank, I'm sure she won't mind if I let you into a little secret – she's actually into the fourth week of a very serious nervous breakdown! Now it's over to Margery, who's been finding out what's available holiday-wise for those of us who aren't going abroad this summer. Hello Margery, what's available holiday-wise for those of us who aren't going abroad this summer?
Margery	Hello, Joan. Well believe it or not, but not every holiday-maker will be flying to Marbella or Alicante with a suitcase full of velour leisure shorts singing 'Y Viva España'.
Joan	And why is that, Margery?
Margery	Possibly because they don't know the words to the second verse, Joan.
Joan	So a lot of people will be looking for a reasonably priced package in this country?
Margery	That's right, Joan.
Joan	OK – so I'm single, I don't have very much money, I can't afford to go abroad, I don't make friends easily, what can I do?
Margery	Look, we had all this out in the wine bar . . . *(Realises her mistake.)* Well, there's lots of, alternatives available, Joan,

the cheapest being a two-week conservation holiday in the West Midlands dragging old bedsteads out of the Grand Union Canal and living on pulses.

Joan And what will I need to take with me?

Margery Well, if they haven't been soaked – a can of air-freshener.

Joan And if I'm a book-lover and would like nothing better than to meet my favourite authors?

Margery Then hie yourself along to the Swan Hotel, Warwick, where you can mingle with popular novelists and have the chance to examine such literary treasures as the original manuscript of *Wuthering Heights,* James Herriot's collection of rubber gloves, and most exciting of all – Jeffrey Archer's very first bank statement.

Joan But you've also been looking at Singles Holidays, haven't you, Margery?

Margery That's right, Joan. Because for every outgoing popular physically attractive swinger like me, there's an emotionally repressed lumpy old pongo like Joan. See how we got on.

Cut to film

A coach bowling along a cliff road.

Joan *(Voice Over)* Margery and I are heading for the three-star Cliff Top Hotel – where single people of all sexes are hoping for sun, fun and a little bit of mountaineering.

Front of Hotel. Coach. Joan on the steps of the coach. Extras collecting luggage at back. Margery seen through the coach window heaving into a sick bag.

Joan *(to camera)* Well, a bumpy five-hour drive on badly tarmacked B roads wouldn't suit everybody. *(Margery appears behind Joan, wiping her mouth.)* But we're both raring to pick up our bags and get going.

Walks to rear of coach. Margery picks up the last case.

Driver   *(as rehearsed)* The blue samsonite, please.
         (closing the boot) Nope, that's the lot – sorry.

Twin-bedded room. Margery holding up racy evening clothes against herself and chucking them on the bed.

Joan   *(on other bed)* Well, I've been told my case will be here in the morning, so till then, Margery and I will be sharing the same toothbrush.

Margery   *(to herself)* That's what you think.

Joan   *(checking timetable)* Well, it's six o'clock, so I'm heading for the TV lounge, for the first event of Singles Week – a Twist 'n' Jive session with the Pauline Mowbray Skiffle Experience. Coming, Margery?

Margery   No thanks. I'm going to the bar.

Bar. Joan leaning up at the bar. Everyone very jolly. Waiter serves Joan a cocktail and moves out of shot.

Joan   Well, after a few of the hotel's speciality cocktails, the ice is well and truly broken. Everyone's having a marvellous time! Over to you, Margery. Cheers!

Another part of the bar. Camera finds Margery performing a drunken dance with a reluctant businessman who's trying to get away.

Margery   You don't need to phone your wife! Come on – forty-two and no bra, not bad, eh?[122]

Back to Joan, immersed in her cocktail.

---

122 Changed to 'forty-two in April and no bra'.

Joan	And I might try that later in the week! Now it's off to bed, because believe you me, tomorrow's going to be a very full day!

Poolside. Joan in towelling robe and extremely elaborate swimming cap.

Joan	Well, I've been shopping, I've visited the local museum and I'm just recovering from a vigorous session of pool-side aerobics, and I imagine that Margery's been pretty busy as well. *(Waves up at a balcony)* Yoo-hoo! Margery!

Margery on a balcony wrapped in a sheet, having been 'at it' all night and just woken up. All messy hair and smudged eye-shadow.

Margery	*(can't think or speak)* Hello, Joan. Yes – er – I've been pretty busy. *(Yawns.)* You know . . .

The businessman in towel stomps out on the balcony from the room, grabs a pair of underpants and goes back in, mumbling.

Man	Can't find your pants.
Margery	What? *(Yawns.)*

Cliff face. Joan is half-way up the cliff dangling on a rope held by Margery, who has reached the top. Both are in full climbing gear. Margery still not with it.

Joan	Well, this is the highlight of the holiday as far as I'm concerned, a two-day course in simple mountaineering. It's a marvellous way for single people to get to know each other, because in a life-and-death situation like this, you're totally dependent on your climbing partner *(tugs the rope)*. Margery, I'm coming up!

Margery   *(yawning)* OK.
Joan   *(starting to climb)* If Margery was to let her concentration
               lapse for just one second, I could literally –

She falls out of shot.

Back to the studio. Joan in neck brace as before.

Margery   Well, that's it – and happy holidays!
Joan   Bye!

Music. Lights fade.

Margery   When are they taking the pins out?
Joan   They're not.
Margery   Bad luck.

ACORN ANTIQUES

EPISODE ONE

Scene One. A tiny set, very artificial looking. An antique shop. Through the back door is a kitchen, with the end of a draining board and then a gap where the flattage has run out. Outside the shop window is a crooked photo of a street. All the actors in this serial are over made-up (women) or speak ironically (men). Babs is blonde, sitting by a blank wall-plan. She's on the phone, holding it well away from her face for the camera. Music.

Babs   Acorn Antiques, can I help you? No, I'm afraid he's out buying antiques, who is it calling?

Mrs Overall, the daily help, comes in with coffee. Babs waves and smiles, then frowns abruptly.

Rowena? From Kuwait? Hello? Hello?

She puts the phone down.

Darn. Oh sorry, Mrs Overall.

Mrs Overall Here's your coffee, Miss Babs. Now what's wrong?

Babs   Oh nothing, just rather a mysterious phone call from the Far East.

Mrs Overall Yes, well, sometimes that's God's way of saying think on and look sharp.[123]

Babs You're right. Gosh. I am awful. Here I am blabbing away about my own troubles and I never asked you about your husband's car crash.

Mrs Overall Oh he's dead, Miss Babs. In fact I was going to ask you if I could have a couple of hours off on Thursday for the funeral.

Babs Of course. Just pop back at five for the hoovering. What happened?

Mrs Overall His heart stopped beating.

Babs Oh, no.

Mrs Overall Yes, well, sometimes that's God's way of telling you you're dead. Not to worry, Bingo tonight. Mr Kenneth not down yet?

Babs Er, no.

Mrs Overall That's not like him, he's not having a nervous breakdown, is he?

Babs To tell you the truth, Mrs Overall, we had a huge row last night, he put the triplets in the Wolsely and I haven't seen him since.

Mrs Overall Men! Oh well, better get on and dust a few antiques.

Babs sips coffee and pulls a face.

Babs Well, they say things go in threes.
Mrs Overall Why, whatever's happened?
Babs You forgot my sweeteners. Ho ho ho.
Mrs Overall Ho ho ho.

They laugh.
Music.

---

123 Changed to 'telling you to think on'.

Scene Two. Babs on the phone.

Babs   Yes, just bring your antiques in. Bye.

Enter an enigmatic man (Clifford).

Clifford Babs?
Babs   Bored with Zurich, or did Zurich get bored with you?
Clifford You always did ask a good question.
Babs   But did I ever get a good answer?
Clifford You look well. Answering the phone in a family an-
            tiques business seems to suit you.
Babs   Thank you, kind sir.
Clifford Babs, can't we . . . ?
Babs   We? Who's we, Clifford? There might have been a we
            before you left me by the handbags in a well-known
            store . . .

Pause.

Clifford Don't say any more. I love you, Babs.
Babs   I've changed, Clifford. I have triplets now.

He lunges at her over the desk.

Clifford Darn your triplets!

*He kisses her, the desk cracks ominously. They corpse silently
while kissing.*
Music.
Credits.
We cut back to close-up of Clifford.

            There's something I haven't told you. I go bell-ringing
            on Wednesday nights.

EPISODE TWO

Scene One. Babs as before on the telephone.

Babs   As I say, it certainly sounds like a genuine Picasso, Martin, but I would have to see it to be sure. Bye.

She looks at the phone and puts it down, smiling. Enter Berta, a Babs look-alike, but brunette where Babs is blonde.

Berta! You look marvellous! So you're out of intensive care!

Berta   I told Doctor Spencer I had to get back and help you out in the shop, so he cured me. So here I am. Ha Ha Ha.

They laugh.

Babs   Coffee, or are you still on your diet?
Berta   Oh, diet be blowed! Ha ha.
Babs   Mrs Overall!

She enters immediately.

Mrs Overall	Well, if it isn't Miss Berta!
Berta	Hello, Mrs O. How's widowhood treating you?
Mrs Overall	Mustn't grumble. I sometimes think being widowed is God's way of telling you to come off the pill.
Berta	Still the same Mrs O!
Mrs Overall	Well, this coffee won't get made on its own.

They all pause, realising a line has been missed.

Babs	Oh yes, two coffees, thank you.
Berta	No milk for me.
Mrs Overall	Well, this coffee won't get made on its own.

Exit Mrs Overall.

Babs	And a plate of your delicious home-made gingerbread, please. Bet you didn't get that in intensive care.
Berta	Oh, I don't know. Money talks, even in hospital, Babs. And though of course it was a dreadful shame Daddy being shot like that in Dhaka, being a millionairess does have its compensations.

Enter Mrs Overall with a tray full of scummy coffee and biscuits.

Mrs Overall	Here we are. It's awfully quiet in here. Anybody would think you were talking about million-pound legacies or something.
Babs	Good heavens, no.
Berta	Oh, come on, Babs. Mrs O's practically one of the family. Daddy's gone and got himself shot in Dhaka, Mrs O.
Mrs Overall	Oh, and he'd only just got over that chill on his kidneys. Well, you know what I think?
Berta	What?

Mrs Overall	I think you better have some milk in your coffee after all! Ha ha.
Berta	I think I had! Ha ha.

They laugh.

Scene Two. Babs and Berta poring over blank papers at the desk.

Berta   Yes, that's much better. If we deliver these antiques on Friday morning, we can take delivery of these antiques in the afternoon.

Babs nods, having no dialogue but waiting for someone to enter. Enter Derek, the handyman.

Derek   Excuse me, Miss Babs and Miss Berta, could I have a word?

Babs   Well, if it's to ask me for another job for your untrustworthy cousin Jacob, then the answer's no. His last little escapade cost me thirty-two pounds in French polish. Not to mention apologising to every Asian grocer between here and Manchesterford.

Derek   No, it's not that – it's your father, Miss Berta, he's been seen in the Post Office.

Berta   But my father's dead!

Music.
Credits.
Back to close-up of Derek.

Derek   He was buying a TV licence stamp and a padded envelope.

EPISODE THREE

Scene One. Trixie is on the phone. She is very flighty and tarty.

Trixie No, I'm sorry, Miss Babs has taken the triplets to see 'Get Carter', they won't be back till this afternoon. No, you won't recognise my voice, this is my first day in the antique shop, I've just been moved up from antique packing. Sorry? Trixie. Trixie Trouble, some people call me. Bye . . .

Mrs Overall enters disapprovingly with a cocktail and some biscuits.

Mrs Overall Here's your cocktail, and don't blame me if you run out of stomach lining.

Trixie I won't. Anyway, I only have to snap my fingers and somebody I know will come running with a dozen stomach linings.

Mrs Overall I suppose you mean Mr Kenneth?

Trixie He's already bought me a leotard and a wet-look wig.

Mrs Overall And what did you have to do in return?

Trixie You'd better ask the receptionist at the Formica Motel.

Mrs Overall Disgusting. And him an ex-Territorial with triplets.

Trixie That's a matter of conjecture. I found out quite a few

things at the Formica Motel; one, that your precious
Miss Babs checked in there nine months to the day
before the triplets were born.

Mrs Overall   Who with?

Enter Derek. Trixie files her nails pointedly.

Derek   It's very quiet in here, I hope you weren't talking about
me.

Scene Two. Babs at the desk with Derek.

Babs   Right, so we'll have those antiques packed up immediately and sent down to the station. Plenty of Sellotape,
we don't want any more accidents.

Derek   Yes, Miss Babs.

Babs   *(over-casually)* How's your girlfriend these days, Derek?
What was her name, Marie-Thérèse Francine Dubois?

Derek   Yes, Miss. She's – back in the convent, Miss.

Babs   Oh, no! After all that trouble you went to, to find her a
pleated skirt. Did she leave a note?

Derek   She left a novel, but I don't think it's very commercial.

They speak together.

                 Miss Babs!

Babs   Derek!

Derek   I still think about you, Miss Babs. When I'm watching
the show-jumping or grilling a tomato.

*She puts out a hand and snatches it back as Trixie enters.
They all crowd into one shot.*

Trixie   Oh, sorry. Hope I'm not interrupting anything.

Babs	Of course not, Trixie. We were just discussing the best way of packing a Spode tea service.
Trixie	Yes, well, we can't afford to have anything broken, can we?
Babs	What do you mean?
Trixie	Like your marriage to Mr Kenneth?

She pulls out some photos from her bag.

It's amazing what you can find in a waterproof packet tied to a lavatory ballcock if you look hard enough.

She tosses them down on the table. Reaction.
Music.
Credits.

Seems like I'm not the only one round here with a birthmark shaped like a moped – Mummy . . .

EPISODE FOUR

Scene One. Trixie and Mrs Overall at the desk.

Mrs Overall Well it's a long time since I've seen a diamond engagement ring as expensive as that. Not since Miss Babs got married.

Trixie Why, this is her ring, Mrs O! Don't forget we just found out Miss Babs is my mother!

Mrs Overall Why, of course. But doesn't that mean you're engaged to your own brother?

Trixie Well, yes, but Mummy spoke to the vicar and he's prepared to make an exception.[124]

Mrs Overall That's a relief. Well, I'd better go and take away Miss Babs's coffee cup. It's a new brand, the last lot tasted a little bit odd apparently.

Enter Babs.

Babs Hello, Mrs O. I thought I'd bring my own coffee cup down today. You know, it still tastes a little bit odd.

Trixie What sort of little bit odd?

Babs Oh, I don't know, almost as if someone was trying to kill me . . .

---

124 Cut and replaced with 'I suppose it does'.

Trixie	Oh Mum, you are an old silly billy – ho ho.

She stops laughing when she notices Babs and Mrs Overall look serious.

Babs	Well, you see, I am the majority shareholder in Acorn Antiques, since Berta's amnesia. If I were to die that would certainly suit Cousin Jerez very well.
Mrs Overall	But he's a notorious gambler and playboy. And anyway, he's in Marbella.

Enter Cousin Jerez with a peculiar accent.

Jerez	Correction, *was* in Marbella. Planes are very quick nowadays, or perhaps here in your world of antiques you did not know this.
Mrs Overall	I'll make some sherry, Miss Babs. *(Exits.)*

Babs corpses slightly at this mistake.

Jerez	And who is this charming young señorita?
Babs	She's my daughter, and she's engaged.
Jerez	Not too engaged to come out dancing this evening, I hope?
Trixie	I, I . . .
Babs	Aren't you and Bobby going crown green bowling this evening?
Trixie	No, he's ricked his wrist. Yes, I'd love to come out dancing.
Jerez	That's settled, then.
Trixie	Can I borrow your long-line bra, Mummy?
Babs	It's in my sideboard.
Jerez	Do you have any dance dresses that fasten with velcro?
Trixie	Yes, a blue one.
Jerez	Wear it.

Reaction from Babs.

*Scene Two. The lounge. A sofa and a standard lamp. Babs
and Jerez are having coffee.*

Jerez That was a delicious five-course meal, thank you. I'd
forgotten how good you were with quails.

Babs I may feed you, Cousin Jerez, but I don't like you. Let's
cut the pleasantries, shall we? Just why do you want to
buy my shares? You don't like antiques and you never
have done.

Jerez True. But I do like motorway service stations.

Babs What do you mean?

Jerez Look out of the window.

Babs There are some council workmen putting a sign up. I
can't quite . . . 'New motorway to be built here, starting
the 25th'. That's tomorrow! Why haven't I had a letter?

Jerez whistles a few notes.

Why are you whistling like that? I know that tune, it's
the one our postman always whistles. Oh I see, it wasn't
a postman at all, it was you!

Enter Mrs Overall.

Mrs Overall Can I clear away now, Miss Babs? The triplets are a bit
fractious and I promised I'd pop up and read them a bit
of Simone de Beauvoir.

Babs Yes, do clear away, Mrs O. In fact, you may as well clear
away the whole darn shop!

Music.
Credits.

Jerez Could you fetch my briefcase, Mrs Overall? I'd like to
show Miss Babs my theodolite.

EPISODE FIVE

Scene One. Derek puffing and panting, having just moved something. Enter Mrs Overall with tea.

Mrs Overall Here's your beef tea, Derek. You've never shifted that 1869 Bechstein all by yourself?

Derek Well, I didn't like to bother Mr Kenneth. He was having his breakfast.

Mrs Overall What was it Muesli? What was it, muesli?

Derek I think so, Mrs O.

Mrs Overall Yes well, I think muesli is God's way of making shredded wheat look exciting.[125]

Derek winces.

It's your heart, isn't it, Derek? You strained it, didn't you, lifting that oil tanker off Miss Berta's handbag?

Derek Well, I knew she was right fond of it. Do you think those revolutionary new tablets will cure her amnesia?

Mrs Overall Well they might, if she could ever remember to take them.

Pause. Enter Trixie in a wedding dress.

---

125 Changed to 'I sometimes think muesli . . .'

Trixie   Honestly, I could kill those triplets!

*Mrs Overall shakes her head. Trixie realises it's not her
entrance and retreats, bumping into Babs.*

Babs   Hello Derek, Mrs O. Honestly, I just don't see how we
can get this wedding ready in a month. Trixie hasn't
even chosen her dress yet.

Derek   What's happened about the new motorway, Miss Babs?

Babs   Oh, I phoned up the Town Hall and they've agreed to
re-route it and knock some poor people's houses down
instead.[126]

Mrs Overall Oh, I am pleased. This calls for some tonic wine and a
sponge finger.

Babs   Yes, Mrs O. I should jolly well think it does.

They all laugh. Derek winces and holds his chest.

I say Derek, your heart's strong enough to put the mar-
quee up all by yourself, isn't it?

Derek   If it's for an Acorn Antiques wedding, Miss Babs, I'll
put it up even if it kills me.

Mrs Overall and Babs look apprehensive.

*Scene Two. The lounge. Berta and Babs on the sofa. Trixie
rushes in as before, in a clean wedding dress.*

Trixie   Honestly, I could kill those triplets!

Babs   Calm down, Trixie, whatever's the matter?

Trixie   They've put jammy fingerprints all over the front – all
over it at the back.

Babs   We'll get Mrs O to sponge it off.

126 This and Derek's preceding line were cut.

Mrs Overall enters as she is being called for.

	Mrs O!
Mrs Overall	What on earth's wrong with the front of your frock? Looks like jam.
Trixie	On the back, yes.
Mrs Overall	*(out of character)* What?
Trixie	There is jam on the back. The triplets didn't put any on the front.

Mrs Overall freezes, completely lost.

| | Shall I come along with you and you'll find something to sponge it with? |
| **Mrs Overall** | Come along with me and I'll find something to sponge it with. |

After a short pause, they leave the room.

Babs	Trixie's going to look gorgeous this afternoon, isn't she, Berta?
Berta	I don't know any Trixies.

Laughs slightly at this odd remark.

I don't know anybody. I live in a world of strangers.

Enter Clifford.

Babs	Clifford! What are you doing here? I thought I made my feelings quite clear last November in the British Home Stores.
Clifford	But I'm here to see Berta.
Babs	Berta? But you hardly know her.
Clifford	You may well be right, Babs, but the fact remains, whether she can remember it or not, Berta and I were

married by the Bishop of Manchesterford the Tuesday before last.

Music.
Credits.

Babs   So that's why there was confetti on her body-warmer!

EPISODE SIX

Scene One. Clifford, face unmarked, is mopping his nose with a bloodstained hanky. Berta and Babs stand by, faces blank. They receive some cue and begin acting.

Babs   Well, Clifford, you came in at exactly the right moment. Trust me to forget Cousin Jerez was an expert knife-thrower.

Clifford   He won't be building any more motorways round here in a hurry.

Babs   What's in your letter, Berta?

Berta   It's from the Bishop of Manchesterford. No, I can't have an annulment, and yes, I did leave my gardening gloves in the vestry.

Short pause. Enter Mrs Overall.

Hear that, Mrs O?

Berta   Look Mrs O, no amnesia!

Mrs Overall   Oh, I am pleased.

Berta   And do you know what was the first thing I remembered, what it was?

Mrs Overall   No, I don't, Miss Berta.

Berta   I remembered that I'm absolutely mad about your[127] delicious home-made gingerbread!

They all laugh.

Mrs Overall Coming right up, Miss Berta.
Clifford   Could Berta and Babs fetch it themselves, Mrs O? I'd, er, like a word.
Babs   Why, of course we could.[128] As Mrs O would say, fetching your own gingerbread is God's way of letting you have an extra piece!

Babs and Berta exit laughing. As Clifford speaks Babs knocks into something off the set.

(Babs   What blithering nuisance left that here?)
(Voice   Ssh!)
Clifford   There's been a new development over Berta's father's will. A new one has been found, dated the day he died . . .
Mrs Overall And who's the sole beneficiary this time?
Clifford   That's the problem. It's a little redhead he met in the blackout in 1943. They had one night of passion and he never saw her again.
Mrs Overall Or he thought he never saw her again!
Clifford   What do you mean, Mrs O?
Mrs Overall Oh, I'm grey now, Mr Clifford, fairly grey indeed, but right up to 1947 my hair was red – as red as a London bus!

Music.

---

127 Cut from 'And do you know what' to here.
128 The rest of Babs' speech was cut.

Scene Two. The lounge. A celebration. Mrs Overall, Trixie, Derek, Babs, Berta and Clifford, all drinking water out of champagne glasses.

Berta I can't believe Mrs O is my mother!

Mrs Overall Well, I am. The doctor said he'd never seen a finer pair of twins.

Berta Twins? But –

Mrs Overall A lovely big boy.

Berta But where is he now?

Mrs Overall I had to give him away – we hadn't room for the two cots.

Babs Oh well, he probably would have turned into a hulking great brute anyway.

She stares at Derek thoughtfully.

Trixie Oh I spoke to our family doctor, Doctor Wimley, today.

Babs And?

Trixie Apparently, being spiteful and having lots of extra-marital affairs could bring back my jaundice, so I'm going to be really nice from now on.

Clifford So we can't call you Trixie Trouble any more.

Trixie No, in fact it's Sister Trixie – I've taken holy orders. Bobby's running me up to the convent in the Wolseley. Bye!

Exit Trixie. The phone rings:

Babs Hello? I thought you'd committed suicide. OK, see you later. That was my so-called husband, not dead at all. He says put the triplets in their body-warmers – he's taking us all to Manchesterford Zoo, if you please!

Mrs Overall It was just a cry for help, Miss Babs. Otherwise why try to slash your wrists with an electric razor?

Babs	I'd better go and find that king-size thermos. Looking at animals can be thirsty work.
Berta	Oh, we'll go and look for it, Babs.
Clifford	Yes, Berta and I have lots to talk about.
Mrs Overall	Well, if it's to be another christening, I'll need plenty of notice, or we won't have nearly enough delicious home-made gingerbread.
Berta	We will!

Clifford and Berta leave, laughing.

Babs	She may find my thermos, but will she ever find her twin brother?
Mrs Overall	All I know is, he's called Derek and he's a handyman in an antiques shop.
Babs	Derek? That's your name, isn't it, Derek?
Derek	Well, yes, Miss Babs.
Babs	And this is an antiques shop and you are a handyman!
Derek	I must be Miss Berta's twin brother then, Miss Babs.
Babs	Yes, run along and tell her, Derek!

Exit Derek.

Babs	Phew – it's been an . . . Sorry, Mrs O, both talking at the same time there.
Mrs Overall	I was just saying, someone had better answer that phone.

Phone begins to ring.

Babs	Oh blow, I suppose I'd better answer it.
Mrs Overall	You answer it and I'll bring you a nice hot cup of coffee.
Babs	You don't have to.

Phone stops ringing.

After all, you are the sole proprietor of Acorn Antiques now. Hello?

Mrs Overall leaves.

The 'Mona Lisa'? Yes, I certainly have heard of it. Yes do, we're open till five. Bye.

Mrs Overall comes back in with coffee.

Looks like we won't have to go out of business after all. I've just been offered Leonardo da Lisa's 'Mona Vinci' at a very reasonable price.

Mrs Overall And Miss Berta's found your thermos, and apparently it's not a thermos at all, it's a very valuable Georgian silver wine cooler!

Babs Well, they say things go in threes.

Mrs Overall Why, whatever's the third thing?

Babs You remembered my sweeteners! Ho ho.

They laugh.
Music.
Credits.

Mrs Overall Oh Miss Babs, I'm awfully sorry, I think I've given you the wrong coffee – that one's full of poison guaranteed to cause agonizing death within minutes!

Reaction from Babs.

EPISODE SEVEN

Film. Ext. Day. Village High Street. Small van labelled 'Acorn Antiques' pulls up in front of a shop bearing no resemblance to the one in the studio. The shop has been hastily and badly re-named 'Acorn Antiques', but the real name of the shop can be seen underneath. Miss Babs gets out of the van, holding an antique, goes over on her ankle as she steps down, and goes into the shop. Small group of interested onlookers nearby stare at the camera throughout.

Scene One. Shop as before. Babs selling an antique to our extras as before. She hands over a large paper bag (printed with 'Acorn Antiques') and some change.

Babs   And fifty-three change. Bye!

Extras leave. Phone rings.

Acorn Antiques, can I help you? Gainsborough's Blue Boy? Yes, I think we have it in mauve, I'll just check.

Flips over blank bits of paper.

Yes, we do; shall I pop it under the counter for you? Not at all, bye!

Puts phone down. Enter Mrs Overall with tray of coffee.

Mrs Overall Here's your coffee, Miss Babs.

Babs Thanks Mrs O, no poison this time I hope.

Mrs Overall Yes, I'm sorry about that – attempting to murder you was just a silly way of trying to draw attention to myself. I shan't need to do it again now you've bought me this lovely blouse.

Babs smiles absently and then sighs. Mrs Overall misses the cue, Babs sighs again, more obviously.

Mrs Overall Why, whatever's the matter, Miss Babs? Have you got an incurable disease, or is it just the sterilized milk?

Babs I wish it were.

Mrs Overall Then what on earth –

Babs I won't beat about the bush, Mrs O. Ever since Mr Kenneth left to become a follower of that weird religious sect, Acorn Antiques has been losing money. And this letter you were just asking me about is to Dorcas and Hincaster.

Mrs Overall The Manchesterford estate agents?

Babs Yes. Pop it into the pillar box on the corner immediately, Mrs O – Acorn Antiques is going up for sale!

Mrs Overall goes out of the door.

Music.

Cut to film. Ext. Day. Street. Mrs Overall, now miraculously attired in coat and hat, comes out of the shop, walks to the post box, takes from the pocket of her coat an entirely different-looking letter, stares at it meaningfully and puts it back in her pocket. All this is watched by gawpers in distance.

Scene Two. Living room. Babs and Clifford. He is snuggling up to Babs on the settee. She is unresponsive.

Clifford   What's wrong, Babs? Last night you were so warm and passionate . . .

Babs   Last night was yesterday, Clifford. I was happy, we had champagne, we danced . . .

Clifford   You danced – magnificently . . .

Babs   Oh, anyone can do the can-can.

Clifford   Not in a snack bar.

As suddenly as he can, Clifford goes down on one knee.

Babs!

A beat late, Mrs Overall enters.

Mrs Overall   There's a visitor, Miss Babs. *(Mumbles absently)* Oh Mrs O.[129]

Babs   Oh, Mrs O, can't you see we're busy?

Clifford gets up, annoyed.

Mrs Overall   But this is important.

Clifford   *This* is important.

Mrs Overall   *(as herself)* Yes, 'this is important', I said that, didn't I?

Babs   Clifford was about to ask me a very important question, Mrs O.

Mrs Overall   In that case, I'll wait outside.

Mrs Overall goes out.

Clifford   Babs – will you marry me?

Babs   Of course, Clifford, but do you know what you're taking on?

---

129 Cut. By the time the script was recorded, it would have been established that Bo Beaumont barely knew her own lines so she could hardly be relied upon to remember anyone else's.

Clifford	A loveable scatterbrain with the nicest lipstick in Manchesterford.
Babs	Lipstick – and debts.
Clifford	Debts?
Babs	Quite frankly, Clifford, I'm flat, flat broke.
Clifford	But you gave me oysters.
Babs	Instant mashed potato and a heck of a lot of nail varnish.
	But money doesn't matter, Clifford. *(Turns round and sees he's gone – or nearly gone)* Clifford? Clifford?

Enter Mrs Overall.

Mrs Overall	Oh Miss Babs, you've never been jilted again.
Babs	I think I jolly well have, Mrs O.
Mrs Overall	Men! If they're not doing that they're becoming world heavyweight boxers.
Babs	Oh – who was the visitor?
Mrs Overall	It was your wicked cousin Jerez, Miss Babs, completely reformed and doing a sandwich course in computer studies at Fuengirola Poly. He dropped in to see if you wanted twenty-five thousand pounds to boost your flagging antiques business.
Babs	Twenty-f– I could fill the place with antiques for that, and fit a new cistern in the downstairs cloakroom into the bargain! Well, where is Cousin Jerez, Mrs O – bring him in!

Music.
Credits (list of credits to end with antiques adviser – Rosamund Crull).

Mrs Overall	Oh, he couldn't wait, Miss Babs. I told him you were having a proposal done and he caught the next plane back to Marbella!

EPISODE EIGHT

Scene One. The shop. Babs, Jerez and Mrs Overall laughing on cue.

Babs   But what I can't understand is why Dorcas and Hincaster –

Mrs Overall   The Manchesterford estate agents, yes?

Babs   Why they never put Acorn Antiques on the property market.

Mrs Overall   Because I never posted the letter.

Babs   So they never got the letter at all.

Mrs Overall   No – because I never posted it.

Jerez   Well, that is too complicated for a simple Spaniard like me, but as they say, All's Well *(The other two are supposed to join in with the second half of this, but aren't sure when to come in)* That Ends Well!

Babs   That ends well.

Mrs Overall   All's well that ends well. Well, this calls for a cup of delicious home-made coffee.

Jerez   Home-made coffee? I'm afraid I do not –

Mrs Overall   Well, we have been economizing and this is Acorn Antiques – so what do you think I've been making the coffee out of?

Babs   I give in.

Mrs Overall   Antiques!

Exit Mrs Overall, laughing. Stops laughing abruptly, and clears throat.

Babs   But seriously, Cousin Jerez – it was marvellous of you to lend me the money – are you sure you don't want anything in return?

Jerez   I would like, how do you say in the English – to marry you.

Babs   Well, that's not quite the correct jargon, but I do get your drift. I'm sorry, Jerez, it's not possible.

Jerez whips round and bangs his face on a camera.

Jerez   Ow. What are you sayin' to me?

Babs   When I married Mr Kenneth I gave birth to three children, all born on the same day, all triplets – two of them had dangerously straight hair and had to be rushed immediately to the hairdressers, nurses worked day and night with curling tongs and heated rollers – and if that's what marriage entails, then quite frankly Cousin Jerez, the answer's no, no –

Mrs Overall opens the door and closes it again.

The answer's no, no, no!

Music.

Cut to film. The shop. Jerez comes out, slams the door, hails a taxi. There is no sound. Clifford collides with him, catapulting from behind the camera.

Scene Two. The shop. The door is now open. Enter Mrs Overall with coffee.

Mrs Overall	Whatever was that terrible bang?
Babs	Cousin Jerez slamming the door. The Spaniards may have enormous onions, but their manners leave a lot to be desired.
Mrs Overall	And their football's deteriorated since the World Cup, if you ask me. *(Pause.)* So no fat cheque.
Babs	In other words, Mrs O, we're right back to square –

Enter Clifford.

Clifford	One?
Babs	Clifford! But –
Clifford	Our friend Jerez seemed in rather a hurry. *(Takes out a piece of paper labelled 'Jerez – cheque'.)* Certainly he never noticed I'd taken this from his overcoat pocket.

(Jerez wasn't wearing an overcoat, at least not in the film.)

Babs	The cheque! Quick, Mrs O, it's three twenty-five, take it to the local branch of the nearest bank and cash it immediately!
Mrs Overall	I certainly will, Miss Babs. *(Setting off)* And on my way back, I'll buy us some ginger bourbons and a lovely new cistern for the downstairs cloakroom.
Babs	You do that.
Clifford	Hey! Don't forget the cheque *(throws a paper dart)*. Catch!

It goes nowhere near her. We hear an urgent voice off saying 'Leave it, just go.' Exit Mrs Overall.

Thought any more about marrying me?

Music.
Credits.

Babs   I can never marry Clifford – I have a terrible disease. I'm allergic to men's pyjamas. One whiff of a pyjama jacket – even a pocket of a pyjama jacket – and I could literally drop – down – dead!

EPISODE NINE

Scene One. Shop. Babs on the phone. Extras as usual.

Babs   Hello – Acorn Antiques, can I help you? I'm sorry – you'll have to speak up – we're having extensive alterations and drastic refurbishments.

Sound of half-hearted laughing.

No, we're sticking with mauve. Look – I'll have to go, Mrs Overall's standing over me with a cup of coffee. Bye!

Babs puts phone down. Mrs Overall catapults in with coffee.

Mrs Overall   I've been standing here so long this coffee's practically congealified!

Babs   Oh Mrs O, nobody would think you had a degree in linguistics and advanced semantics.

Mrs Overall   Well, I had to do something while I was recovering from that transplant.

Babs   Yes, we were grateful to you for donating all that bone marrow to Miss Berta.

Mrs Overall   I hope she got it all right.

Babs   I'm afraid some of it had leaked out of the Jiffy bag.

Mrs Overall   Men!

Slight hiatus.

Babs	Yes, the doctors are very pleased with her.
Mrs Overall	I heard she may never play the gramophone again.
Babs	Oh, that sounds like the postman. That looks like an important letter.

Props boy tries to stuff large envelope through the letter box – it won't go – he pushes it through the side of the door.

I'll get it, Mrs O – oh, you're too quick for me – I can never lift a finger when you're around.

Mrs Overall sets off very slowly for the door.

Mrs Overall	*(pronouncing it correctly)* It's your decree nisi, Miss Babs.
Babs	*(pronouncing it the same way)* 'Nisi', Mrs O.
Mrs Overall	'Nisi'. I always get that word wrong.
Babs	I can't bear to look – have I got custody of the triplets?
Mrs Overall	I'm afraid not, Miss Babs, but you have won a weekend for two in the Peak District and a deep fat fryer.
Babs	Do you think those triplets were really mine, Mrs O? After all, I did only go into hospital to have my ears pierced.
Mrs Overall	Well, look at it this way – you can't break an omelette without beating eggs. Eating eggs.

Babs sighs ruefully.

Music.

Film. Ext. Day. Hospital. Berta comes out, sees a crawling mini-cab, hails it and gets in.

Int. Back of cab. Berta is actually saying something like 'I'll just pretend to be saying something'.

Berta   *(dubbed on later)* Acorn Antiques, please.

Scene Two. Dining Room. A dining table with chairs along one side only, to leave room for the cameras at the other side of the table. Babs, Clifford and Trixie sit facing the camera. Trixie dressed as a nun, loads of eye make-up etc. On cue, they all put down their spoons as if they've just finished their pudding.

Trixie   Oh Mummy, that was a truly delicious Prune Melba.
Babs   High praise indeed from a Mother Superior!
Trixie   Oh Mummy, you know I've been expelled from the convent. I'm only wearing this old habit because I forgot to collect my dry cleaning.
Clifford   Yes, why did you get expelled?
Trixie   *(off-hand)* Oh, I just broke a few things.
Clifford   Like what?
Trixie   Oh, just a few vows.
Babs   Listen!

Sound of black cab.

Clifford   *(very slowly)* It sounds like –
Babs   *(jumping in)* I think you're right.
Clifford   *(determined to finish his line)* A taxi.
Babs   Derek can't be back from the clinic this early.

Enter Berta with a carry-cot, tilted at a dangerous angle.

                   Berta!
Berta   You may as well know, I've discharged myself.
Babs   Come and sit down, you're just in time for coffee. Clifford, run and fetch Mrs O.

Berta sits down.

She's in the scullery stuffing an aubergine. Trixie – show him the way.

Clifford leaves very slowly, Trixie can't get past him.

Now, I couldn't help noticing – what's in the carry-cot?

Berta See for yourself.

Cut to library film of a baby in a different carry-cot.

Babs A baby! Where did that come from? And while we're on the subject – where's your eighty per cent lambswool eau-de-nil donkey jacket?

Berta I, I . . .

Mrs Overall appears in shot without having come through the door.

Mrs Overall Miss Berta! You've never gone and done one of your silly, silly swaps!

Music.
Credits.

Berta But that's enough about me, what's all this building work I saw as I came in?

Babs I should have sent you a telemessage –

Mrs Overall The fact is, Miss Berta, Acorn Antiques is re-opening as a health club and leisure centre.

Reaction from Berta. Screen goes blank.

Mrs Overall *(Voice Over)* With sun beds! *(In own voice)* Why, why, why do I always forget those darn sun beds, anybody know?

EPISODE TEN

Scene One. The shop. Extras as before but now dressed in towelling dressing gowns with 'AA' on the back, and flippers. Babs is in her usual gear, with a sweatband round her wig.

Babs   Enjoy your swim – just leave your antiques in the cubicle – they'll be perfectly safe.

Extras nod and smile without speaking. Enter Berta from another door in top half of suit, tracksuit pants and court shoes.

Berta! Feel better for your run?

Berta   I certainly do. After all, running does keep you fit and could be a considerable contributory factory in reducing heart disease. Where's Mrs O? It was only the thought of her macaroons that kept me going.

Babs   *(pressing buttons on new intercom)* Mrs Overall, coffee for two in reception, please. Now *(leaves button pressed down, strange female voice comes from it)*

Voice   – went all the way to Nottingham, all the way back.

Babs switches it off.

Babs	Now – there's something I've been meaning to –

Enter Derek and Trixie in judo gear. Trixie with lots of jewellery and high heels.

Babs	Ah! Derek and Trixie, how did you get on in the international judo competition?
Derek	We came third, Miss Babs. Tibet was first, then Manchesterford.
Babs	Well done. Now get along to Maintenance, Derek, please. A parcel's just arrived and we haven't a clue if it's a Henry Moore or part of the central heating.
Derek	Right away, Miss Babs *(doesn't move)*.
Babs	*(supposedly stopping him in the doorway)* Oh, Derek –
Derek	Yes, Miss Babs?
Babs	Oh, nothing, it doesn't matter.
Trixie	Mummy?
Babs	Yes, darling?
Trixie	Oh, nothing, it doesn't matter.
Berta	Mrs O is being a long time with those macaroons. I hope –
Babs	What?
Berta	Oh, nothing – it doesn't matter.

Enter Mrs Overall.

Babs	Mrs O, you have been a long time, I hope there's nothing wrong.
Mrs Overall	Why should there be anything wrong, Miss Babs?
Babs	No reason, it's just –
Mrs Overall	Except of course that –
Babs	That?
Berta	Go on.
Trixie	Yes?
Mrs Overall	Except that – oh, it's nothing, it doesn't matter.

Reaction from other three. Music.

Film. Usual street. Babs walking along, reaches a doctor's house, looks up at the name plate, checks it on the piece of paper she's carrying (cut in close-up of piece of paper held by hairy male hand), checks the name plate again, steels herself and goes in.

Scene Two. Sitting room. Babs, Berta (still with sweat-bands) and Clifford (in tennis gear with tan make-up stopping just below the chin). Enter Mrs Overall in leotard and tights, and carrying tray.

Mrs Overall   Here we are. A nice tray of decaffeinated coffee with low-fate milk and sugar-free sugar.

Babs   Goodness, how healthy.

Mrs Overall   Oh, I enjoyed myself.

Babs   And how was the aerobics class?

Mrs Overall   Oh, I enjoyed myself. The correct footwear, a supportive brassière to prevent chafing and plenty of individual attention from a qualified instructor.

Babs   It sounds ideal *(suddenly looks worried)*.

Mrs Overall   It was only the exercises I didn't take to.

Clifford   Babs? You look pensive.

Babs   No I'm not, I was just thinking.

Berta   *(getting up with difficulty, wedged in the sofa)* Well, I think I'll go for a ten-mile bicycle ride.

Babs   Well, don't forget your florescent clothing and protective headgear.

Berta   I won't.

Babs   And Berta –

Berta   Ah – ha?

Babs   Oh, nothing – it doesn't matter.

Exit Berta.

Look, you two, this isn't easy to say . . .

Mrs Overall I knew it – the mysterious man with the bins seen lurk-
ing by the binoculars – it's Trixie's twin cousin, isn't it,
he won't rest until Acorn Antiques Leisure Centre and
Sunbed Centre has been closed down.

Music.
Credits.

Babs *(The table is now covered in milk dripping everywhere.)*
No, it's not that. I went to see our family doctor, Dr
Wimley, today.

Mrs Overall Oh, Miss Babs, what did he say?

Clifford Yes, for heck's sake Babs, what did the doctor say?

Babs He said he was sorry about the noise but there were
men outside digging up the pavement.

EPISODE ELEVEN

Scene One. Shop. Extras as before (no dressing gowns). Babs staring at letter. Enter Berta from the house.

Berta	Is that the bill from the wholesalers?
Babs	Yes, and it's rather puzzling.
Berta	Why, what does it say?
Babs	See for yourself.

Babs breathes huge sigh and blows it off the table.

Berta	*(trying to appear to read it and still stay in shot)* That's ridiculous. They've charged us for seven Laughing Cavaliers!
Babs	It must be a misprint, I'm sure we only ordered four.

Enter Mrs Overall.

Mrs Overall	I know it's only a quarter to, but I've just this minute whipped my coconut buns out of the microwave. Miss Berta?
Berta	Well, you know me and coconut.
Mrs Overall	Not to worry. We got it all out of the carpet last time. How's the baby, Miss Berta? Still breastfeeding?
Berta	Well, I know I should be passing on my immunities, but with a bra-slip and a jersey two-piece it's just not on.

Babs   Clifford should have been here by now.

*Clifford can be seen through the window of the shop,
laughing animatedly, talking to a stage-hand.*

Mrs Overall He's been looking very strange these past few days. I
hope he hasn't done anything silly.
Babs   Anything silly?
Berta   Like what?
Mrs Overall Like putting on a false nose and learning the banjulele.
Berta   No, it's all right, I can hear his car.
Babs   Yes, thank heavens he has such a distinctive horn.

*Clifford stubs out his fag on the set, and acting ponderously
as before, comes into the shop.*

Clifford! What's wrong, you're as white as a sheet! *(He's
as brown as ever.)*
Clifford   I have something to tell you, Babs.
Berta   Shall I go?
Clifford   No, stay. And please come back, Mrs O. *(She hasn't
moved but does so on his line.)* What I have to say con-
cerns everybody.

*Sits down heavily on a small ornate table, the leg crunches
and he slips sideways a few inches.*

---

*Film. Street. Derek pacing up and down outside the shop
door. He comes to a decision and walks away.*[130]

---

*Scene Two. Sitting Room. Mrs Overall standing. Clifford
sitting.*

---

130 Cut.

Mrs Overall Come on, Mr Clifford – while Miss Babs and Miss Berta are sellotaping that bit back onto Michelangelo's 'David', why don't you tell me all about it?

Clifford The fact is, Mrs O, my life seems completely grey, bleak and pointless.

Mrs Overall Yes well, sometimes that's God's way of getting you to enjoy 'Gardener's World'.

Clifford stands up suddenly, catching the boom operator unawares, hits his head on it, and collapses in pain, moaning. Mrs Overall is oblivious to all this.

Mrs Overall You see, you're smiling, things can't be all that bad, out with it!

Clifford *(in pain)* Bloody Norah. Oh, blimey.

Mrs Overall Oh, you're not! Mr Clifford, what shocking news!

Enter Babs and Berta.

Well, I finally winkled it out of him, Miss Babs, and it took some winkling.

Babs Don't say any more, Mrs O. The baby alarm was on in the antiques packing department, and Berta and I heard the whole darn thing!

Music.
Credits.

Enter Derek in street clothes, nearly the same as in the film. Clifford has left the set.

Babs Yes, come in Derek, we all know your sordid little secret. Why don't you and Clifford have a session right here and now?

Derek That's what I came to tell your Mr Clifford. The accordion and the banjulele – they've disappeared into thin air!

Reaction from Clifford's chair.

EPISODE TWELVE

Scene One. The sitting room. Berta ironing a shirt. Clifford, Trixie and Derek are all jammed on the sofa.

Berta   So you and Derek weren't having an affair after all?

Trixie   Oh, no. He was just lying on top of me to get the creases out of my negligée.

Berta   I knew there must be a perfectly reasonable explanation.

Trixie   *(struggling up from the sofa)* Anyway, I have to get back to the convent.

Berta   The convent? Why?

Trixie   I forgot my teapot.

Derek   I'll give you a lift.

Trixie   Well, all right, but don't crash through a grocer's window this time. Those tinned pears really hurt me. Bye!

Exit Derek and Trixie.

Berta   Bye! *(having completely mangled the shirt).*

Berta   There, that looks a bit better.

Clifford   Perfect. Berta – I've been meaning to –

Berta   Just unplug the iron for me, could you?

Clifford   A pleasure *(he bends to do so).*

Berta   Only don't touch it with your bare hands because . . .

Clifford	Argggh!
Berta	Because . . . it's faulty . . .

Enter Mrs Overall with a tray.

Mrs Overall	Whatever was that heartrending scream, Miss Berta? I thought somebody was being electrocuted.
Berta	Look!
Mrs Overall	Oh, my good golliwog!

She drops the tray on Clifford's foot.

Clifford	Ow!
Berta	Is he – dead?
Mrs Overall	Well, put it this way, Miss Berta, I needn't have bothered rinsing out the extra mug.
Berta	No, Clifford will never touch your macaroons again!

Enter Babs.

Babs	What was that terrible noise? It sounded like a tray of coffee being dropped on someone who's just been electrocuted.
Mrs Overall **Berta**	*(nearly together)* Look!
Babs	He's dead. *(Bursts into tears.)*
Mrs Overall	Crying won't bring him back, Miss Babs.
Babs	*(cheering up)* No, that's true.
Mrs Overall	Why don't we all have a mug of my delicious home-made sherry and a couple of sausage dumplings?
Babs	Yes, Mrs O, why don't we?

They all laugh. Music.

Film. Street. Derek and Trixie bring out from the back of the Acorn Antiques van a large cardboard carton labelled

'Venus de Milo. Fragile. This way up. Use no Hooks' etc.
They take it into the shop.

Scene Two. The shop. Extras leaving as usual, Babs on the
phone.

Babs   *(waving goodbye to extras)* Ah oui, bien sûr, j'aime beau-
coup le World Cup, aussi. Naturellement. Au revoir.

Babs puts the phone down. Derek and Trixie come in with
carton, now upside down. Next dialogue at high speed.

Derek   We've brought the 'Venus de Milo', Miss Babs.
Trixie And we want to say goodbye.
Babs   Goodbye? But why?
Derek   We're going away.
Babs   Away? Where?
Trixie Together.
Babs   Together? When?
Derek   We're going overland to Morocco.
Babs   You're going overland to Morocco? Why?

Enter Berta from street.

Berta   What's wrong, Babs?
Babs   It's Derek and Trixie; they're going away, travelling
overland to Morocco, together.
Berta   Derek and Trixie are overland travelling away to Mo-
rocco, together. But why?
Trixie Everyone says you can get really nice jumpsuits. Bye!

Trixie and Derek leave.

Babs   Right – back to business – these antiques.

Babs draws Berta away to one side as the focus of the scene changes to Mrs Overall, who enters stealthily from the street and tiptoes past them. We are not supposed to hear their dialogue but the mike is in the wrong place.

Babs	I'll just go blah blah blah blah.
Berta	And I'll nod back blah blah blah blah . . .
Babs	Give the blithering old nuisance time to get to the table. Chippendale.
Berta	Mahogany.
Babs	Da da de dum. Right. Mrs O! We never heard you come in. What happened to the body?
Mrs Overall	Mr Clifford? He's gone nice and stiff, so I've propped him up by the ironing board.
Babs	How lovely.
Mrs Overall	Well he was that tall, there was no room to hoover.
Berta	Mmm, what's that delicious smell?
Mrs Overall	That must be my macaroons. I've had them on a low light since Wednesday.
Berta	I'll get them.

Exit Berta.

Mrs Overall	Slice them finely, or someone might choke to death . . . I don't think she heard me. *(Pulls face to indicate sudden worry.)*
Babs	What's wrong, Mrs O?
Mrs Overall	The tea-leaves in my cup this morning, something's wrong somewhere.
Babs	Why?
Mrs Overall	It was a cup of Horlicks.
Babs	It's strange to think of Clifford lying in the sitting room, all alone.

Clifford seen in outdoor clothes crossing the back of the set with a bag, waving goodbye to someone unseen, miming 'Let's have a drink', etc.

Mrs Overall Not to worry. When Mr Overall (no relation) was dying, he said, 'Well, Boadicea, I shall never have to play another game of Travel Scrabble.'

Babs Why did he call you Boadicea?

Mrs Overall He was barmy, Miss Babs.

Berta comes in with the tray.

Berta Your macaroons smell delicious.

Babs Yes, Mrs O, you sample the first one.

Mrs Overall Well, I will, but just in case anything should happen when I bite into it *(music)* I just want to say what I feel for Acorn Antiques and the folk who work there. I'm only a simple woman, I haven't any 'O' levels or life-saving certificates, I've never been abroad or fully participated in a Summit Conference, but I have feelings . . .

Babs and Berta gradually stop acting and get bored.

. . . and what I feel for Acorn Antiques and you Miss Babs and you Miss Berta *(turns macaroon over, it has a few scribbled lines pasted on it)* is nothing more or less than plain simple *(squints at macaroon)* cove – love.

She bites into it, chokes to death, and carefully lowers herself to the floor, avoiding the furniture and pulling down her skirt.

Babs She's choking on her own macaroon. Quick, get Dr Wimley, the family doctor!

Berta I can't, he's being blackmailed in the Sudan.

Babs   Oh, darn. Well quite frankly, Berta, as far as Mrs O is
                     concerned, it's far too late.

                     Abrupt change from mood music to theme music.
                     Credits.
                     Cut back to Babs and Berta in tears crouched uncomfort-
                     ably by Mrs Overall.

Babs   Mrs Overall – that macaroon you just choked on – I'm
                     going to send the recipe to the *Weekly News*.
Mrs Overall   Oh, I am pleased.

                     She dies. Pause.

                     (In own voice) Are we off? I thought that went quite
                     well, didn't you?
Voice Off   Still on air!

                     She dies again reluctantly.

                     THE END

THE MAKING OF ACORN ANTIQUES

THE MAKING OF ACORN ANTIQUES

*Int. Office. Day. Opening sequence of 'Acorn Antiques' –
entirely as usual. Camera pulls back – we are watching a
TV screen in the 'Acorn Antiques' production office. Paul
Heiney is sitting on a desk watching it. He switches it off
with his remote control and swivels to camera.*

Paul How many people tune in to hear that oh-so-familiar
music every evening? About fifty-four. But what goes on
behind the scenes? What *don't* the public see? *(He runs the
sentence through again in his head, then carries on.)*

Walks over to a door marked 'Script Conference In Progress'

Let's find out what exactly does or doesn't go into the
making of 'Acorn Antiques'.

CAPTION 'THE MAKING OF "ACORN ANTIQUES"'

Paul taps on the door.

Marion *(out of vision)* Get out!

*Conference room. Day. Marion Clune, at the head of the
table, is checking through that week's scripts, talking into
a phone jammed into her neck and checking a wallplan*

> *behind her, all at the same time. Round the table are Simon,*
> *the weedy director, and a few writers including Roberts and*
> *Watkins.*

Paul   *(out of vision)* It's seven o'clock on Monday morning and
                Marion Clune, 'Acorn Antiques'' much feared executive
                producer, is knocking the week's scripts into shape.

Marion   *(tossing the scripts back like homework)* Blake, Thursday's
                not bad, Roberts, Monday's script – not totally bananas
                about the AIDS story – would Mrs Overall really know
                what a condom is?

Simon   *(eagerly)* She could call it a 'Comdon'.

Marion   *(seriously)* Yes, that's very funny, we'll use it. No, this
                AIDS idea[131] has been an itsy bit overplayed – let's box
                a wee bit dangerous – I'm talking off the top of my
                hairdo now – let's really go for it – earwax – I've never
                seen it tackled – it's an issue, it's health – suppose Berta
                gets earwax – no – she finds a syringe.

Roberts   Could I just throw something in here, Marion?

Marion   Feel free, mucho libre[132] –

Roberts   I think perhaps AIDS has more potential, dramatically,
                than earwax.

Marion   *(not even looking up)*[133] Right, you're fired. Don't talk
                to the press if you like having kneecaps *(tossing another
                script back as Roberts leaves, stunned).* Tuesday's script,
                very good,[134] Watkins – funny way to spell 'Acorn'.
                Friday's . . .

Ext. Church hall. Day.

Paul   And those very scripts end up here, where the actors

---

131 Changed to 'No, I really think this AIDS idea . . .'
132 Changed to 'multo libre'.
133 In the recording, Marion Clune does look up.
134 Cut.

and director sweat to produce the magic that *is* 'Acorn Antiques'.

He goes inside.

Church hall. The floor is marked up. A few odd pieces of furniture. Thermoses in a corner where Albert and Michaela are sitting. Far away from them sits Mrs Overall in lovely tailored slacks. Clifford sits alone, embroidering a tray cloth. In the middle of rehearsing stand Babs in jaunty casuals and unfamiliar hairdo and Derek resplendent in an off-the-shoulder overcoat and toupé. Simon watches intently, making squares of his fingers to represent the camera lens.

Babs	*(mumbling to herself)* Put the phone down. Down it goes, turn to Derek . . . Simon? Yes?
Derek	And I'll look sort of questioningly at you.
Babs	*(off-hand)* Will you? So turn to Derek. 'That was the Immigration Authority, Derek.'

He gasps.

	Are you going to do that, because I'll leave a gap.
Derek	No, it was my tooth again.
Babs	Poor you. 'Immigration Authority, Derek. It's not good news, I'm afraid.'
Derek	Miss Babs?
Babs	Can't we cut that 'Miss Babs'? It's Bab Bab Bab every two minutes. Anyone mind? Simon? No? OK. 'Good news, I'm afraid. You're being repatriated, you've to catch the first train to Kirkcudbright tomorrow morning.'
Derek	It's Kirkcudbright.
Babs	I know that – Babs wouldn't. Simon? Agreed?
Derek	Then I'll look – because he's quite stunned by this news, isn't he?
Babs	No idea.

Derek	Then I'll turn and go *(starts to do it very slowly and dramatically)*.
Babs	*(walking off the set)* The camera's on me there anyway, isn't it? Simon? Yes? Tea break? Simon? Yes? Black coffee please, Albert!

Calls from everyone else for tea and coffee.
Berta dashes in.

Berta	Hello![135]

They all gather round concernedly, cries of 'Darling!' 'How is everything?', etc.

Mrs Overall	Oh darling, how did you get on?
Babs	Oh yes darling, any luck?
Berta	Not bad *(waves carrier bag)*. No éclairs, but a lot of those nice long doughnuts.

Cries of 'well done', 'how marvellous', etc.

Same. Paul, Mrs Overall and Kenny sitting a little way off from the others.

Paul	Are you like the part you play? Are you in fact Mrs Overall?
Mrs Overall	I think Bo and I are rather alike, Paul, yes . . .
Paul	Bo?
Mrs Overall	Boadicea. We're both rather gutsy ladies, very determined, strong moral sense, we've both had rather difficult lives, a certain amount of personal loss . . . *(She loses her thread as she dwells on this.)*
Derek	They're both very warm and very giving.
Mrs Overall	*(patting his hand)* Bless you for that, my darling. And of course I'm rather younger and I hope rather more attractive!

---

135 This line and the rest of the scene were cut.

They all laugh.

Paul   *(laughing)* So the famous lumpy tights and, er, varicose veins are just something that goes on with the make-up?

Mrs Overall   *(after nasty silence)* Have you got the crossword, Kenny my darling?

Same. Clifford and Paul

Paul   Are you all one big happy family? Do you all get on well?

Clifford   *(thinks)* I should say, on the whole, no.

Same. Mrs Overall, Derek and Paul.

Paul   There's been rather a lot made in the Press of a feud between you and certain younger members of the cast – any truth in that?

Mrs Overall   *(shrugging enigmatically)* Dear Paul, I'm a huge, huge star – this is the price I pay. Look how the Press treated poor Yorky.

Derek   Fergie.

Mrs Overall   Fergie.

Ext. The location shop front and street. Day.

Marion and Simon in earnest conversation as the camera is being set up for a shot of Mrs Overall leaving the shop with a letter. Paul is hanging around, not liking to interrupt.

Paul   *(out of vision)* Thursday is set aside for outside filming, and here on the 'Acorn Antiques' lot a tricky shot is being discussed.

Marion   So Mrs Overall comes out, takes out the letter, posts it, goes back in. Bueno. Let's shoot it.

Simon   Except we haven't got the letter box.

Paul	Ah – so –
Marion	*(furious)* Mickey! Here! Now! *(The props boy Mickey runs up.)*
Mickey	Yes, Miss Clune?
Marion	*(slapping him on each side of the head in turn)* You don't – chew – gum. *(Holding hand out)* Take it out. Give it to me. You're fired. What say, Simon?
Simon	*(agitated)* No letter box, she can't post the letter.
Marion	No problem. Nila problemo. Slip in a line 'Oh Miss Babs the letter box has been stolen by international terrorists, what a palaver . . .'

Mrs Overall with a fur coat over her costume, supported by Derek, totters up.

Simon	What, and pick that up in another story later?
Marion	No *(concerned)*. How are they, Bo?[136]
Mrs Overall	They're fine, I'm fine. Kenny – if you could hover with my Veganin?
Kenny	*(taking her coat)* I'll be here.
Paul	Is there some sort of problem –
Marion	*(back to business)* Small change, Bo – the letter box has been stolen –
Mrs Overall	So I come out –
Marion	Come out –
Mrs Overall	Walk walk walk to the pillar box –
Marion	Blimey oh fiddledebob – no pillar box.
Mrs Overall	React react react.
Marion	That's it.
Simon	Oh fantastic, it's here!

Man in anorak dumps down pillar box.

Marion	Right – back to plan A – there is now a pillar box.
Mrs Overall	Oh, there is a pillar box. First there's no pillar box, then

---

136 Added in the recording: 'Has this terrible rain brought them on again?'

one appears. What next, no pavement, no shop? *(She notices Paul and the film crew.)* Sorry, do you mind – this is rather a tricky manoeuvre – rather fussing to be filming as one's working.

Paul   OK. Cut it.

Make-up room. Babs and Berta larding it on. Clifford being made up by girl, Derek hanging round chatting to him.

Paul   *(out of vision)* It's Friday, just time for a quick make-up check before the cameras finally roll.

Girl   I thought perhaps as Mr Clifford has been in prison for a year, he perhaps would be quite pasty, so I thought I'd use this instead of the Cool Copper.[137]

Clifford   No, I'll stick with the usual, I think.

Paul   So where will I find Mrs Overall?

Babs   In her dressing room, I expect.

Derek   *(out of vision)* I said 'Excuse me – I had leather shorts before George Formby had a ukulele' –

Paul   So you've all got a dressing room to relax in, have you?

Berta   No, not all of us.

Mrs Overall's cosy dressing room. The room is full of flowers, cards, photos of Russell Grant, Derek and Mrs Overall's mother, stuffed toys etc.

Paul   And these are all presents?

Mrs Overall   People are so so so kind. I'm just a jobbing actress, who scraped to put herself through the RADA and yet somehow I've captured the hearts of the nation – it's almost frightening.

Paul   *(sniffing at fancy jar)* And what's this?

Mrs Overall   It's a haemorrhoid preparation to be brutally frank, Paul *(winces as she takes it from him)*.

---

137 This line and Mr Clifford's reply were cut.

Studio, the usual set. Albert and Michaela position themselves by their antique. Babs, Berta and Clifford sort themselves out by the desk.

Paul   *(out of vision)* This is it. This is the moment when all that hard work pays off. As the actors stand by on the studio floor . . .

Int. Gallery. Day. Marion, Simon and batty PA.

Paul   *(out of vision)* . . . Marion and Simon get ready to record episode 1,573 of 'Acorn Antiques'.

Marion   *(into mike)* OK, running up recording. You've done a marvellous week's work – relax, enjoy it, but above all – don't touch the antiques – I want them back in my lounge in one piece. Stand by.

Simon   Cue titles.

Opening sequence comes up on monitors.

Side of set. Mrs Overall with Paul, waiting to enter with tray.

Paul   How are you feeling?

Mrs Overall I won't talk, Paul my darling, I just have to gather myself in, focus . . . 'be' . . .

Gallery (as before).

Simon   Cue Albert and Michaela.

PA   Coming to 2. No . . . 3. No, it *was* 2. Now coming to 3. Oh . . .

Simon   And in on Babs!

Babs   *(on monitor)* I've had a most peculiar letter . . .

Marion   Good and close camera 2. Love those nostrils.

Side of set (as before).

Mrs Overall	*(in full flow)* And Princess Margaret is so like me, give, give, give *(hands Paul the tray)*. Do you mind, I did promise the specialist – well –

Gallery (as before).

Berta	*(on monitor)* I don't know about you Clifford, but I could jolly well do with a nice cup of tea and a chocolate bhaji.
Babs	So could jolly well I.
Marion	*(over Babs's line)* Nice nod to the Asians there.
PA	Coming to 3. Oh, what page are we on now?[138]
Simon	Stand by, Mrs Overall, steady on the doorway 3.

Side of set (as before).

Mrs Overall	I said – for you Lord Delfont[139] –

Assistant Floor Manager runs up frantically waving.

I'm talking Sally – for you, Lord Delfont it will be a pleasure and an honour.

Gallery (as before). Monitor: Babs, Clifford and Berta wait silently.[140]

Simon	Where is she? Cue her!
Marion	She'll be there, be calm, be calm. *(Screaming)* COME ON!

Side of set (as before).

---

138 This line, as well as those from Berta, Babs and Marion, were cut.
139 Bernard Delfont, theatrical impresario who for twenty years presented the Royal Variety Performance. Created a life peer in 1976.
140 Added in the recording:
  Babs: She won't be long.

AFM   You're on!
Mrs Overall   I'm aware of that, Sally, after thirty years in the business.

Goes on, leaving Paul with the tray.

Gallery (as before).

Simon   No tray! Where's the bloody tray?
Marion   We'll cope.
Simon   It's mentioned!
Marion   Mentioned?

Cut to close-up of monitor.

Babs   Mrs Overall, we could smell your bhajis a mile away!
Berta   And do I spy a new tray?

Silence.

Marion   She'll get us out of it, come on, Bo. Improvise!

Back to monitor.

Mrs Overall Yes, I just had to bring it in and show you. Take it, isn't it light?
Babs   *(miming)* Mmm, and such a lovely shade of mauve. Look, Clifford!
Clifford   It's magnificent.
Simon   *(overlapping Babs's line)* Shall we cut? Go back?
Marion   No, we professionals notice these things, but[141] Joe Public never clocks a darn thing.

She sits happily watching the monitor as Paul appears in the doorway with the tray.

---

141 'these things, but' was cut.

STILL BARMY

SPAGHETTI

Lunchtime in a small Italian restaurant. Philippa and Faith drinking wine.

Philippa   Cheers.

Faith   Cheers. How's things?

Philippa   Oh, its been a terrible week. Monday I thought I was having an early menopause.

Faith   And were you?

Philippa   No, the dog had been beggaring about with the thermostat.

Faith   I didn't know you had a dog.

Philippa   It's my mother's. She's in Marbella for the winter.[142] Twelve pounds a week all in.

Faith   That's very cheap.

Philippa   She's sharing a room with two dustmen.

Faith   Does she like Spain?

Philippa   She likes the majesty and grandeur of the landscape, but she's not keen on the bacon.

Faith   What sort of dog is it?

Philippa   Oh, performing. Rolls round the kitchen on a beach ball *(is interrupted by arrival of cheeky Italian waiter who serves two pasta dishes).* Thank you.

---

142 Changed to 'for the summer'.

Waiter	Pasta – bit fattening, hey? Something to grab hold of . . . nice one *(They half-smile, he leaves.)*
Philippa	They're all like that here. Jamming their groins into your tortellini. Then on Tuesday, Nick left home.
Faith	What, for good?
Philippa	He's taken the toolshed.
Faith	I thought you were so well-suited.
Philippa	We were – especially physically. Every time I gave him the old come hither, he came hither.
Faith	You were quite experimental, weren't you?
Philippa	Oh yes, outdoors; three in a bed –
Faith	With the man next door?
Philippa	I don't recommend it. They got on to politics and I ended up watching 'Take the High Road'[143] with the sound off.

Waiter in.

Waiter	Parmesan?
Philippa	Thank you.
Faith	Thank you.
Waiter	Yum, yum, very nice, very cheesy.

Makes kissing noises and leaves.

Philippa	We should have gone to the Snacketeria. One thing about self-service is no one tries to arouse your sexuality. No, Nick, apparently, is in love with someone else.
Faith	How long's that been going on?
Philippa	Must be yonks, because he told me 'their tune' was 'Chirpy Chirpy Cheep Cheep'.
Faith	Who is it?
Philippa	You know I mentioned a very small neighbour of mine – buys children's clothes and spends the VAT on tequila?
Faith	Mmm.

---

143 Scottish soap opera. VW named Mrs Overall after Mrs Mack, one of its main characters.

Philippa   It's her. I wondered why he'd had that cat-flap widened.

Waiter in with huge pepper mill.

Waiter   Pepper, ladies? Make you nice and hot.
Both   Thank you.
Waiter   Nice big one, eh? I know what you ladies like *(leaves)*.
Philippa   Thank heavens the sausage was off. So I'm totally disillu-
               sioned. No more sex, I'm going to become a nun.
Faith   I thought you had to be able to play billiards.
Philippa   Oh no, that's all changed. I'm joining a convent in
               Smethwick[144] on Friday. I have to take one small suitcase
               and a jigsaw.
Faith   What's the habit like?
Philippa   Hot pants.
Faith   They're very outdated.
Philippa   Well, you have to make some sacrifices.
Faith   Won't you miss the physical side of life?
Philippa   No, Faith, because I'm basically a very cerebral and
               spiritual person – I don't go round panting for bodily
               intimacy like a misguided poodle.

Waiter nuzzles up to Philippa.

Waiter   You like to come and be very naughty with me in the
               staff washroom? Lots of sexy fun with nice big Italian
               boy?
Philippa   *(hesitating slightly)* Oh, go on then. Faith?
Faith   Just a black coffee, thank you.

---

144 Where JW grew up.

MEDICAL SCHOOL

An interview room. Two men and a woman behind a table. Paralytically nervous girl in suit sitting down. All the interviewers are completely non-committal throughout.

First man Sit down, er, Sarah.

Sarah Thank you.

First man It's only an interview, we're not going to eat you.

Sarah Ha ha ha.

First man I see you're taking Biology, Physics, Chemistry and English, all good A levels for medical school. How do you think you're going to do?

Sarah Well, I might get an A for physics, I might get an A, two Bs and a C for biology or I might get a B for physics, what I get very much depends . . .

First man Thank you.

Second man I see you're doing the Duke of Edinburgh's Award Scheme – do you think that's character-building?

Sarah Yes, I think it builds character, it is character building, yes, it is a character building thing, yes.

Second man In what way does it build character, do you think?

Sarah In what way – I think in the way that – just the way you'd expect, really.

Second man Thank you.

First man	Sarah – do you think there's any link between environment and disease?
Sarah	Do you mean *the* environment?
First man	Living conditions – do you think living conditions can affect health?
Sarah	Yes, I think they probably can.
First man	In what way?
Sarah	If you shared a bedroom with someone who had measles then you might get measles, or if you were very rich and had very thick carpets you might trip and break your ankle, it would affect you in that way.
First man	What about if you were very poor?
Sarah	If you were very poor, then you wouldn't have that kind of carpet.
First man	Do you think poor housing would have an adverse effect on health?
Sarah	Yes, I think it would have an adverse effect on health because, because it would affect people's health adversely.
First man	Thank you.
Woman	Sarah – do you think there's a gap between the media's portrayal of doctors and doctors in real life?
Sarah	Yes I think there is a gap because the doctor in East Enders has bushy eyebrows and it might make people think that if you're a doctor you have to have bushy eyebrows and you might not have bushy eyebrows but you might want to be a doctor, and that's not really fair . . .
Woman	Thank you.
First man	What do you think about the National Health Service?
Sarah	In what way, 'think'?
First man	Do you think it's crumbling, or doing very well, or . . .
Sarah	I think that probably that parts of it are crumbling, and parts of it are doing very well, I think you have to look at both sides.
First man	Go on.
Sarah	Of course some people say well oh let's close casualty departments and spend the money on nuclear weapons

> but I think you have to sit back and say if there is a
> nuclear war then we'll need casualty departments.

Second man   You don't think in a nuclear war we'll all be annihilat-
ed?

Sarah   No.

Woman   What qualities do you think you'll bring to the medical
profession? *(Pause.)* Are you particularly warm, or com-
passionate?

Sarah   I'm quite tidy.

Woman   Thank you.

First man   What was the last book you read, Sarah?

Sarah   *Othello.* It's a book by William Shakespeare of the Royal
Shakespeare Company. I've got the book, and I've got it
on little cards as well.

First man   What do you think is the main theme of *Othello*?

Sarah   I don't think it's got one, really. It's just various people
talking, and sometimes they do things in brackets.

First man   And do you think Othello was ill –

Sarah   *(quickly)* No.

First man   To act in the way he did – was he suffering from anything, when he discovered Desdemona's handkerchief?

Sarah   I think he might have been suffering from a cold.

First man   Right Sarah, thank you very much indeed.

Sarah goes out. They write.

I thought she was jolly good, didn't you?

Woman   Excellent.

Second man   Very astute.

First man   Unconditional offer?

Woman   Absolutely.

Second man   Definitely.

HE DIDN'T: ONE[145]

Bus stop. Kelly-Marie Tunstall and her pal.

Kelly So he walked over, right, big 'I am' and he had tattoos up his arms right, an anchor here and a microwave here.

Pal He didn't.

Kelly He did. He said do you want a drink or do you want a kick up the bum with an open-toed sandal. I said get you Eamonn Andrews.

Pal You didn't.

Kelly I did. I said I'll have a pint of babycham, some pork scratchings and a yellow cherry and if I'm not here when you get back I'll be in t' toilet putting hide and heal on my love bites.

Pal You didn't.

Kelly I did. So I come out of toilets, right, and he says hey scallop face your skirt's all caught up in your knickers at back, I said I pity you do you know why, he says why, I says 'cos it happens to be the latest fashion, I read it in a book, he says what book, I said Vogue that's what book, he said oh likely likely when do you read Vogue, I said when I'm in the hospital having exploratory surgery that's when. So he said oh.

---

145 The second half of this script was slightly cut and greatly rearranged.

Pal	He didn't.
Kelly	He did. And he sits there, right, picking the quiz off his beer-mat, and he says what were they exploring for, I said well it wasn't the Left Bank of the blinking Limpopo.
Pal	You didn't.
Kelly	I did. I said if you must know Magnus Magnusson[146] I was rushed in last Wednesday when I swallowed the upholstery attachment of an Electrolux 567. He said how did you do that, I said I were hoovering a pelmet with my mouth open. Like that.
Pal	You weren't.
Kelly	I was. He said was it a long operation, I said it was a bit longer than normal because while they were stitching me I said could they put a new zip in my drainpipes.
Pal	You didn't.
Kelly	I did. Anyway, he stands up and he says do you want to come for a Chinese or do you want a clip round the ear with a wrestler's braces? I said I'll come for a Chinese because I've had a clip round the ear with a wrestler's braces and there's nowt to it.
Pal	You didn't.
Kelly	I did. He fell about laughing. Like this. I could see all cheese and onion crisps in his fillings.
Pal	You couldn't.
Kelly	I could. So we sit down and he says right I'm bloke I'm ordering, I says haven't you ever heard of Women's Lib he says no, I said oh. Anyway, we get t'end of meal, right, he's having a crack at burping and I'm chasing a lychee round a saucer, he says can I walk you home?
Pal	He didn't.
Kelly	He did. I said what's brought this on, bird bath? I said you needn't get any funny ideas because my mum and

---

146 Presenter and author, best known for asking the questions on *Mastermind* for 25 years from 1972.

dad'll be up, I don't fancy you, and the surgeon says I can't joggle[147] about for a fortnight.

Pal   He didn't.

Kelly   Who?

Pal   Surgeon.

Kelly   He did. So I said you can walk me home, but you're not pressing me up against the doorbell. So he puts down his banana fritter, he says Kelly-Marie Tunstall, just because I have tattoos and a hairy navel button does not mean I do not have the instincts of an English gentleman. Please believe me when I say I will be happy to escort you to your abode of residence, asking nothing in return but the chance of seeing you again.

Pal   He didn't.

Kelly   No, he didn't. He caught his bus and I had to pay for my own lychees.

---

147 Changed to 'says I haven't to joggle'.

TATTOO PARLOUR

Small shop, a few sample designs on the wall, and electric equipment. Two young slightly drunk sailors come in, ring the bell for service and stand shoving each other and laughing. Enter nice cosy woman.

Woman	Can I help you, boys?
Eric	Isn't there a feller?
Woman	Mr Armstrong's having a lie down, I'm afraid. I'd rather not wake him. He's just done flags of all nations on a twelve-stone Wren.
Eric	Shall we go, Paul?
Woman	I'm a qualified tattooist as well as my husband. That's how we met. I had the shop next door, and he used to pop over if I needed an extra hand with a tricky buttock.
Paul	There's another shop up the road, isn't there?
Woman	Harry Abraham's? You should be all right there, they do have marvellous antibiotics these days, don't they?
Paul	How do you mean?
Woman	Apart from which he bolts his food.
Eric	Eh?
Woman	One hiccup halfway through the execution of a naked woman, and you're going through life with a bicep full of hermaphrodite.
Eric	OK, well we'll stay here then, shall we?

Woman	Lovely, right.[148] Have a seat. What designs had you in mind?
Eric	Don't know – we only came in because we couldn't get into 'Bambi'.
Paul	What about a name? My girlfriend's name.
Woman	What is her name, dear?
Paul	Pat.
Woman	Not much to get your teeth into there. Hardly worth plugging the needle in for. I should leave that till you meet a girl who'll pay for a good bit of scrolling.
Eric	My girl at home's called Suzannah Margaret Mary.
Woman	Is it a steady relationship?
Paul	Not really.
Woman	You see, by the time I was up to the double 'n' you could have split up. Then you're either scouting round for another Suzannah Margaret Mary, or you find a girl with another name altogether who's broadminded, illiterate or never reads in bed. No, if you're stuck on having a name, boys, have something that can't cause embarrassment in later life, like 'Mother' or 'Miriam Stoppard'[149].
Eric	No . . .
Paul	What about an anchor and 'HMS Indestructible'? On my arm.
Woman	Yes, but what happens when you leave the Navy? It's going to look very incongruous if you go into the antiques business and have to roll your sleeves up to manoeuvre a Chesterfield.
Paul	I never thought of that.[150]
Woman	This is what I'm here for – we don't want you to roll in here drunk and wake up the next morning covered in inappropriate remarks.

---

148 Cut from 'There's another shop up the road' to here.
149 Doctor and presenter of medical and scientific programmes.
150 This line and Woman's reply were cut.

Eric	Hey – daggers! A pointed dagger, and it's dripping blood – like in three drops.
Woman	Not very cheerful, a dagger. If you're set on dripping, how about a leaky teapot?
Eric	No . . .
Paul	Hey – a panther! No, a cheetah – pouncing – right across my back – like that! *(Points to picture.)*
Woman	Stand up. Mmm. You've not really got the breadth of back for a fully successful cheetah. Have to be something a bit smaller. How about a Chihuahua?
Paul	Chihuahuas don't pounce.
Woman	They do if you tread on them.
Eric	*(ripping his shirt off and posing)* I've got a big back – I could have a cheetah.
Woman	Yes, but you see, dear, by the time I'd woven its paws in and out of your acne, it wouldn't be pouncing so much as waving.
Paul	*(laughing)* Tell her what you said to me on the way in.
Eric	What?
Paul	You know!
Eric	I didn't know it were a woman then, did I?
Woman	Oh, I've seen it all before dear – think of me as an usherette.
Paul	He said he wanted a Ferrari on his – thingy.
Woman	Well I'm happy to do that, though you must understand in moments of excitement it will distort. And[151] if you're posted to a cold climate it may tend to look more like a Reliant Robin. *(They sit dejected.)* Look, why not have one of our set pieces? *(Demonstrating on one of them:)* The Parthenon across here, rambling roses to the elbow, two naked women either side of the spinal column, Caucasian or Oriental depending on what ink there is in the stockroom, a map of the London underground

---

151 'it will distort. And' was cut.

down each leg, finishing across here with an illustrated recipe for Baked Alaska.

Paul   That's sounds great, doesn't it, Eric? How much is that?

Woman   Eight colours and a no-fade warranty – 350 pounds.

Eric   We can't afford it.

Woman   Never mind boys, how much money have you got?

They sift through their pockets.

Paul   We spent a lot on booze, didn't we?

Eric   *(sheepishly)* About four quid.

Woman   And you want a tattoo for that?

Eric   Yes.

Woman   OK, Boys. *(Slapping a transfer on the back of his hand)* Lick that.

PARTLY POLITICAL
BROADCAST

Caption: 'Jean and Barbara'.

Barbara	Just to say if Jean and I are elected, we're obviously going to do our best to serve the constituency. I'm going to serve it Monday through Wednesday.
Jean	And I'll do Thursday through Saturday.
Barbara	And we'll do alternative[152] Sundays, because I like to worship on that day.
Jean	And I like to have a good go at the kitchen cupboards.
Barbara	We both know this area pretty well, don't we.
Jean	Yes, in fact we can remember when the Old Malthouse Arts Centre used to be a Bingo Hall.
Barbara	That's right, and, and[153] the Co-op used to do coffee and a little bun-ny-type snack for forty pence, do you remember?
Jean	Yes, because that's where you knocked into that stand of ovenproof tableware with your wonky buggy.

---

152 This was possibly a typo. Changed to 'alternate'.

153 Cut from 'in fact we can remember' and replaced with 'because we were here when the Co-Op . . .'. This meant the next three speeches were swapped around, Jean saying Barbara's and vice versa. After 'pity it wasn't buggy-proof', it continues as per the script.

Barbara	And we said pity it wasn't buggy-proof! *(Laughs.)* Anyway. We're both quite political, aren't we?
Jean	Reasonably political. I was originally Liberal, and still think David Steel has a lot of credibility, popping up to the Borders every weekend to chop logs.
Barbara	And I was a Conservative, but looking back I think I was swayed by their rhetoric. And of course their garden parties had the best bran tubs.
Jean	You had those secateurs for years, didn't you?[154]
Barbara	But we've both broken away, haven't we? Rather like Shirley Williams[155], whom we both admire, on the whole.
Jean	We feel she needs a little updating, eyeshadow-wise, but —
Barbara	And we've formed a new political party.
Jean	It's just called the Jean and Barbara Political Party.
Barbara	It's got its own colour.
Jean	The mainstream parties seem to have left the field clear as far as pastels are concerned.
Barbara	So we plumped for taupe.
Jean	Mushroom.
Barbara	Can we just say we've always been very active in local politics, haven't we?
Jean	Oh yes, I wrote to the papers and said now the dustmen didn't have to hump the actual bins, should we still tip?
Barbara	And we both boycotted a restaurant once where there was a strike.
Jean	That's right. The waiters were holding placards up outside asking you not to go in.
Barbara	So we didn't.
Jean	We never went in anyway.
Barbara	No, but we were still making a firm political stance. In

---

154 Cut from 'And of course their garden parties' to here.

155 The era's most prominent female politician on the left. In 1981, the former Labour education secretary defected to form the Social Democrat Party. After the general election in 1987, when *Barmy* was published, the joke acquired an extra layer as she supported the SDP's merger with the Liberal Party.

fact we popped back after we'd done our shopping and boycotted it again, didn't we?[156]

Jean But we definitely know what people in this area want, don't we? Have you got our manifesto, Ba?

Barbara *(rooting in handbag)* No, I think I used it to jam my quarterlight.

Jean Well, anyway. It was – libraries. More Large Print novels, especially Jackie Collins.

Barbara That's for my grandad. He likes smut and he can't focus.

Jean More ramps. Ramp access – very very important for the wheelchair-bound.

Barbara And for the able-bodied, it's a lovely tone-up for the calves and thighs *(slapping them)*.[157]

Jean Proper sugar bowls on each table at The Swiss Cottage, not packets by the till.

Barbara Free dental treatment for old and sundry alike.

Jean Especially the woman on the pastry counter at Lewis's because she's just upsetting, I won't go in.

Barbara We want an increase in Family Income Supplement; we want a more frequent bus service.

Jean And we want a much bigger hut at the Sauna Centre, it's nose to nipple in there.

Barbara Mixed Wednesdays you have to beat them with twigs to get them to come out! But seriously . . .

Jean Yes. *(Pause.)* Well, that's about it. I'd better go, Ba, I'm doing something out of a book with sweetbreads.

They gather up their things.

Barbara Anyway, so vote for us if you feel like it next Thursday.
Jean Only if you're out anyway.
Barbara Oh yes, don't go specially.

---

156 Cut from 'Can we just say' to here.
157 This and the preceding line were cut.

They put coats on etc.

Jean	Lennons' sale previews Thursday.
Barbara	You could gen up on the reductions and then vote . . .
Voice Over	That was a partly political broadcast on behalf of Jean and Barbara.
Barbara	*(Voice Over)* Oh call me Ba, everyone else does!

SUSIE (CONTINUITY)

Susie   *(behind her is a map of Britain with flashing lights)* And Employment Update. Job losses – three thousand in Paisley and eight hundred in Sunderland with the closure of GK Metalworks. Job gains – good news in Hove is that Mrs Mason of the Sea Breeze Restaurant is taking on somebody to peel the potatoes.

MR RIGHT

Film. A tidy dull suburban street of semis and front gardens. A small neat woman, Pam, with a shopping trolley, waving to an occasional front window as she passes. She lets herself into one of the houses.

Pam   *(Voice Over)* I believe there's one man in this world that's meant for me, and I'm looking for him quite assiduously, and I'd really quite like him not to be Mexican, just because of the sombrero, it would give us all sorts of problems with the serving-hatch.

The hall of Pam's house, as she takes off her coat, calls hello to her mother, and takes the shopping trolley into the kitchen.

Pam   *(Voice Over)* I've got everything else, suede coat, two-speed hammer drill, and all I need now is Mr Right.

TITLE 'MR RIGHT'

Pam's kitchen. Pam is at the kitchen table, apparently peeling potatoes.

Corin   *(Voice Over)* Pamela Twill is forty-seven. She's never been married, she's never been engaged, she's never been to a

	Spinners concert[158] with anyone called Roger.
Corin	*(In camera. To Pam)* Has anyone ever proposed, Pam?
Pam	Oh yes, lots of people. A lot of widowers, a deckchair attendant, an anaesthetist, someone who made lamp-shades out of thermal underwear . . .
Corin	But you've never said yes.
Pam	I've never said yes. I'm looking for Mr Right, Corin. I've met Mr Wrong, I've met several Mr Reasonably OKs, and I've spent a very long afternoon in a bus shelter with Mr Halitosis but –
Corin	Do you think you're too choosy, pernickety?
Pam	No.
Corin	What are you doing with those potatoes?
Pam	Well, before I put them on to boil, I'm just carving them into the faces of minor celebrities, Corin. I've done Cliff Michelmore,[159] here, and Anona Winn,[160] and I'm just having a crack at Jeremy Beadle[161].
Corin	And do you do this every time you have boiled potatoes?
Pam	Oh yes, though I wouldn't normally do Jeremy Beadle, because of his perm, but –

Pam's lounge. Pam and her mother, an over-made-up drunken, chainsmoking old tart in a wheelchair. Pam has a coffee, mother has all the makings for a gin and tonic on the tray of her chair.

Mother	You'll never get a man dressed like that anyway, Pam.
Pam	I don't want a man dressed like this. *(Winks at Corin.)*

---

158 Changed to 'a bowling alley'.

159 Ubiquitous broadcaster who covered the moon landings, the assassination of President Kennedy and the investiture of Charles as the Prince of Wales.

160 Australian-born soprano and broadcaster who was a popular figure on BBC radio shows such as *Twenty Questions* and *Petticoat Line*.

161 Hyper-jolly presenter of LWT's *Game for a Laugh* and *Beadle's About*. From VW's 1993 live show: 'Mind you, if laughter is the best medicine, there must have been something terribly wrong with Jeremy Beadle.'

Mother	When I was your age I wore my blouses so tight my bosoms applied for a transfer. Any more gin?
Pam	In the pantry.

Mother wheels menacingly towards the camera.

Mother	Get out of my bloody way!
Corin	Has your mother always been in a wheelchair?
Pam	Oh, no. She was a very active nymphomaniac for many years, and eventually of course, something snapped . . .
Corin	Is that partly why you've never married – you feel you can't leave her?
Pam	I can't stick her, never mind leave her. No, I'm only – she's still quite insatiable, even now. I mean it's not nice, is it, someone kerb-crawling in an invalid car?
Mother	*(Off)* Well, whereabouts, you sexless dodo?
Pam	Next to the weedkiller! *(Winks at Corin.)* Some hopes!¹⁶²

Pam's office. Three desks. Pam, Margaret and Poll. All very similar, hanging up coats, gloves etc., putting on office cardi's and settling down at their desks.

Pam	*(Voice Over)* I share an office with Margaret and Poll. We dovetail pretty neatly together in the frantic hustle of a typical high-pressure, big-business situation.
Poll	*(reading from newspaper)* Right. Pam – Aquarius. This is a good day for buying a beige headscarf, but make sure it goes into the tumble dryer because you have been caught like that before. Margaret – Aries – your haemorrhoids should be on the wane . . .

Fade out Poll, fade up Corin.

Corin	*(Voice Over)* But today brings a break for Pam from office

---

162 This and Mother's preceding line were cut.

routine, for, in her ceaseless search for the man of her dreams, she has made an appointment with a computer dating agency.

Poll   (*still reading*) and be particularly wary of salesmen offering low-priced tweezers and denture tablets. Right . . .[163]

Dating agency. Walls covered in wedding photos. Dim girl nervously feeding Pam's details into a computer.

Girl   So what is it – meeting a man with a view to marriage?

Pam   Yes.

Girl   Some of our ladies just want someone to repoint the brickwork. Any particular colour of man?

Pam   No, I don't think so. I'm not nuts on freckles.

Girl   No freckles. What type of personality?

Pam   What type have you?

Girl   Outgoing, homeloving, miserable. You'll find there's quite a big choice at the miserable end of the market.

Pam   Dull, I think. Dull-ish.

Girl   Does he have to be able to –

Pam   Sorry?

Girl   Oosiswhat inter-thingy. Do you wish the marriage to be constipated?

Pam   I –

Girl   Are you looking for physical fill-fullment?

Pam   Yes.

Girl   It's just that some of our gentlemen can't manage that type of activity. They tend to be the miserable ones . . . It's now searching, and with any luck should come up with the name of your computer date just about now. Ooh, I'm new – it's flashing a recipe for flaky pastry. Mrs Lomax!

Town hall clock (or similar landmark). Pam waiting in her best clothes.

---

163 Cut.

Corin	*(Voice Over)* Pam is waiting for her first glimpse of her computer date, Donald Renshaw.

Donald, a perfectly normal-looking fifty-ish businessman, approaches Pam, shakes hands and leads her away.

Corin	*(Voice Over)* On paper he's perfect; will Mr Renshaw turn out to be Mr Right?

Restaurant. Pam and Donald being seated at a table. Waiter pulls out Pam's chair as she is sitting down, she falls under the table. He helps her up and gives them both a menu.

Donald	Soup of the day, please.
Waiter	Yes sir, which one?
Donald	Thursday.
Pam	*(pointing to item on menu)* Sorry, what are these?
Waiter	Grilled mushrooms with garlic, white wine and chopped parsley.
Pam	Do you think I could have them without the garlic?
Waiter	No garlic.
Pam	And no white wine.
Waiter	No wine.
Pam	And I won't have the mushrooms.
Waiter	How would you like the parsley?
Pam	Just how it comes, thank you *(waiter leaves),* but not too chopped.

Time lapse.

Corin	*(Voice Over)* Half-way through the main course. How are they getting on?
Pam	No, I think you're right. I think that tablecloth is a slightly different colour.
Donald	Slightly more of an off-white.

Pam   That's right. Sort of white with a hint of beige, as they
             say.[164]

             They fall silent.

             Time lapse.

Corin   *(Voice Over)* We're nearing the end of the pudding; has
             romance flourished over the meringue glacé?
Pam   I think one just has this idea, doesn't one, that in a
             restaurant like this, all the tablecloths will be the same
             colour, but –
Donald   It's remarkable how many shades of tablecloth there are
             just in this one room.
Pam   One room – I agree. As I say – but – er . . .

             They fall silent.

             _____

             *Ladies' powder-room. Pam enters, and immediately backs
             away.*

Pam   Oh I'm sorry, I – oh, we're filming.
Corin   Well, to me, Donald seems dull, obsessive, repetitive,
             humourless and crass. Would you agree?
Pam   Oh definitely – I'm hooked – that's my man!

             _____

             Doctor's waiting room. Pam sits reading Brides Magazine.[165]

Corin   *(Voice Over)* With Pam's marriage to Donald only a week
             away, she feels the time is right for a little chat with the
             doctor.

             *The surgery door opens. A man is ushered out by the doctor,
             frothing at the mouth, bouncing against the walls like a*

---

164 Cut from 'Half-way through the main course' to here. Over the voiceover, Pam can be heard
talking about 'pinky beige . . . with flowers in the carpet'.
165 This scene was cut, as were the scenes in the surgery and Pam's back garden.

mad moth etc.

Doctor   As I say, Jim, some people do get a very slight reaction with that one – enjoy your holiday anyway. Miss Twill?

Pam steps over the man who is now staggering to the door on all fours.

Surgery.

Pam   – so I just wanted a little chat before the wedding night, Doctor.
Doctor   Very sensible. What about?
Pam   Well, I've never had physical fill-fullment, and I thought I'd just pop in and get the gen, Doctor.
Doctor   Very wise. Well it's quite simple. The woman has an egg in her waterworks, and this comes to an arrangement with the man's plumbing, and Bob's your uncle. *(Standing up)* Any problems, just pop back and see me.
Pam   Thank you, Doctor.

Pam's back garden. Through the window we can see Donald and mother. Pam and Colin in deckchairs.

Corin   *(Voice Over)* And the final obstacle. Will Pam's mother and Donald get on, or will she turn against him and ban next Thursday's wedding?
Corin   They seem to be getting on quite well.
Pam   Mmmm.
Corin   How do you envisage married life?
Pam   Rather like single, I suppose. I think in my mind's eye I can see a bigger teapot.
Corin   And the intimate side of things?
Pam   Well, I must admit it'll be the first time I've seen a man's pyjama case.

A burst of laughter from inside the house. Ripping noise from Corin's deckchair and he sinks half-way through it. Pam looks at him.

Church. Corin waiting on the steps.

Corin   (*to camera*) Well, it's the big day. Pam asked us not to film the ceremony itself, and with a sensitivity rare amongst documentary film-makers, we've agreed.

Organ music heard from church.

Here they come! Any minute now we'll get our first glimpse of Mr and Mrs Donald Renshaw.

Donald comes out of the church pushing mother in her chair, in a mad wedding dress. Pam, in a neat suit, throws confetti over them.

Corin   Sorry – Donald – you haven't married Pam's mother?
Mother Yes, he bloody has! He knows a bit of a swinger when he sees one. Now put your foot down and get me to the bubbly!

Donald wheels mother away. Pam sweeps up the confetti.

Corin   Pam – this is awful – how do you feel?
Pam   Little bit disappointed, obviously.
Corin   Don't you feel bitter?
Pam   Not really.
Corin   To be their bridesmaid, so generous, and to throw confetti. . .
Pam   It's poisoned.
Corin   Sorry?
Pam   The confetti. They won't get far.

Pam winks at Corin.

HE DIDN'T: TWO[166]

Kelly	So I get to work, right – and I'm just sitting on t'photocopier having a crack at my earwax and in walks Mr Fisher.
Pal	He didn't.
Kelly	He did. Right grumpy. Reeking of Rennies. He says Kelly-Marie Tunstall do you know what time it is? I said yeah I do ta very much.
Pal	You didn't.
Kelly	I did. So he gets right mad and he starts shaking, I love it when he does that 'cos all his dandruff drops into his top pocket. He said it's ten-fifteen and I want an explanation. I said all right five minutes ago it was ten past ten, that do yer?
Pal	You didn't.
Kelly	I did. He said I'm waiting, so I parked my chewy on my bra strap and I said – well – I was just posting this coupon for me mam, right – competition – I drink toilet cleaner because . . . okey dokey and this right rabid dog came bounding across the road and bit me right in the pedal-pushers.
Pal	It didn't.

---

166 Not broadcast. A slightly cut version was performed solo in *Victoria Wood As Seen at Christmas*, a run of three shows in St David's Hall, Cardiff in December 1986.

Kelly   It did. So there's somewhat of a commotion, right, and this man came up and he said you know what you've got I said what he said hydrophobia, I said that's that morbid fear of a Cross Channel Ferry and he laughed. Like this. I could see his uvula.

Pal   You couldn't.

Kelly   I could. It were just like the adverts. And he said hydrophobia means you can never ever imbibe water – I said I'm not bothered I only drink Pony – he said no it's right incredibly dangerous and you have to have an operation right now!

Pal   He didn't.

Kelly   He did. And he said and fortunately I'm qualified to do it, though I'm actually a tree surgeon and I've only ever done it on a sycamore. Well, he hadn't got any anaesthetic so I had a right big whiff of *Rive Gauche* and next thing I knew I was on the ten o'clock bus completely cured.

Pal   You weren't.

Kelly   I was. But Mr Fisher's gone a bit puce, right. I said you want to study the heart disease statistics in the British Medical Journal, you do. He said Kelly-Marie Tunstall you have been repeatedly warned for persistent lateness and coming to work in a nightie, I've a good mind to fire you on the spot.

Pal   He didn't.

Kelly   He did. I said you can fire away, but I'm not leaving otherwise I'll tell everyone what happened on Christmas Eve when you drank two pints of correcting fluid and sexually harassed me with an outsize party squeaker.

Pal   He didn't.

Kelly   No he didn't – he nibbled my Twiglets and passed out – but it shut him up.

WE'RE HALF ASLEEP[167]

Logo and signature tune 'We're Half Asleep!'. Bleak little studio. Girl presenter, fiddling with her hair, realises she's on air but isn't too bothered.

Girl   Oh, right. OK. Well, a lot of you have been to zoos I suppose, and seen a lot of ezotic, sorry, exoktic, God I can't talk this morning, exotic animals. Right? But have you ever thought of keeping one in your back garden? Well, someone who has, or does rather, has thought of it, does do it, whatever, is er Louise erm Louise, God I've been getting this name wrong all morning – Louise Kazinski.

She strolls over to po-faced thirteen-year-old.

Hello, Louise.
Louise   Hello.
Girl   It is Kazinski – I got that right, didn't I?
Louise   Not really.
Girl   So, what have you brought along to show us?
Louise   What?
Girl   Weren't you bringing something, or something?

---

167 Not broadcast.

Louise	No, you can't travel them about really.
Girl	What's that?
Louise	Alligators.
Girl	Oh right, got you. Alligators. Dummee. No, you see *(to camera)* someone had scribbled over my running-order thing and there was a word beginning with 'a' and I thought it said animals but it said alligators so there we go. Right, Louise, alligators – how many have you got?
Louise	Ten, at the moment.
Girl	Ten, gosh, it must be quite a problem finding room for them all, what do you do, keep them in the bath?
Louise	No, we've built an artificial environment –
Girl	Really, gosh, that must be quite difficult. And how many have you got?
Louise	Ten – I –
Girl	Gosh, that's quite a lot. And are they little tiny ones, they're presumably not the great big ones?
Louise	Well, up to five feet long.
Girl	Gosh, that's quite big. They must take up quite a lot of space, where on earth do you keep them all?
Louise	My father's built a kind of art –
Girl	Dad's sorted something out has he, that's good. Fathers do have their uses, though not if they glug away at the old gin bottle like mine does, anyway, shouldn't have said that really, never mind, er – right, so – how big actually are they, actually?
Louise	Well, in the wild they can grow up to ten feet, but they don't grow that much in captivity.
Girl	Ten feet, gosh, that's quite a lot of feet isn't it, and how many have you got of those?
Louise	Well, ten, but like I said – our ones –
Girl	*(interrupting)* Yes, well, ten times ten, says she doing her maths bit, one hundred feet, just about isn't it, quite a lot of crocodile.
Louise	Yes.
Girl	Really? Well, thanks very much for coming along Louise

          – I'm sure we've all learnt a lot of new things we didn't already know. One thing I must ask you – how many alligators have you actually got?

Louise   Ten.

Girl   Gosh, as many as that.

Lights fade but not sound.

Right, that's it – we just have to look as if we're talking now, it just makes a better picture. So where do you find room for them all anyway, in the bath?

THE TROLLEY

Restaurant – lunchtime – businessmen. Two completely straight businessmen, waiting for pudding.

Alan	Well, those figures sound very promising, Tim – how's Plymouth looking?
Tim	*(waggling hand)* Plymouth? Either way, Alan, either way – it's on hold – I feel personally Plymouth could be another Exeter.
Alan	Really? That's interesting.
Tim	We're very much keeping an ear to the ground with Plymouth.
Alan	I think what the regional boys tend to forget –

He breaks off as extremely dim waitress arrives with sweet trolley.

	Tim?
Tim	Alan?
Alan	Just coffee thank you – yeah, the regional boys –
Tim	Yes, just coffee for me too please – regional boys?
Alan	Is that we have to consider the Isle of Wight as well.

They notice the waitress is still there with the trolley.

	Two coffees, yes?
Waitress	Coffees what?
Alan	What?
Waitress	Have you seen it?
Alan	*(completely lost but trying not to lose face)* Erm –
Waitress	Have you seen it on the trolley?
Alan	Just two coffees, no sweet.
Waitress	Just two coffees no sweet?
Alan	That's it. What was I – the Isle of Wight –
Waitress	Have you seen it on the trolley?
Alan	*(no idea what she's talking about)* No, yes, thank you.
Waitress	Is it a sorbet?
Alan	Just the coffees, thank you. Now, er, Plymouth –
Waitress	Can you point at it?
Alan	No, we don't want anything on the trolley.
Waitress	Oh, anything on the trolley.
Alan	No, just take the trolley away dear, thank you, and we'll just have coffee, thank you.

She wheels it away.

Tim	*(to cover a sticky moment)* I must give you the print-out from Expo – it came out pretty much as you predicted –

The waitress wheels the trolley back.

Alan	Yes, so I believe . . .
Waitress	They're good castors, aren't they? I been right over to cutlery.
Alan	We don't want a pudding, we have a lot to discuss –
Waitress	You don't want a pudding.
Alan	Right.
Waitress	But you're having a sweet.
Tim	Er love – we're just having the old 'café', coffee.
Alan	I'll handle this Tim, thanks very much.
Waitress	Coffee.

Alan	Coffee.
Waitress	Is it on the trolley?
Alan	I asked you to take the trolley away.
Waitress	I did do.
Alan	Then you brought it back.
Waitress	Then I brought it back.
Alan	Now – take it away –
Waitress	Take it away what?
Alan	The trolley.
Waitress	The trolley. Take it away, the trolley.
Alan	And don't bring it back.
Waitress	What? The trolley!

She wheels it away

Tim	That sorted that out anyway, Alan.
Alan	Yes, well, just don't butt in next time OK, promotion's not automatic, you know.[168]

Pause.

Yes, there, er, Expo figures – Colin phoned them through to the top floor –

Tim	Now I didn't know that.
Alan	Oh yes, that's fairly automatic since the shake-up –

She wheels it back in.

Waitress	What did you say after take the trolley away?
Alan	Get me the bill.
Waitress	Get me the bill. No, it wasn't that.
Alan	I want the bill.
Waitress	Can you point at it?

---

168 Cut. Removing this line made the hierarchy between the two men less clear and, as a result, the testiness of Alan as he tries to dominate the waitress is even funnier.

Alan   Listen to me.

The Waitress listens intently.

        Are you listening to me?

Waitress   I was just then – have I to carry on?

Alan   I am not going to stand up and make a scene. Please fetch, to this table, now, the headwaiter, the man in the dark jacket pouring the wine. Just bring him here, please.

Waitress   Can you mind my trolley?

Alan   Yes.

She goes. They sit in tense silence. The head waiter arrives, suave Italian.

Head waiter   Is everything all right for you, sir? I trust the meal was to your liking, and how can I be of assistance?

Alan   I would like the bloody bill, please.

Head waiter   The bloody bill. *(In waitress's voice, with her expression)* Is it on the trolley?

HE DIDN'T: THREE

Kelly   Anyway, so. I'm stretched out in my new swimming costume, right – cut up here, cut down here, keyhole *(indicating leg, chest and midriff)* and I'm boiling hot and the light's burning my eyes and my mam comes up and says Kelly-Marie Tunstall will you switch that cooker off and get off that ironing board.

Pal   She didn't.

Kelly   She did. And we're having our tea, right, pommes lyonnaise and spam nuggets – and she said you'd better know – I'm running away with a nuclear physicist and if you look behind the clock you'll find fifteen quid and a bag of oven chips.

Pal   She didn't.

Kelly   She did. She said when your dad comes in tell him not to try and find me 'cos I'm changing my name, cutting my hair and laughing on the other side of my face.

Pal   She didn't.

Kelly   She did. And she laughed. Like this. I said I hope that's not hereditary 'cos it hurts your eyeballs. She said well actually you're adopted – you were left on my doorstep wrapped in the business section of the *Sunday Times*.

Pal   You weren't.

Kelly   I was. And it's right embarrassing when you're fourteen. She said your real father is a right prominent rhythm

	guitarist and your mother does the ironing for University Challenge.

Pal   She doesn't.

Kelly   She does. Then I got this letter, right, all typed – loads of spelling – it said Kelly-Marie Tunstall your father has been killed whilst falling under a bus, and you might be in for one million pounds and half-shares in a stationary caravan at Cleveleys.

Pal   It didn't.

Kelly   It did. So I went to see the solicitor, right, all dressed up – black bondage outfit, tan accessories, and he said Kelly-Marie Tunstall, I'm going to give you a cheque for one million pounds, and all you have to do is give up Babycham, learn the oboe, and have one thigh tattooed with a crude caricature of Rupert Murdoch.

Pal   He didn't.

Kelly   He did! *(Shows tattooed thigh.)* So I had that done, learnt the oboe and then I phoned up and told him to stuff it. What's the point of having a million pounds if you can't get legless on Babycham? Eh?

LADY POLICE SERIAL[169]

Juliet and Wilberforce, the desk sergeant, chatting at the front desk. They both have their hats on.

Juliet	Wilberforce.
Wilberforce	Ma'am?
Juliet	Do you mind if I ask you something?
Wilberforce	I don't, no.
Juliet	Do you know how to make a cup of tea?
Wilberforce	No, I don't, ma'am.
Juliet	No, neither do I. *(Bangs on desk.)* And I should know! Wilberforce – I've just had a call from Harry Potter.[170]
Wilberforce	Harry Potter the safebreaker? Little feller? Black 'tache, hangs round The Mop and Bucket, easily led but unexpectedly generous?
Juliet	That's him. Do you know him?
Wilberforce	No. What did he want, ma'am?
Juliet	I don't know, we were cut off before he could tell me. He might have been murdered – I'll pop round on my way home. What happened about the brick that went missing from the building site, Wilberforce?

---

169 Not broadcast.

170 Is this where J. K. Rowling got the name from? On the day VW died, she posted a video of 'The Reincarnation Song'.

Wilberforce	It's been found, ma'am. It's chipped along one corner, but they think it's going to be all right.
Juliet	That's good. Our Asian friends – are they still being racially harrassed?
Wilberforce	No. Those National Front skinheads have completely changed their tune, thanks to you. In fact, they're throwing a party for the entire Asian community to-morrow.
Juliet	Right. I thought that new ping-pong table would do the trick. I might go to the party, Wilberforce – I've got a serge sari – where is it being held?
Wilberforce	Kitchener Street, ma'am – five streets away from the old playground where someone who did some shoplifting's mother was found wandering in a confused state – do you know it?
Juliet	Yes, I do. It backs on to the Cut where old Barney the tramp drowned himself because his dog had been run over by a Bedford van – I forget the registration number.
Wilberforce	We all had a whip-round, ma'am, as you suggested, and bought him a new puppy.
Juliet	Did it work?
Wilberforce	Yes, the old tramp's alive again now. In fact, he's think-ing of doing social sciences at the Open University.

Message comes through on the radio.

Voice	Oscar Delta Tango Charlie Farnsbarns to base, over.

Juliet grabs the mike.

Juliet	I'll deal with this, Wilberforce. You go and check on Garstang's Television and Video Rental shop in the High Street. I passed there this morning and some of those televisions looked like they were about to be stolen.

Wilberforce   Right away, ma'am. *(Leaves.)* I've just got to get some after-dinner mints and change my library books.

Juliet   Good lad.

Wilberforce   *(stopping in doorway)* Where is the High Street, ma'am?

Juliet   Not sure, Wilberforce. Ask when you get there.

He leaves. She speaks into mike.

Oscar Delta Tango Charlie Farnsbarns, come in please – this is Bippetty Boppetty Eggwhisk Goulash Pantie-girdle, over.

Voice   There's an incident taking place on the moors, ma'am.

Juliet   Got that. Anything else I should know?

Voice   It's quite windy.

Juliet   Will I need a poncho?

Voice   You might need a sheepskin coat.

Juliet   I'm on my way. Don't do anything stupid, Constable.

Voice   Like what, ma'am?

Juliet   Hot air ballooning. It can be very dangerous given bad weather conditions like those you've described. I'll be with you as soon as I've had a good cry, because I'm only a woman and from time to time the pressure gets to me, tough as I am. Over and out. Wah!

SELF-SERVICE

Department store, upmarket self-service counter. Extremely long slow queue. A couple of girls serving behind. Our two nice ladies are at the end of the queue by the trays. Enid has a beret and no hair visible.

Enid   *(taking a tray)* Do you know, I've scoured this store from top to bottom, can I find a side-winding thermal body belt, can I buffalo.

Wyn   What did you want one for?

Enid   *(handing her tray over the counter)* Excuse me – I think you'll find there's spam on that. *(Taking another tray)* That gippy kidney.

Wyn   Flared up?

Enid   I'll say – it's like being continually poked – can you imagine that? *(Wyn can't.)* [171] Dr Brewster says if I don't keep it lagged for the winter I could be spending a penny every twenty minutes come March.

Wyn   Can't they operate?

Enid   I haven't time to go in. I'm on the phone day and night about that carpet. What's the soup, dear?

Girl   Country vegetable.

Enid   What country – Taiwan?

---

171 In the broadcast version, Wyn says 'No', securing VW her only laugh in the entire sketch.

Wyn	Have they not sent it? Your carpet. *(Rootles round the counter.)* There's croutons.
Enid	With my molars? Filthy French habit. Oh they sent it – I sent it back. I said, 'Do I look like a woman who would grace her lobby with a bordered Axminster?' I've told them time beyond number I'm the wall-to-wall elephant.[172]
Wyn	Is that steak?
Enid	I would doubt it. Probably some poor beast that came a cropper at Beechers Brook. Er, dear – is this fish boned?
Girl	No.
Enid	I should check your insurance. Then I had a huge to-do and hoohah at the hairdressers.
Wyn	What about these Dublin prawns?
Enid	Never touch prawns. Do you know, they hang round sewage outlet pipes treading water with their mouths open – they love it!
Wyn	Still going to Maison Renée?
Enid	Chez Maurice was putting out feelers . . .
Wyn	Oh no, he reeks of neutraliser.
Enid	And he's forever dabbing at his cold sores with *Old Spice*_[173]
Wyn	Aren't prawns an aphrodisiac?
Enid	I wouldn't put it past them. Well, I'm at Renée's – waiting to be shampooed – flicking through a *Woman's Weekly* – lovely piece on Alma Cogan.[174] *(They've now reached veg, and the queue's stopped.)* Sorry – what's the hold-up here, dear?
Girl	We're waiting for fresh cauli . . .
Enid	Fresh! You might as well wait for Maurice Chevalier.[175] So I'm called into the cubicle – it's all separate at Renée's

---

172 Cut from 'Have they not sent it' to here.

173 Cut from 'Still going to' to here and replaced with 'So anyway, I'm at Maison Renée.'

174 Singer and highest paid female UK entertainer of the 1950s. No figure in the public eye is mentioned more regularly in VW's comedy, partly because she found the name irresistibly funny. *DL*: 'You practise for ages an' all you get asked for is Alma piggin' Cogan.'

175 French crooner.

– not like these terrible modern places where you find yourself sharing a perm trolley with two footballers – *(annoyed at the delay)* this is ridiculous *(pushing past the veg waiters).* Can I thrust by – I'm a diabetic.

They are now at the sweet section.

	So in comes Renée.
Wyn	She must be getting on.
Enid	Well, this is the trouble. If she leans too far forward with a sponge roller she topples out of her walking frame – and you really have to shout up – I don't particularly want the whole world knowing I'm not a natural conker.
Wyn	Is that trifle?
Enid	It may have been in a previous existence. *(Elaborately casually looking away)* Don't have the gateaux – I just saw her scratching her armpit with the cake slice. And Renée's very set in her ways, style-wise – I don't mind – I'm a great admirer of Phyllis Calvert.[176]
Wyn	So why hence the hoohah?
Enid	Well, I decided to go a shade mad because we've the Smoked Meat Purveyors Buffet 'n' Mingle at the weekend.

Irate voice from a woman a couple of people further down the queue.

| **Woman** | Could we get by please; we're not having a sweet. |

Woman and friend push by our two.

Enid	Very wise, with those hips. So I said, 'Skip the conker, Renée – I'll have burnished beech-nut and to heck with it.'
Wyn	So?
Enid	Well, you know she's colour blind and they've only a gas mantle round the back?

176 Actress whose heyday was in British films of the 1940s. She was later cast in *Staying In*.

Wyn	Colour blind?
Enid	Can't tell red from blue. Once tottered into a brothel thinking it was a police station.

They reach Tea, Coffee and the Till.

Second girl	Tea, Coffee?
Enid	No.
Wyn	She didn't.
Enid	Oh, it was all right – one of the girls came out and helped her pump her tyres up.
Second girl	Sorry, are you still waiting for something?
Enid	Yes, a small mineral water and an orange squash, please.
Second girl	Water and squash back down the end by the trays. *(To next customer)* Tea, Coffee?

Enid and Wyn leave their trays behind and push past every-body back to the starting point. They pick up two trays and rejoin the queue.

Enid	You've a look of Eva Braun, did you know?[177] Well – what Renée mixed up in the back – burnished beech-nut it was not – more like varicose violet – I could have wept.

Engrossed, they move off again – past the water and squash – people behind them as before.

Wyn	Did you have to pay?
Enid	Well, she knocked off my bourbons but – *(they move along)*. Then in comes Maxine, waving her whitlow . . .
Wyn	Is she the bodybuilder?
Enid	No that's Lois *(start to fade)*. No, Maxine's the one I told you about – excuse me – grey eggs – is that an Arab custom?

---

177 In the shooting script, VW crossed out the original line, 'I've always wondered if Eva Braun died in that bunker', and made this indelible improvement (see note on 'Cleaning', p. 84).

Right Down the Middle

Nice, easy, middle-of-the-book humour for all you folks who aren't getting any funnier.

INTRODUCTION

In September 1996, in the same month as the publication of *Chunky*, Victoria returned to the Royal Albert Hall. This was her second residency there, and it reconfirmed her place at the very pinnacle of stand-up. With live comedy on her mind, she submitted three character monologues from her previous tour to pad out the compendium and offer readers something extra.

The monologues had a specific function in an evening's entertainment. They were there to break up the show and offer some visual variety too. Victoria would come on in costume at the start of the second half and in the encore. A note at the end of *Chunky* advised that the three monologues included in the volume came from *Victoria Wood Live in Your Own Home*, broadcast in 1994. Actually 'Toupee Time' was never seen on TV, while 'Madeline' was written for *Victoria Wood's All Day Breakfast* in 1992, but there wasn't room for it, so she took it out on tour the following year instead.

'Fattitude' was a challenge. Victoria had been coming on after the interval as a comic character since *Lucky Bag* in 1983. This was how audiences first encountered Kimberley's friend. But now she added an extra dimension and incorporated an exercise class. It was hugely successful and a wonderful way to kick off the second half of the show. But in later tours, when she invented similar characters, she held them back till the encore, having learned from experience that it didn't make sense to knacker herself with half the show still to perform.

FATTITUDE[178]

Pumping music. Madge addresses her aerobics class, clad in a bright pink leotard displaying her fine figure.

Madge   Come in everybody, find a space. Hi Betty, hi Dot. Dot, Dotty, how did you get on last night? Did he not? Was he not? Could he not? No. He was probably threatened by your newfound physicality. All right, spread out everybody, nice arm's reach between every person. Hi, are you new? Have you got any trainers? Well, just do the best you can with those. They're not ideal, stilettos. Connie, Connie, come away from the air-conditioning. No, because when we go leaping and springing you're going to give yourself a sort of mini lobotomy on the corner of that. You what, you've had one already and they only gave you a support stocking? You should have said something. Okay we're ready, marching on the spot. Connie, both feet. Now, I see we have quite a few newies here today, so is there anything I should know about? Bad backs, injuries, funny knees? Yes, you what, your leg? What's wrong with it? It's plastic? No that's fine, no it's nice. It's nicer than your other one. All right, bit

---

178 The script makes no reference to the fact that VW does a full workout. She starts at 'marching on the spot' and ratchets it up at 'let's funky it up a little'. And she did all this in a padded suit.

more vigorous. What I say to everybody is go at your own pace. If you can't do the legs, do the arms. If you can't do the arms, do the breathing. If you can't do the breathing, you don't deserve to live. Ha, ha, ha, ha, ha. No, I'm only kidding, I'm very wacky in my style, you'll get used to me. A bit more vigorous. Now, I'll just launch into my usual preamble. Bear down with me if you've heard it before. I'm Madge, obviously, oh no sorry, not obviously, I've usually got it written on. I've got a new leotard on tonight. Do you like it? It's flattering, isn't it? I wasn't sure when I got it home. I thought, hmm, a bit subtle. Okay, stepping side to side. Stepping to the left, Connie, to the *left*, no because you're actually hurting her foot doing that. Where's the lady with the plastic leg? Can you stand next to Connie for me? Okay, I'm Madge. Welcome to my Friday night low impact class for fatties with attitude. Welcome to FATTITUDE! Okay, let's funkyit up a little. Because you can do any diet you like, girls, but if you don't do those exercises you are up that shopping centre without a credit card. And I should know, I've been there. I used to have a weight problem. Oh yes, I was quite hippy at one point. Okay, put a bit of a kick into it now. Very gently kicking the buttock, giving it a nice stretch to the front of the thigh there, Connie, kick your own buttock. Okay, steady on down into a plié. Plie on down now. Now what we're doing here, I'll just explain, carry on doing it. What we're doing here, we're working this muscle here. It's the glutonius maxitive and it's the biggest muscle in the entire body and it's actually directly connected to the brain. So when we're working it we're actually improving our circulation and our breathing and our ability to follow a knitting pattern. And punch. Punching across. Punching, raising the heartbeat, getting ready to burn fat. Now don't get me wrong, we're not all looking to be skinny, we don't all want to be Madonna do we? No, some of us want to be Petula Clark, don't we? And who else, yes, Michelle Pffiefferfiffer, yes, she's nice. Who? Kylie Minogue, no, sorry to me Kylie is too much petite-o.[179] I think there is a point with skinny where it can tip over into scrawny. And I should know because I'm dangerously near it myself. Okay. Raising the heartbeat now, getting ready for the aerobics section. Now don't back off on this girls, because when we do aerobics we produce a hormone in the body called phenophonometamorphenone. And you can get hooked on this. Has anybody heard the expression, the jogger's? Yes, there is a jogger's nipple, the jogger's high, that's right. So let's get high! What we're aiming to do in this section, is raise the pulse rate to eighty per cent of one hundred and eighty per cent of the resting pulse for twenty-two minutes. Now don't attempt to compete with me. I'm a very experienced exerciser and after so many years in aerobics I am a superb physical specimen. I did run the London Marathon with a chicken on my head. On the other hand, we don't really know if any of this is doing us any good. Connie, have you got those doughnuts?

179 In the early years of her stardom, Kylie's diminutive size proved irresistible to VW. From her 1990 live show: 'There was some talk of Kylie Minogue coming but she's had an accident. She knocked some things off the dressing table and was pinned to the ground by a kirby grip. Little Kylie. I sometimes think, what do you get if you crossed Kylie Minogue and Mussolini? What would you get? Anne Diamond, I suppose.'

TOUPEE TIME[180]

Charlene   Hello. And you're back with me, Charlene Dawson,
coasting right down the middle of that road till four
o'clock in the a.m. So whether you're a trucker, a trucker's mucker, or a plain old insomniac, stick with me,
Charlene Dawson. I'll be with you till four o'clock when
I'll be handing you over to the very capable hands of my
very good friend, Conrad Meredith. With his very popular blend of two hours of organ music, prayer, and plenty
of that old anti-abortion chit-chat. So stick with me,
Charlene Dawson, I'll be putting the wee into the wee
small hours. Well, that's enough blarney from me, Charlene, let's get straight on with the nitty, not forgetting
the gritty, let's plunge right on in with *Toupee Time*. Yes,
this is the part of the show dedicated to toupee wearers,
toupee collectors and toupee fans from as far away as the
Netherlands. And I've a letter here from Ginger Parsons
of Hathersage. He writes to say, 'I have a black Crown
Topper. Side parting – needs some attention. Would exchange for similar in dark chestnut, or portable Olivetti
typewriter.' Mrs Ivy Smith of Medway writes to say, 'My
husband died recently.' Oh, lots of regrets and oodles

---

180 Charlene Dawson was closely based on Julie Dawn, a popular singer with big bands after the
war who for ten years from 1977 presented *Julie Dawn's Penfriends Programme* on Radio 2.

of sympathy from me, Charlene Dawson, on that one.
No, death is quite an upheaval, and I should know, I've
had four cats since 1978. One good thing, Mrs Smith, I
don't suppose you had to carry your husband through
the house on a shovel and bury him in the back garden.
She goes on to say, 'My husband died recently and
left, among many other valuable articles, eight toupees
dating from 1954. The old elasticated sort rather than the
stick-on variety which later became popular.' She says
one in particular has interesting historical associations as
it was blown off during the state opening of Parliament,
1958. Whoo hoo! Toupee requests now. Arthur Tomato
of Scullduggery writes to say, 'Excuse my wobbly hand-
writing, Charlene, I'm writing with my left hand to raise
money for charity – in aid of Toupee Concern.' Arthur is
very keen to track down that very popular make of hair
piece, the 'Undetectable'. He says, 'I do not mind which
shade, Charlene, but styles preferred are the Clifford or
the Pedro.' On a more serious note, folks, many many
listeners have phoned in to me, Charlene Dawson, to
let me know that old 'chain toupee' has reared itself up
again, so if anybody does send you a toupee asking you
to wear it for a week and pass it on, please don't. Just
send it to me, Charlene Dawson, I'll get rid of it for you.
Honestly, I think if these jokers can't find something
better to do with their time then they should be executed. Well, I know you say those days have long gone
but I don't know, there was something nice about capital
punishment. It meant never having to say you were
sorry. Well, it's nearly time for the four o'clock news now,
nearly time for Charlene to say goodbye. We may hear
a little bit more on that Saddam Hussein story we heard
at three. Now, I don't know Saddam myself personally
though I do have friends who rented a holiday bungalow
from him and they found him very reasonable, with
quite a fondness for the records of Jackie Trent and Tony

Hatch, apparently.[181] So no one's all bad, are they, folks? Well, I'm going to close the show in my usual way with a little bit of music. Not Jackie Trent tonight, I'm going to close the show with one of my own ditties[182] because I do know from my postbag that Charlene's ditties are the biggest things in the show. So this is Charlene Dawson saying good night, God bless, drive safely – and if you *do* hear about any miscarriages of justice – keep your mouths shut. Ciao!

---

181 Married couple and co-composers whose best-known song over a thirty-year songwriting partnership is the theme from *Neighbours*. Trent had a minor career as a singer. Hatch was a regular judge on the ATV talent show *New Faces*, though not, despite what VW claimed in *LB*, in the 1974 heat she made her network debut in: 'I went on and I sang a song and Mickie Most said it was awful and Tony Hatch said it was dreadful and Clifford Davis said it was terrible and Arthur Askey said could he have something to sit on?'

182 In the live version, Charlene glides over to the piano and introduces 'The Paradise Where Dreams Come True' as 'a little song which paints a picture of my ideal world'. The spoken verses begin thus:

I was chatting to some lady friends of mine the other day

About how life was better years ago

There was ballroom dancing, discipline and snow on Christmas Day

And hanging was quite common then you know.

MADELINE

Madeline   Carlene, can you do my lady a shampoo, please. She won't keep you a moment. Yes, I think what we'll do is take it up and over and back round the sides. Very free and easy but quite structured. Yes, what I was saying to you previous was my friend worked in hairdressing and my cousin worked in hairdressing and my mother (that's her on wall in't sponge rollers), she said to me what are you planning on doing, our Madeline. And I said modelling, and she said modelling Madeline. And I said yeah, and she said ooh Madeline you'd be very middling at modelling. I said would I. She said yes if you go muddling with modelling you'll be middling our Madeline. I said you're meddling. Meddling, Madeline, me? Well, this was in the middle of a wedding so she's spitting tuna vol-au-vents on me plus her bra wire has poked up through her costume and is picking up the soundtrack of *Going For Gold*.[183] Well, she's never nice to me my mother, well no, tell an untruth, she was in a documentary on debt once and she was pleasant to me then. She said you are modelling Madeline over my dead body. Well, that was comical for a kick-off. You couldn't do nothing over a body her size, except possibly volley ball.

---

183 BBC One game show aired between 1987 and 1996.

Well, I'd had half a Mackinson's so I was feeling quite
Frank Brunoish[184] so I told her a few home truths. I said
Mother, nobody likes you, me father's having an affair
with a dental receptionist, and you've just sat in some
Black Forest gateau. Well, she didn't like that. Nolena,
can you do my lady a tea please. Yeah, take the teabag out
this time. Yeah, put it back in the steriliser. So then she
did what she always does when she can't get her own way,
she fell down frothing. Well, this was bang in the middle
of *Agga Do* so nobody cottoned on till twenty past.[185] So
we're all gathered round her bed in hospital, she's kicking
up merry behaviour because the catering's been priva-
tised and she's only got croutons. She's looking at me
like that woman out of *A Hundred And One Dalmatians*.
She said I will not have this modelling Madeline. I said
give me a for-instance why not. She said oh well, I knew
a girl that went in for modelling. By the time she was
twenty-one she was smoking metholated cigarillos and
getting engaged to goal keepers. Well, there was a nasty
silence then right round the cubicle. You could hear
the woman in the next-door bed's Lucozade popping.
I said all right, scrap the modelling, forget it, suppose I
go demonstrating time shares in Fuengirola. Well, that
was even worse. She starts hyperventilating then, we
have to waft her up the cleavage with an *Exchange and
Mart*. Not that nothing good came out of it because we
spotted an advert for one of those chairs that goes up
your staircase, and fair do's to me mother, at top speed
with the radio on it's very like Alton Towers. Carlene,

184 The British heavyweight boxer was a huge celebrity in the 1980s. In *ASOTV*, he played
himself in a spoof of the gameshow *Tell the Truth*. Three panellists, faced with three guests, had to
identify the Labour politician from Denis Healey, Claire Rayner and Frank Bruno.
185 'Agadoo' was a novelty hit for Black Lace in 1984. Voted the worst song of all time by music
writers for *Q* magazine in 2003, it was much loved by VW. Petula Gordeno in *DL*: 'She knows
all the old tunes – Agadoo, Coconut Airways, Shaft.' And in *ATT*: 'OK, lads, Agadoo,' says the
conductor at the end of 'Brassed Up'.

are you doing this shampoo for my lady, sorry, she's just
doing somebody more important. Anyway, it was all
sorted out over a family get-together. We went to that
mediaeval banqueting hall outside Tesco's, yeah, we get
in half price because my dad's sister-in-law is a wench.
Oh no, she was a wench but there was some trouble over
a low-cut blouse and two tankards so now she's on gravy.
Anyway, it was all agreed en family that I should go back
to hairdressing. My mother was up the moon. She drank
a bottle of Mateus Rosé without even taking the lamp-
shade off it. I beg your pardon? *(Pause.)* Well, it will take
quite a long time to do your hair, yes, well because of
the way it's been neglected. *(Pause.)* Well, there's the cut,
the colour, the condition, I mean really it's what we in
the world of hair would call quite diabolically cruddy. I
mean, where were you previous to coming to us, I mean
who actually did this for you? *(Pause.)* Oh did I. It suits
you.

Mens Sana in Thingummydoodah

AND FIVE OTHER NUGGETS OF HOMELY FUN

To all the Old Bags in Equity, most of whom were in this series

INTRODUCTION

By the end of the 1980s, Victoria had conquered the sketch show and delivered a stand-up masterclass in *An Audience with Victoria Wood*. Laden with BAFTAs, and now a mother, she itched to attempt something new in 1989. But what?

For most of the decade, she had been quietly trying her hand at cinema and theatre. Because they didn't bear fruit, the public never found out about these projects. She was in a morose mood in January 1989 when she wrote to the West End producer Michael Codron, who had commissioned her last play *Good Fun* ten years earlier. 'This play is not going to work out,' she wrote. 'This is the 3rd play I've attempted in the last few years, and I think I must accept I've lost the knack, or I'm out of tune with the theatre, and should just stop doing it. It's too miserable scrabbling about like this, when I'm actually good at other things like telling jokes and writing for TV . . . I'm not a playwright – I'm no good at it.'

It was with this self-criticism running through her head that she set about writing the half-dozen half-hour comedies that would be collectively broadcast under the title *Victoria Wood*. They were a stylistic compromise, mixing the zip of sketch comedy with the broader arc of drama. She dubbed them playletinos. Half were set in environments that she knew well – daytime TV, a spa, the moors. The others explored worlds that she had less experience of and indeed love for – agency dating, package holidays and, most alien of all, smart cocktail parties.

What all six films had in common was a semi-fictional character called 'Victoria', sometimes referred to as 'Vicki' as she herself had been in childhood. (Only Celia Imrie, playing her hiking partner in *Val de Ree*, addresses her as 'Vic'.) Across the series, Victoria had to find six ways of making this 'Victoria' part of the story. She manages it better in some than others. In *We'd Quite Like to Apologise*, she is essentially just the feed. In other scripts, she is the friend who tags along before leaping into the heart of the story in a comic voice and disguise. Morphing, as it were, from Wise into Morecambe made for a fun way for Victoria to portray the divide between her very private self and her public role as an entertainer, the woman who hated crowds but loved audiences.

The series was a bold experiment. Most unusual of all was the way Victoria stepped out of the story to address the viewer directly in the style of stand-up. In *Miranda* and *Fleabag*, we've grown used to female characters using the camera as a confidante. Back then, it hadn't been done. Nor had any comedian played a version of themselves, in a style that US audiences were familiar with from *I Love Lucy*, *The Mary Tyler Moore Show* and *Rhoda*.

Victoria would come to feel that the series hadn't quite hit the spot, especially after BBC higher-ups insisted that laughter be added. But being on BBC One would earn Victoria her biggest viewing figures yet, and when *Mens Sana in Thingummy Doodah and Five Other Nuggets of Homely Fun* was published a year on, her playletinos sat well on the page, and sold well too.

Dedicating the book 'to all the Old Bags in Equity, most of whom were in this series', was her way of heralding the unsung stalwarts of her regular company. Glimpsed in many smaller roles in *Victoria Wood As Seen on TV*, now the likes of Lill Roughley, Kay Adshead, Deborah Grant, Meg Johnson and Georgia Allen had a greater chance to glitter. Then there were the stars of yesteryear, two of whom were so much a part of Victoria's cultural upbringing that they are even name-dropped in her scripts. Phyllis Calvert, who had been referred to in 'Self-Service', then appeared in *Staying In*, while Joan Sims, mentioned in *Staying In*, starred in *Val de Ree*. We would now describe such a hall of mirrors as all very meta. Victoria didn't think in those terms. She had grown up watching these people on television and, now that she was on it herself, invited them to join her world as seen on *Victoria Wood*.

HOW A TELEVISION SERIES IS MADE

Hello! I thought I would tell you all about how a television series is made. It's very exciting! It all begins a long time ago when the Writer – she is an irritable person with bitten nails – gets a Red Telephone Bill. This sets the Writer thinking, and not so very long later she has written a television series! This is a collection of six 'programmes', either with a gap in the middle for a cup of tea, or a guaranteed repeat, depending on whether it is a commercial 'programme' or a BBC one. This particular television series is a BBC one, so we will have to wait till it is over for our cup of tea, won't we?

Once the Writer has finished writing, she takes the 'script' and drives through a traffic jam in the rain to the Typist. The Typist is a grim woman in a balaclava who makes jokes like, 'Well it doesn't make me laugh,' and, 'Don't mind the dog, it should come off with a nailbrush.'

When 'scripts' are typed, the Writer takes them to the BBC where a seventeen-year-old Secretary spills coffee on them and leaves them behind the photocopier. When the Secretary leaves the BBC to become a full-time sunbather it can sometimes be a jolly long time before those 'scripts' come to light! And sometimes when they do they have been hidden for such a long time they have become 'dated' and 'unrealistic'. But fortunately, the BBC will still make them into 'programmes'.

Then the fun begins! All is hustle and bustle in the office as the 'production team' begins to assemble. Oh look – there is the Production Secretary. My goodness, she's busy! She knows everything about the show that is about to be made. Surrounded by wallplans and telephones, she is a real hub of activity. She has three fags going in the ashtray, and a fourth is singeing her bi-focals, but we'd better not tell her, had we? We would get our heads bitten off!

Here come the Producer and the Director. They are both men, and my goodness they drink a lot of tea! Thank heavens they have a Production Secretary or they'd have to make it themselves! And that would never do!

Hello, here's the Designer. He is bringing in a 'model' of the 'set'. The Writer has written a programme 'set' in a Welsh kitchen. The 'model' is of a shopping centre and multi-storey carpark. Oh well, never mind!

Well, now everyone has had plenty of tea and hidden the cups all round the office. The Production Secretary will have fun trying to find them all! Shall we help her? No. We would get our heads bitten off!

Now the fun really begins! We have to find some 'Actors and Actresses' to appear in our 'programmes'. The Production Secretary could do this perfectly well, but she's busy washing up so let's phone up the 'Casting Director'. She is a lady in funny shoes who can remember some of the names of half of the people she's seen in the theatre. While she's trying to remember the others, let's have another cup of tea! Oh honestly, where on earth is that Production Secretary? She'd better turn up soon, or the Producer will be cross!

Well, now we have some Actors and Actresses. The ones we really wanted were all busy or asked for lots of money, but I expect these ones will do jolly well, don't you?

Now the fun is really hotting up! Everybody meets up in a condemned council block called the BBC Rehearsal Rooms. This morning we are having a 'read through', but first we have to get past the Security Man. And, oh dear, he's not in a very good mood this morning. He hasn't heard of any of our Actors and Actresses! Never mind, let's leave the Production Secretary to sort it out while we have a nice cup of tea!

Now fun is really on the agenda! Everybody sits round a big table. They are all very nervous but the Producer goes to the lavatory and soon everyone is chatting away like billy-oh! It's time to read out the whole script from top to bottom. It is a long time since the Writer first had that Red Telephone Bill and she is dying to hear how the 'dialogue' will sound when acted by real Actors and Actresses. When they have finished everyone is very pleased. Didn't they think of some nice funny voices? Everybody has been so clever, the Writer has had to go to the window and think what a long way it would be to jump down onto the main road. Ouch! That would hurt, wouldn't it?

Now 'rehearsals' are all over, and it's nearly time for the 'recording'. What fun that will be! Now we will find out exactly how funny our 'programme' is! Look – here comes the audience! Hurry up, slow-coaches! Goodness me, what a lot of walking frames! Somebody is grumbling that his hearing aid is faulty and he didn't want to come out anyway. Never mind, the Actors will just have to speak up, won't they?

Now the 'warm-up' starts. And oh, it is fun! What nice slacks the Warm-up Man is wearing! The audience do enjoy his jokes. You can see them nudging each other. 'What is a pouf?' they ask.

Now the 'recording' is underway and the audience is having a lovely time. They are looking at the cameras, the lights, the doorway, in fact everywhere except at the poor Actors and Actresses. Never mind; let's all shout louder and see if we can make them laugh that way.

Once the 'programme' is 'in the can' the fun really begins! Our audience were having such a good time they forgot to laugh! Never mind, let's switch on this clever machine that sounds almost like an audience laughing. Let's turn it up really loud, then everyone will know just how funny our 'programme' is. The Writer is pleased. Now no one can hear the Actors and Actresses getting their 'dialogue' wrong. That's a relief!

Now the 'programme' is on the 'television'. I hope everybody likes it. Thank heavens there are three other channels! James Bond is on one of them. I wonder which channel people will watch tonight?

Now 'television' has closed down for the night, and all the people who write for the newspapers are settling down to tell everybody just what they think of our 'programme'. Now the fun really begins!

MENS SANA IN THINGUMMY DOODAH

Old country house in its grounds, very imposing but maybe a little run down. Signboard says Pinkney Hydro – Your Gateway to to Health. *Lill and Victoria are getting their bags out of the car, locking it, and going up the steps to the front entrance. Lill is a bit overweight; a bit run down and frazzled-looking.*

Entrance hall of the Hydro: modern reception desk amidst chipped statuary and grubbily carpeted staircase. Lill and Victoria stand with their bags, looking around.

Lill   It looked nice in the brochure.

Victoria Chernobyl looked nice in the brochure.

Lill   Well – somewhere through there is a team of dedicated professionals, lean, fit, health conscious, ready to help me achieve my full potential in mind and body.

Dana, huge, nineteen, in filthy overall, thunders down the staircase holding a washing-up bowl full of wet greens and a sink plunger. She is shouting up to someone on the upper landing (unseen).

Dana   If the lard comes, put it next to the pig-bin. *(Stops. Looks* *up.) Eh? (Pause.)* Well just blow the hairs off it. Sorry – I didn't see you. Is it Miss Wood and Miss Sutcliffe?

Victoria   Yes

Dana   D'you want to come up? Everyone's out ont' Health and Nature Trail.

Lill   Oh that sounds nice, doesn't it?

Dana   It's just a load of hopping over logs really.

She goes upstairs, they follow her.

Anyway, I'm Dana.

Lill   Unusual name.

Dana   My mother's favourite singer[186] when she fell pregnant. I were lucky. My brother's called Harry Secombe.[187] Anyway, I'm head cook and carrot scrubber – so – *(stops outside door and opens it)* this is it. Your bathroom's *en suite* with it all; there's no emergency bell but we can be summoned by a thump. Er, your flush is dicky, but it responds to patience and don't run the bidet and that cold tap simultaneous or you'll scorch your nancy. Any chocolates, booze, fags?

Both   No.

Dana   Right. Calorie-wise, you're now under orders till check-out.

Lill   Right. Good.

Dana   And we'll see you downstairs in half an hour for an introductory blah-blah – yeah?

Victoria   OK.

Dana   *(leaving, singing)* Oooh-eee, chirpy chirpy cheep cheep . . .

---

186 Irish singer.

187 Welsh singer and comedian, star of *The Goon Show* in the 1950s and latterly a presenter of religious programmes, including *Highway*, a clip from which became a staple of VW's Christmas viewing. In 1987, from a shopping centre in Ipswich, Secombe introduced a group of female singers performing an eye-popping rendition of 'Who Will Buy' from *Oliver!*

They go into the room. It is a twin-bedded, smallish, nastyish hotel room; modern fittings with old windows and curtains etc. Victoria is on the bed looking out of the window; Lill is unpacking.

Victoria   What's it for?

Lill   What?

Victoria   Candlewick.

Lill   What do you mean?

Victoria   Well it doesn't look nice, or feel nice – it must have *some* other purpose. I think it was probably invented in the war –

Lill   Like Spam?

Victoria   No. Like Morse Code. As a method of passing cryptic messages – it's all in the pattern – two tufts and a wiggly bit mean 'Watch Out – Vera Lynn is touring North Africa'.

Lill   I shouldn't have said Spam.

Victoria   Why?

Lill   Well I want some, now I know I can't have any.

Victoria   Well go and get some.

Lill   This is a health farm! I'm here to detoxify, lose weight. It's not going to work very well if I'm nipping out every two minutes for a quarter of potted meat.

Victoria   Sorry.

Lill   This week is crucial to my whole future way of life, and I will need your full and unstinting support and encouragement to make this vital project a success.

Victoria   Right.

Lill   Do you understand?

Victoria   Yep.

Lill   Do you have anything to say?

Victoria   Yep.

Lill   What?

Victoria   Spam Spam Spam Spam Spam! Chips! Nougat! Chocolate!

The main reception room has also seen better days. Oil paintings, ping-pong table, sofas, coffee tables abound. A group of residents, including Victoria, Lill, Connie, Enid, and various rheumatic and overweight older people, are listening to Nicola who is slim, thirty-five-ish, very sincere and softly-spoken.

Nicola OK, everybody, I'm Nicola. I'm just calling you 'everybody' because I don't know everybody's name as yet, and until me doing that, 'everybody' as a sort of termitude will have to huffice. I'm Nicola, as I say; if you should need me at all during the periodical which you're with us, just examine a member of staff who's approximate, say 'Where's Nicola' and that will find me. This is the Pinkney Hydro, as you'll have gathered, the gateway *to* health. I don't know if you're familiar with the old Latin saying – I only speak a little Latin myself, just enough to buy a paper – the saying 'Mens Sana Incorporises'. And I think we can learn a lot from that. I've only recently taken over as head of Pinkneys, but don't despair, I do have a full and variable business career behind of me, including hands-on salon experience galore plus two years of prosthetic nail work. I'm Nicola, as I say, and this here standing alongside of myself is Judy. Judy is more to deal with the physical aspects of the body; aerobics, jogging and our very own Pinkneys specialité de la hydro, Ping-pong Mobility. Judy will be explaining of that as and when and so forth . . . As well as Judy and myself we do have a highly professional team of, of professionals, who will be intending to your needs should they arise. *(Looks down at notes.)*

Victoria *(mouthing to Lill)* Where are they?

Nicola Our aim here at Pinkneys is very simple, erm, it's to do with intoxifying the body, treating the body as a temple, I hope that doesn't offend anybody, I say 'temple' but I could just have easily as said 'garden centre' – they're very

popular of a Sunday, aren't they; and losing weight and
perhaps trying a face pack or something – anyway – I'm
Nicola. Thank you. As I say.

*The dining room: tables for four and five scattered about.
A few people are already sitting waiting, including Victoria
and Lill at a table for four. Lill is in a dressing gown, Victoria in a track suit.*

Lill	Well, my massage was marvellous. I feel really relaxed. And my masseur, Harold –
Victoria	You can't have a masseur called Harold. It's like having a member of the Royal Family called Ena.
Lill	Harold says that underneath my fat, I'm actually very slim.
Victoria	He sounds very intelligent.
Lill	And an extra daily massage with him –
Victoria	At twenty pounds.
Lill	At twenty pounds – should really make a difference.
Victoria	Well my girl was hopeless. She's only here because she didn't get enough CSEs to work in a pet shop. Every time she said S she spat on my hair.
Lill	That doesn't matter.
Victoria	It does if she's telling you about Somerset. I had to change the subject to Peterborough.

*Connie and Enid come over to the table; fiftyish, glamorous,
in track suits and high-heeled mules.*

Connie	Can we park? Are you bothered?
Victoria	Help yourselves.
Connie	Connie and Enid. We're old Pinkney partners from way back.
Victoria	You've been here before?
Connie	Bushels of occasions, haven't we?
Enid	Oh, at least.

Connie	First time since it changed hands, but last year it really was fandabbidozy and how.
Lill	Do you come to lose weight?
Enid	And tone.
Connie	Trim and tone. Enid has underarm swoop and I have runaway midriff.
Lill	You look very good to me, actually; both of you.
Enid	Well, I like to keep at it. I was Slimmer of the Month in February.
Connie	The February we went decimal.
Enid	It isn't food with me, like it is with Connie, I have water retention.
Connie	You've perhaps heard Hereford's missing a reservoir?
Enid	Connie's having acupuncture. For stress-related gobbling.
Connie	Enid's not been offered it, naturally. Well, acupuncture and water retention – you'd be forever swabbing the lino. How about you?
Lill	Well – today is the first day of the rest of my life.
Connie	Oh! It's the first day of Lewis's sale. Beggar. Go on.
Lill	I want a complete new start – hair, face, body, psyche . . .
Enid	Are you?
Lill	Sorry?
Enid	Are you psychic?
Lill	No I'm not.
Enid	Oh. Only my mother's haunting our spare-room blanket box and I could do with having it exorcised.
Connie	Trust your mother. Whole of Paradise to choose from, she plumps for your blanket box. She was the same in Fuengirola. Five-bedroom luxury villa, girls. Spent the whole holiday rinsing dishcloths.

Dana comes in with four small glass bowls of brown slop.

Victoria	Thanks.
Dana	Don't leave it all at once.

Victoria	What is it?
Dana	Bran, another sort of bran, wheatgerm, apple juice and sultana.
Enid	Sultanas?
Dana	Sultana.
Victoria	Is it good for you?
Dana	Haven't a clue, but don't spill it – it sets. *(She leaves, singing.)* All kinds of everything, remind me of you . . .

They eat, gingerly.

Their bedroom. Lill is staring at her face in the dressing-table mirror. Victoria is on the bed with a chart.

Victoria	Lill!
Lill	I'm sorry; it's the wheatgerm. What have we got this afternoon?
Victoria	I'm having twenty minutes in the thermal cabinet and you're having your legs waxed, then we're meeting up for passive exercise.
Lill	I'm going to be a new woman when I leave here – this is going to be the turnround in my relationship with Marcus.
Victoria	Why?
Lill	Well, I think when he sees me all well-groomed and slim, and confident, I really think he might re-consider divorcing Petra.
Victoria	But why do you want him to?
Lill	I've been in love with Marcus for twelve years, you know.
Victoria	But he's awful, Lill. His wife is called Petra; he chose to spend his life with a woman who has the same name as John Noakes's labrador.[188]

---

188 Longest-serving presenter of *Blue Peter*. Petra, a mongrel, was actually the dog of co-presenter Peter Purves. Noakes looked after a Border collie called Shep. The name Petra was evidently on VW's mind as it turns up in *The Library* and *Over to Pam*. From her 1990 live show: 'The post

Lill	He loves me. He's just waiting till the children are settled.
Victoria	What in – sheltered housing? God, I'm starving – how many calories in a pillowcase?
Lill	Plain or Oxford.
Victoria	What's for dinner?
Lill	*(consulting the plan)* Clear vegetable soup and crudities.
Victoria	Bum, willy, toilet –

Lill looks at her.

Sorry, I'm so hungry I'm having mine now.

The Gym. Lill and Victoria are both on passive exercisers – electronically controlled couches that do all the exercise for you. Lill's is doing sit ups and Victoria's is working her legs. Sallyanne, a model, is sitting on a rowing machine examining her split ends.

Lill	So what's the diet?
Sallyanne	Well, what it is you do – you eat a hard-boiled egg before every meal, and the hard-boiled egg actually eats some of that meal for you. And so you lose weight.

They all think about this.

Victoria	You don't want to lose weight, do you?
Sallyanne	I do, Victoria. My agent says if I can't taper my hips to quite an extent I can say bye-bye lingerie, hello bakeware.
Victoria	Are you a model?
Sallyanne	Catalogues, glamour and promos. Have you seen the Car Parts Calendar?
Victoria	Er –
Sallyanne	I'm August. I'm pointing at a fanbelt.

---

is hopeless . . . I had a letter last week from John Noakes saying my new design for a threepenny stamp had come third.'

Victoria	Was that topless?
Sallyanne	Not really, I was holding quite a big spanner.
Lill	Course, they say you shouldn't eat a lot of eggs now, don't they?
Sallyanne	Quite honestly, Lill, if you believed everything they tell you – like all this 'other people smoking can give you cancer' – I mean how can it – if you read a book, Victoria, that's not going to make me more intelligent, is it?
Victoria	I wouldn't have thought so.
Sallyanne	No. And look at the moaning over the Greenhouse Effect – the terrible weather we have in this country, you'd think people would be pleased – I'm buying a barbecue. People knock Mrs Thatcher but, good heavens, Victoria, three hours' sleep a night and her suits are immaculate, and that new hairstyle gives her whole face a lift – I think we could do with something like the Falklands again actually, don't you – something British – give us all a rally round . . . *(She gets up.)*
Victoria	See you later.
Sallyanne	In a while, alligator. *(Leaves.)*
Victoria	I can't believe we're doing this, Lill. I can't believe we've paid three hundred and fifty pounds to drink hot water and be strapped to an out-of-control sofa.
Lill	Well if it gives me a waist like Sallyanne, it's absolutely worth it.
Victoria	If it gives you a brain like Sallyanne you'll have room for a handbag under your skull.
Lill	*(getting off her machine)* Right, that's me finished. You're on this one now.
Victoria	Am I? *(Gets on it.)* What does this one do for me?
Lill	It narrows the waist and flattens the abdomen.
Victoria	Oh yeah?
Lill	If you stay on it long enough.
Victoria	Could be a long time. I can see all the chaps at the Central Electicity Generating Board with their coats on, going 'Oh blimey – is she still on it?'

Judy marches in, clipboard at the ready.

Judy	Early morning jog: takers?
Lill	Now, what does jogging do for you exactly?
Judy	*(miming)* Circulation, stamina, hah hah hah hah and muscle. *(She slaps her stomach.)*
Lill	Really? Which muscles is it good for then?
Judy	Tip top for hams, gluts, pecs, abs –
Victoria	And you speak Esperanto!
Lill	Sorry, I didn't catch all the names –
Judy	Well, pop into my eyrie if you'd like more gen.
Lill	OK.
Judy	I've a selection of full-colour diagrams of the major muscle groups – thrilling!
Lill	Right. So you think jogging's definitely a good thing?
Judy	Not a doubt in my mind. I jog – I'm strong, I'm fit. I haven't blown my nose since 1973 and I have an extremely regular and satisfactory bowel movement.
Victoria	Got any diagrams of that?
Judy	So – yes to jogging?
Lill	Yes, I think I should.
Judy	I agree. *(Pokes Lill's leg.)* Tighten these wobblers.

Victoria laughs.

Lill	Put us both down.

Judy moves to the door.

Victoria	What?
Judy	*(stopping in doorway)* Six forty-five – patio – warm up – yes?
Victoria	What are you trying to do to me? Six forty-five is a time for dreaming that Woody Allen has popped round with a picnic hamper: it is not a time for assembling on a patio with a load of eager beavers in mesh sleeveless blouses.

Lill   It'll release all your tensions.

Victoria   It will not. I shall be all knotted up wondering how I can
                  kick you up the bum without breaking my stride.

Lill   *(switching Vic's machine on)* I shall see you at Happy Hour.

She leaves.

Victoria   Happy Hour? Huh! Two cups of Marmite for the price
                  of one.

*A pause while the machine works. Two maintenance men
come in; a big middle-aged one and a lad. They stare at
Victoria's machine intently, bending down to look at the
mechanism. They take no notice of her.*

Older Man Thought so . . .

He straightens up and looks at watch.

Come on, Allardyce; brew time.

They leave. Victoria is left on the machine.

Victoria   I see that was Allardyce.

*The dining room. Victoria, Lill, Sallyanne, Connie and
Enid are finishing their meal. They're at the herb tea stage.
Dana comes to their table with a Thermos jug.*

Dana   More hot water, slaves?

Victoria   Can I have another tea bag?

Dana   Can you bog roll. Nothing more now till brekkers.

Enid   You can top me up, Dana.

Lill   Oh, we're on early breakfast.

Victoria   Oh yes, miss, early breakfast for us, miss, we're going
                  jogging.

Connie	Catch me.
Enid	You've come adrift, Dana, cleavage-wise.
Dana	*(buttoning herself up)* Blinking Allardyce. I said to him, I don't mind what you do with them but put them back after. Tuh. *(She goes off singing:)* Gimme gimme gimme dat, gimme dat ding . . . *(She turns at the doorway.)* I mean, I'd do the same with his flies, wouldn't I? *(Sings:)* Gimme dat ding . . .
Victoria	And she chops our coleslaw!
Connie	Talk about Now Wash Your Hands.
Sallyanne	I've seen that somewhere. Is it a film?

Nicola comes in.

Nicola	Oh hello – everybody. I hope you all enjoyed your crudities. Nicola here. I'm afraid we don't have an organised activity as such on the agendum. We were hoping to have a twilight display of mouth-to-mouth resuscitation in the treatment lobby.
Connie	*(knowingly)* Resus.
Nicola	But Mrs Fernihough can't be here, she had a slight accident and scratched her Volvo. But activities will have resumed by tomorrow and we'll be circling a pamphlet to that intention so you can exercise your choosing as and whenever. I hope you haven't found the first day's regiment too astringent – I know camomile isn't everyone's cup of tea – but do stick with it and results will turn themselves up shortly. So. Bye.

She goes out.

Connie	Nice enough woman, but nothing on sale in the brain department.
Enid	Not even a special purchase.
Sallyanne	I'm going to wash my hair again. I've got a shampoo with herbs in that mends split ends.

Victoria	How can it?
Sallyanne	How can it?
Victoria	How can it mend them?
Sallyanne	How can it mend what? Sorry?
Victoria	How can it mend split ends?
Sallyanne	My shampoo?
Victoria	Yes. How can it mend them?
Sallyanne	It's got herbs in.
Victoria	What do they do?
Sallyanne	They mend the split ends. See you later.

Sallyanne leaves.

Victoria	What's on telly tonight?
Connie	There's no telly at Pinkneys.
Enid	You're supposed to be getting away from it all. The hurly-burly of modern living.
Victoria	But I like hurly-burly. Especially burly.
Lill	Well, I'm going on the rowing machine, I think.
Connie	Come on, Enid; face-pack time.
Lill	*(eagerly)* Are they good?
Connie	It shuts her up yapping, so it suits me.

Connie, Enid and Lill prepare to go.

Victoria	Are there any books?
Connie	There's a *Reader's Digest* in the treatment lobby. What was that piece, Enid? –
Enid	'How I scaled Kilimanjaro without a Spleen'. Night night.

The three of them leave. Victoria spots a forgotten cauliflower floret and eats it.

Victoria	I'm fed up.

The patio, early next morning. Victoria, Lill, a couple of silent men and one very fit-looking elderly lady are bending and stretching to Judy's orders.

Judy	OK. Follow me. Brisk walk to begin.[189]
Victoria	I hate you, Lillian Sutcliffe. I hate everybody here. I hate the sky. I hate my eyelids.
Lill	It'll get you fit.
Victoria	What am I getting fit for? I'm never going to do this again. Jogging is for people who aren't intelligent enough to watch breakfast television.
Judy	And *jog*!
Lill	Suppose you have to run for a bus?
Victoria	I'll wait for the next one.
Lill	It lifts your buttocks.
Victoria	I don't want them lifted; I'm quite happy with them bobbling along where they are.
Lill	Well I know Marcus would prefer mine a little higher.
Victoria	Well have plastic surgery. They could probably convert them into shoulder pads.

(Both are getting out of breath.)

	And anyway, Marcus is hardly Michelangelo's David. And as for that thing he wears on his head . . .
Lill	It's a very expensive hairpiece.
Victoria	He should ask for a refund. I've seen more convincing toupés grown on a wet flannel.

Judy and the others forge ahead.

Judy	Come on, slackers – put your backs in.

They stagger on. Victoria looks at Lill.

---

189 Cut.

Victoria   Oh, Lill, you haven't! Not again!

Lill   It must be the raw broccoli.

Victoria   I wouldn't mind, I can't even open a window.

The dining room a little later. Dana is laying tables. Victoria and Lill stagger up to their table, breathless.

Victoria   Where's breakfast?

Dana   There.

Lill   Where?

Dana   On t' table.

Victoria   There's only hot water here.

Dana   That's it.

Victoria   That's breakfast?

Dana   You're fasting today; did Nicola not say?

Victoria   No.

Dana   Ne'er mind. Tomorrow's Grape Nuts. *(She sings:)* Every sha la la la la, Every who oh oh oh . . .

Lill   Well – when I stand in the registry office with Marcus by my side this will all be worth it.

Victoria   While you're there – could you register my death?

The sauna. Connie, Enid and Victoria are laid out on shelves. Lill comes in and arranges herself.

Lill   You know, I think Sallyanne's shampoo really works – I don't seem to have half so many split ends today.

Victoria   Oh please, Lill. You'll be holding your sheets up to the window next.

Enid   *(reading from a magazine)* What's wrong with this? Problem page: I am at the end of my tether – my husband is important.

Connie   Impotent!

Enid   What's that when it's gone shopping?

Connie   No oomph. Bed-wise.

Enid   Eh?

Connie	The escalator doesn't reach the underpant department.
Enid	Not with it.
Connie	Explain, Victoria.
Victoria	Well, you know celery –
Enid	Do I know celery? Widnes Central Slimmer of the Month – I could make an edge-to-edge jerkin out of celery and still have enough to stiffen a roller blind. What do you mean, though, re celery?
Lill	It's a sexual problem, Enid.
Enid	*(losing interest)* Oh. I thought it was something interesting.
Lill	Marcus can't always . . . you know.
Victoria	Well you can't concentrate when you're wearing a toupé. It's like trying to play *Monopoly* with a paper hat on.
Connie	Is this your chap, Lill? Marcus?
Lill	I'm hoping he'll divorce his wife.
Connie	Mm, I kept hoping mine would – and I *was* his wife. He passed away in Cleveleys, so that saved a solicitor.[190]
Lill	Don't you miss him?
Connie	I prefer my independence.
Victoria	See!
Connie	I've never done anything with a man that was more fun than rummy.

Lill sighs.

Victoria	What's on tonight, Enid?
Enid	*(looking at pamphlet)* A talk – 'Corsetry Thro' the Ages'. Nicola gave me a taster over breakfast. Apparently Mary Queen of Scots –
Connie	What – *the* Mary Queen of Scots?
Enid	Mm – her in the necklace. She apparently was wearing something very like our modern brassière the day she was beheaded.

---

190 Changed to 'passed on'.

Connie	That's pitiful, isn't it. If it had been halter-neck the chopper might have bounced off the elastic.
Enid	I love historical people, don't you? Cleopatra, Florence Nightingale, Noële Gordon[191] –
Victoria	She wasn't historical. She was an actress.
Enid	I don't mean Noële Gordon. I mean Edith Cavell.[192]
Victoria	What's on tomorrow night?
Enid	Barndancing with Kirsty.
Connie	They can stuff that, for me: barndancing. They can stuff it in a pastry case and glaze it. For me.
Enid	And me. That Kirsty's never set foot in a barn. Obviously been no nearer a barn than a gingham wrap around. Kirsty's much more of a hip hop and scratch merchant.
Connie	You'll be hip hop and scratch if you don't shift it – herbal rubs at half past.

Connie and Enid prepare to leave.

Victoria	What's that?
Connie	Gordon only knows. I just hope it's not parsley.
Enid	Ooh so do I. Parsley's my pet noir.

They start to leave, mumbling.

Enid	Where's my bandanna, Connie?
Connie	How the figgy pudding should I know – I'm not a bandanna warden . . .

Judy bursts in.

Judy	Come on, come on! Aerobics! Gymnasium two minutes! *(She claps her hands.)* Far too lax.

---

191 The star, it almost goes without saying, of *Crossroads*.
192 British nurse who helped save the lives of combatants on both sides in the First World War. Found guilty of treason and executed by a German firing squad in 1915.

Judy goes out. They get up.

Victoria   She makes Mussolini look disorganised.
Lill   Marvellous figure though.
Victoria   Shut up.

The main recreation room. Disgruntled guests are moving about including Victoria, Lill, Connie, Enid and Sally-anne. A few people sing 'Why are we waiting?' quietly.

Connie   Why are we waiting . . . ?
Enid   Why are we waiting . . . ?
Lill   Will you test me on my calorie values?
Victoria   No. What's the matter with you?
Lill   I want to get thin.
Victoria   Why? Because of Marcus? He'll still be married. You'll just be hanging around, waiting in smaller trousers.
Lill   Marcus prefers petite women.
Victoria   Yes, because they're easier to tread on.

Nicola comes in.

Nicola   Erm! Could I just pronounce a change of itinament? As you know, this evening's recreational fertility was to have the barndancing; but I'm afraid as of lately it has had to have been – not happening. Kirsty, who recently attended an intensive two-day Dosey Doe[193] workshop in Lincolnshire has had to cry off for presently. She lost concentration whilst tossing a medicine ball earlier; they think the kneecap's not too bad, but they may have to splice-in a new floorboard. So as an alternative we've decided to temporarily break our no-television Pinkney's embargo *(excited mumbles of* Eastenders *and* Bob Monkhouse *from guests)* and show a very instructative

---

193 Form of square dancing.

video tape featuring various slimmers; each with their own inspiring slimming story, of how they slimmed, and what it was like to slim, get slim, stay slim . . . not to be fat. *(She tails off.)* Dana! Could you wheel through now, please?

Dana, wonderfully dressed for a night out, wheels in a TV and video, and plugs it in.

Nicola   So I'm sorry about the barndancing. We're still hoping tomorrow night's activity will go ahead: it's just a question of whether the blood donors' van will fit thro' the main gateway.

Dana puts in the video.

Nicola   OK? Lovely. Bye!

Nicola goes out. Dana switches on the video.

Dana   Right, that's me off, slaves. Going to get down the Yellow Ferret and get boogying. *(She leaves, singing:)* When I need you . . .

The video begins. It's very old and poor quality from the early 70s. Music title with logo of 'Acorn Enterprises' cuts straight to an awful 70s girl in tank top and huge trousers squinting into the sunlight. She speaks stiltedly.

Girl on video Hello, I'm Melanie Dickinson, Swedacrisp Slimmer of the Year. I used to be nineteen stone seven. You wouldn't believe it now, would you? I can wear bikinis, lacy feminine underwear and – yes – even hot pants.

Victoria is amused at this.

And it wasn't so hard sticking to 800 calories a day for fourteen months – let me tell you how I did it.

Victoria nudges Lill.

Girl	Lemon juice in hot water was my biggest treat . . .
Victoria	Lill!
Lill	*(poised with notebook and pen)* Sshh!

Lill and Victoria's bedroom. Victoria comes in. Lill is hopping about in a vaguely aerobic way.

Victoria	I'm so starving I've just eaten two inches of fluoride toothpaste.
Lill	That was a good tip on that slimming video, actually. Every time you want to eat something, brush your teeth.
Victoria	If I brushed my teeth every time I wanted to eat something, I'd have gums up to my sinuses. Can you just stop a minute?
Lill	No I can't.
Victoria	Well it's driving me mad.
Lill	*(stopping)* Look – I've got something to tell you.
Victoria	*(apprehensively)* What?
Lill	Well, while I was here on my own I did something absolutely unforgiveable; I despise myself.
Victoria	What?
Lill	You know that squashed chocolate raisin we found in the wastepaper basket.
Victoria	Yeah?
Lill	I've been thinking about it since yesterday and as soon as you'd gone I took it out of the wastepaper basket and ate it.
Victoria	So what?
Lill	It's thirteen calories – I've been exercising since I swallowed it but I can't be sure I've burnt it all off *(jogging)*. I don't know what to do – I'll have to tell Nicola. Heaven knows what I'll weigh in the morning –

Victoria Lill –

Lill Marcus'll never marry me now. They'll have to wheel me into the registry office at this rate – I don't even know if they have a ramp!

Victoria *(sitting her down)* Lill – stop it a minute. If you really want to go and tell Nicola –

Lill I do; I have to.

Victoria Well we'll find her in a minute. But listen – you've been going out with a married man for twelve years.

Lill Yes.

Victoria And some of the time you've been thin and some of the time you haven't.

Lill Yes.

Victoria And which ever you've been, he's never mentioned divorce.

Lill No.

Victoria And he has got twins and a Shetland pony.

Lill Yes.

Victoria So, chances are, even if you weighed less than a Pot Noodle, he'd still stay happily married.

Lill Yes.

Victoria And he collects beermats.

Lill Yes. *(Pause.)* I know. But I'm thirty-nine. I know I'm silly to have carried it on this long, but I kept thinking he might change his mind. If I could just flatten this and raise these.

Victoria But if he loved you he wouldn't care, would he? You could have a bum that only just cleared the pile on an Axminster carpet and it wouldn't matter.

Lill I know. And then I was thinking, if I did finish with him, I'd need to look good or nobody else would fancy me.

Victoria You look good now. You can't pass a building site without some poor hunk losing his grip on the scaffolding. Come on – let's go and confess to Nicola about the chocolate raisin. Say three Hail Mary's and a Ryvita.

A corridor with the treatment room off it. Victoria and Lill pass and look through the door at Judy exercising fiercely with dumbells.

Lill Oh but, Vic, to be all tanned and lean and disciplined like Judy.

Vic Judy's not a person: she's worked by a computer in Milford Haven. Anyway – she's not attractive. If a man flung himself on to her in a fit of passion he'd break something.

Lill All right – but wouldn't you like to look like Sallyanne?

Vic No, cos then I'd have to be a topless model and stand around all day. 'Jason, can you powder my nipples?'

The recreation room. Victoria and Lill looking through a window to where a small car is parked. The strip over the windscreen reads 'Allardyce' and 'Dana'.[194] It is rocking somewhat.

Victoria And look at Dana – she's twice the size of you and she has a fantastic time. Dresses up, goes out, and I don't know what she's doing in the back of that car but I bet she's not working out the calories in a chocolate raisin.

Lill You're right.

Victoria She just has fun.

Lill That's true, actually.

Victoria Mind you, she's knackering the suspension.

The corridor leading to Nicola's office. Lill and Victoria are walking along.

---

194 VW was fond of this sight gag. In *Nearly a Happy Ending*, the single Maureen has her own name up in the windscreen of her Mini. In *Pat and Margaret*, Jim starts peeling the names of Jim and Margeret [sic] from his windscreen when he thinks they've split up.

Lill	All right – so weight's not important – but don't you think it's worth persevering with this Pinkney's regime: no caffeine, no additives, raw vegetables.
Victoria	Not with the effect they have on you. It's like sharing a room with a whoopee cushion.
Lill	Pure food, mineral water, no television.

They stop outside Nicola's door. From inside the office comes the theme music from 'Emmerdale Farm'. Lill knocks.

Nicola	*(Voice Over)* Just a memento. *(The music snaps off.)* Come through.

They go into her tiny office. Nicola is seated guiltily behind the desk, a large blank TV screen nearby.

Nicola	Can I help, ladies?
Victoria	Lill's having a fit of conscience because she's eaten a chocolate raisin and ruined her detoxification programme.
Nicola	Oh sit down.
Lill	And I do believe absolutely in everything you're trying to do here.
Nicola	What would that be?
Lill	Treating the body as a temple, pure food, no stimulants –
Nicola	Oh that.
Lill	You look marvellous on it.
Nicola	Well, to be painful, I couldn't run this healthy farm if I didn't have a few stimulants. It takes me three cups of black coffee to get my mascara on. And I don't care what they say, I like monosodium glutamate. I've got a monosodium glutamate recipe book.
Victoria	You don't eat raw broccoli?
Nicola	I can't. It has an unfortunate effect on me wind-wise. And I have to share this office.
Lill	So you don't believe in any of it?

Nicola   *(Thinks.)* I like ping-pong – *(She pauses and opens her desk drawer.)* Marshmallow?

The sauna. Connie, Enid, Lill and Victoria, all clothed, are sharing a bottle of champagne out of triangular water cups.

Lill   I never knew you'd brought a bottle of champagne in.

Victoria   You never knew about the chocolate raisins either.

Connie   *(slightly the worse for wear)* What we'll do, Lill. Lill! We'll throw a party for you – and I'll invite every man I know in Widnes.

Enid   She doesn't know any.

Connie   I figgy do, lady.

Enid   Name one.

Connie   Robin Sutherland.

Enid   In the antique shop? He'd be no use to Lill. She'd need quite a different frontal arrangement to catch *his* fancy.

Lill   Oh bother them all. Let's just have a good time.

Victoria   Hear hear.

Lill   Come on, we're going jogging.

Victoria   Oh, Lill, I thought you'd dropped all that.

Lill   We're not going far. Come on!

Night. The village street. Victoria, Connie and Enid, led by Lill, are jogging, with many complaints.

Victoria   Oh Lill!

Lill   Not much further. Onward and upward!

A small café of the egg and chip variety hoves into view. Lill leads them all towards it.

In the café. The four are standing at the counter, behind which stands a greasy man.

Lill   So that's sausage, egg and chips, sausage, beans and chips, double egg and chips twice, four teas and four rounds of bread and butter.

Man   White or brown?

Lill   White. With additives.

Victoria   And germs on.

Four eager faces stare up at him expectantly.

THE LIBRARY

Inside an Edwardian library in a large-ish town. It is open-plan, with Fiction, Children's and a Reference section, study tables, video machine etc. Pinned up with other local posters is one – 'Tape Your Memories', showing some old dear jabbering away into a tape recorder. Victoria is browsing round the shelves.

Victoria   *(to us)* This is the dreariest library in the whole world. They haven't got anything new. I think they're waiting for the Domesday Book to come out in paperback. It's run by this terrible woman called Madge, awfully narrow-minded, makes Mary Whitehouse[195] look like a topless waitress. Never mind Salman Rushdie – she'd have the Swan Vestas to a Catherine Cookson given half a chance. She thinks book-burning is a sensible alternative to oil-fired central heating. Of course they have to order all the newspapers but if it was up to her it would just be *Nursing Mirror* and *Slimming for Nuns*. She can't bear Page Three – in fact she cuts the girls out and replaces them with a knitting pattern. Quite sad seeing all those old blokes sitting around trying to ogle a sleeveless pully.

---

195 Moral campaigner.

She encounters Ted, a dirty old man, round a corner. He winks and she retreats.

Madge's taste in fiction; half of these are hospital romances – 'their eyes met over a diseased kidney' – and everything else is in large print. You try reading one with good eyesight. It's like being shouted at for three and a half hours.

She moves into Children's.

And it smells. That typical library aroma of damp gabardine and luncheon meat. And every book's got something scribbled in the margin – things like 'Oh I agree', and 'We washed everything by hand too'. I mean it's a bit disconcerting to flick through a copy of *Hamlet* to find 'This happened to me' scrawled all over Act Four.

Madge appears from nowhere, a large frightening woman.

Madge	You know this is Children's?
Victoria	I know.
Madge	Very well. *(She leaves disapprovingly.)*
Victoria	*(crossing to reference)* She's put me off now. I was just going to squander my ticket on a nice career book:[196] *Wendy Carstairs – Receptionist* or *Petra – Forecourt Attendant.*

She sees Sheila, a thin anxious woman fortyish but dressed older, being shown how to work the video by John the nondescript fortyish assistant librarian.

Hiyah. What are you doing?

Sheila waves her over.

---

196 Changed to 'a nice career novel'.

John	And when you've finished, press 'Eject' and your tape comes out, and Bob's your Uncle.
Sheila	Yes he is. Thank you. I know it's a saying. But he is my uncle. Thank you.

John goes away.

Victoria	What are you doing?
Sheila	This is the new video machine.
Victoria	You can watch videos in the library? Where are they? Have they got *Petra, Forecourt Attendant – The Movie*?
Sheila	*(glancing around)* I've joined an agency.
Victoria	Have you?
Sheila	And they've sent me these videos to watch.
Victoria	What? Blue videos?

Madge is now hanging around Ted, seated at a table, snatching up papers and folding them with a lot of noise.

	You'd better not watch them here. You know what Madge is like. I've seen her go through a breastfeeding manual crayonning bras on the women.
Sheila	I've made a decision, Victoria. I'm coming out of the wardrobe.
Victoria	Are you?
Sheila	Since Mother died – oh, and thank you for the flowers, we had tributes from everywhere, even the optician – I've taken stock – what do they call it? – stocktaking?
Victoria	Yeah?
Sheila	And I saw this advertisement in the post office – because I'm trying to sell my stairlift – it's in very good condition, and as I said on the postcard even if you're not disabled, it's FUN! It's called video dating. You've heard of computer dating?
Victoria	Yeah!
Sheila	Well that's gone by the roof, it's completely blasé now;

so the upshot is, they send you six[197] men on a tape and
John, the assistant librarian – he used to pick me out
something historical for mother – 'Bring me something
where nobody dies, Sheila,' she used to say – well, that's
the point of history – they're all dead – he's been through
the mechanicals with me; I view the men and then contact
Valerie.

Victoria   Valerie?

Sheila   She runs the agency. I've only spoken with her briefly – I
had a ten pence stuck – but from the sound of her voice
I think she was wearing a tie-neck blouse.

Victoria   So you pick a man?

Sheila   That's right. Well, I'm free now, it's about time I turned
over a new leaf[198].

Victoria   Put it in then, let's have a look.

Sheila   Arrow pointing this way, and press 'PLAY'. *(Nothing happens.)* It's broken, I knew it, it's me *(pressing all buttons).*
I was the same with the spin drier – wet underskirts all
over my next-door neighbour, and she's Nigerian – not
much of a welcome.

The picture comes up.

*The museum tea bar. It is a small, dreary, slightly whole-
foody place. Victoria and Sheila are finishing tea.*

Victoria   I thought you said they did a good date and apple flap-
jack.

Sheila   You just need to work it round your mouth a bit first.
(She roots in her bag.) Find my notes.

Victoria   Nice little book.

Sheila   Made by disadvantaged Oriental widows. You can see here
where they were too depressed to stick down the edges.

---

197 Changed to 'eight'.
198 Changed to 'leap'.

Victoria	So who did you fancy?
Sheila	Oh I'm no judge of character, Victoria.
Victoria	Do you think *I* am? I've had my drive tarmacked eight times.
Sheila	Give me your views on Rodney.
Victoria	Well, Rodney had white towelling socks, didn't he? Which in my book makes him unreliable, untrustworthy and prone to vaseline jokes. Mark . . .
Sheila	The solicitor.
Victoria	He was OK – but, as he says himself, he does a lot of conveyancing so that'll be seventeen phone calls just to meet him for a cup of coffee.
Sheila	I was rather taken with Simon – the gynaecologist.
Victoria	No – too inhibiting. You can't flirt with someone who can visualise your Fallopian tubes.
Sheila	Now Malcolm – what do you think he meant by 'lively social life'?
Victoria	Drink.
Sheila	He wants a breezy, uninhibited companion.
Victoria	To drink with.
Sheila	And what do you think he meant by 'life peppered with personal tragedy'?
Victoria	Hangovers.
Sheila	I think you're right. He had half an Alka Seltzer stuck in his moustache. Robert.
Victoria	Robert?
Sheila	In radiators.
Victoria	Radiators.
Sheila	The blue bri-nylon with the polo collar.
Victoria	Oh, the one with the bust! He was creepy. He looked like the sort of man who hangs around outside television shops watching 'Challenge Anneka' with his flies undone.[199]

---

199 This was a very contemporary reference. 'The Library' was recorded in mid-October. The first episode of *Challenge Anneka* was broadcast on BBC One a month earlier.

Sheila	Terry was interesting.
Victoria	Yes, wasn't he? It's not every night watchman who can wear a poncho.
Sheila	I liked him. He very much put me in mind of someone. Singer – dark curly hair – outgoing . . .
Victoria	Tom Jones?
Sheila	Alma Cogan. And Kenneth – I've put 'very rushed and jerky'.
Victoria	You had him on fast-forward.
Sheila	Well I disliked his epaulettes.
Victoria	Right.
Sheila	So that leaves Keith.
Victoria	Well he was all right, wasn't he? What did you put for him?
Sheila	Soft, sensitive, a bit woolly.
Victoria	Should be all right as long as you don't put him in the washing machine. Where are you going to meet him?
Sheila	I thought I'd do him an egg salad at home.
Victoria	Are you mad?
Sheila	Why?
Victoria	Because that's terribly dangerous.
Sheila	No, I'd boil them for twenty minutes.
Victoria	Inviting a strange man to your home: he could be an axe murderer.
Sheila	Oh no – he's got a degree in mechanical engineering.
Victoria	Meet him in a restaurant.
Sheila	*(panicking)* Oh I'm sending it back. I can't meet him anywhere. I'm no good with men – really. I can't even tackle the milkman face-to-face. I have to bob behind the ironing board and call through. And then he takes advantage. The times I've been saddled with an unrequested bilberry yoghourt.
Victoria	Meet him here for a cup of tea.
Sheila	I'll clam up, Victoria. I'm no good on my own – I clam up like – what are those things –
Victoria	Clams.
Sheila	Oysters.

Victoria	You won't – you'll be fine.
Sheila	After all those years stuck with Mother, I can't just sit down with a man and come up with the bandage. Suppose he chucks in Giscard d'Estaing – how do I respond?[200] I'll be stumped.
Victoria	Well – do you want me to come with you?
Sheila	Oh if you could just get the ball bowling – that would be marvellous.
Victoria	Well I'll just stay and see that you're all right, shall I?
Sheila	Mm. Just shush him out.
Victoria	And if he looks like being an axe-murderer you keep him talking and I'll immobilise him with the date and apple flapjack. Yep?

The museum tea bar again, on another day. Victoria and Sheila are sitting in readiness with a tray of tea. Sheila is smartly dressed and extremely nervous.

Sheila	*(suddenly)* Take off your jacket.
Victoria	Eh?
Sheila	It's too interesting. Take it off.
Victoria	*(taking it off)* What are you worried about?
Sheila	Well, as soon as he hears you're in television he's not going to squint my way, is he? He'll be querying left right and centre for insider gossip. He won't want to delve into my doings if he can get the lowdown on Patti Caldwell.[201]
Victoria	He's come to meet you.
Sheila	What have I ever done? I've never even been mugged.
Victoria	You've been burgled.
Sheila	And what did they take? Nothing! Two apostle spoons and a bobbing bird. Robbed – I was snubbed.
Victoria	Well I'll go then, shall I?

---

200 Valéry Giscard d'Estaing was president of France from 1974 to 1981.

201 Lancashire broadcaster. Her name, Pattie, was misspelt in the original edition, perhaps to indicate that Sheila might get the name wrong herself.

Sheila	No don't – he might get the wrong idea; he might think I'm a high class call-girl.
Victoria	In a museum tea room?
Sheila	He may be a pervert.[202] He may have come here specifically for the purpose of rubbing up against a scale model of Saxon Fortifications.
Victoria	Well I'll stay for a few minutes.
Sheila	Well, dull yourself down a bit. Set me off. Every beautiful painting needs an understated frame.
Victoria	Every sizzling casserole needs an oven glove.
Sheila	He's here! I recognise his hush puppies. You pour the tea and I'll sparkle.

Keith, early middle-aged in a jacket and sweater, shirt and tie, comes in and looks around vaguely.

Victoria	He hasn't seen us – wave at him.
Sheila	I can't. I've frozen. I'm like this. I was the same with Sacha Distel in Boots.[203] You wave.
Victoria	OK.
Sheila	Nothing too provocative or sensual.
Victoria	*(Waves awkwardly.)* Here he comes. Good luck.
Keith	Is it Sheila?
Sheila	Mmmm.
Keith	I wasn't sure if I had the correct museum.
Victoria	Would you like to sit down?
Keith	Yes I would. *(Sits slowly.)* Well I'm Keith, you're Sheila. Who's the gooseberry?
Victoria	I'm Victoria – I have to go in a minute.
Keith	Now if you were from Dewsbury, Victoria, you'd be the gooseberry from Dewsbury.
Victoria	Ah ha ha.

---

202 Change to 'pervern'.
203 French crooner.

Keith sits quietly, pleased with this joke. Sheila pours the tea with much rattling.

Keith   When I said I was unsure as to whether I'd found the correct museum, the circumstances were these: your note, Sheila, for which much thanks, told me to expect a large building with stone pillars to my left on entering the city centre. *(Pause.)* Now would I be correct in thinking you are not familiar with the workings of the internal combustion engine?

Sheila   A with the workings, what, begging?

Victoria   You don't drive.

Sheila   Oh no. I've been shown around a tank.

Keith   And so, not being cognisant with the traffic lay-out as seen, so to speak, from the steering wheel, it will have escaped your attention that the very first building on the left is not the museum and municipal library, but the Edgar Bentley Treatment Hospital for Tropical Diseases.

Both   Ah ah.

Keith   Now, having got that off my chest, I will just equip myself with a smallish biscuit to accompany my tea and return forthwith.

Keith leaves. Significant silence.

Sheila   *He* nursed an elderly mother.

Victoria   I hope she was deaf.

Sheila   Well I don't think he's an axe-murderer.

Victoria   He doesn't need to be. Hey up.

Keith comes back in.

Keith   Well, I'm familiar with Sheila's hobbies and lifestyle as laid out in the video but what's your line of country, Vicky?

Victoria   You don't want to hear about me. Sheila's the fascinating one – she writes poems – she's a wonderful cook . . .

Keith   No – I'm an orderly fellow. Ask a question, get the reply, that's my handlebar. So, how do you rake in the shekels?

Victoria   Oh I've got such a boring job. I can hardly remember what it is.

Keith   Well let's not forget three million people in this country would *like* to be bored in that fashion.

Pause.

Victoria   I work in an office.

Keith   Now, call me a dashingly romantic sentimental old soft-heart, Vicky . . .

Victoria   I haven't got time.

Keith   But to me an office is more than a place of work – it's a microcosm of everyday society.

Sheila   Goodness.

Keith   What do you say to that, Vicky?

Victoria   I say – ah ha ha.

Keith   I thought so. And what office position do you hold?

Victoria   I just answer the phone.

Keith   Now therein if I may presume – we've taken tea together so we're halfway to being pals – therein lies the cardinal error of the average telephone receptionist.

Victoria pulls a face at Sheila.

Sheila   I see in the paper today Mrs Thatcher's sporting a new brooch.

Keith   I'll ignore that, Sheila, for reasons I'll come to in a moment. The telephone receptionist of any company, be it British Telecom or Joe Bloggs of down the road Ltd, holds a unique position in the business framework. Let me clarify myself – this plate is the managing director, and this shortbread finger is the retail customer – what comes in between them?

Sheila   A doiley?

Keith   The telephone receptionist. Now take a typical day in the office . . .

Inside the library, in the video section, a few days later. Victoria and Sheila are checking their notes. Ted is reading the paper at a nearby table.

Victoria   Right – so we're going to Richard this time.

Sheila   You're sure I shouldn't persevere with Keith?

Victoria   He's boring. You've been bored for twenty years. It would be out of the frying pan into the microwave.

Madge   *(appears from afar and calls)* You two! This is not a zoo!

Victoria   So you can't help me locate the elephant house?

Madge   Quiet study or leave, please.

Madge leaves and Ted winks juicily at Victoria.

Ted   Heck of a rump on that. By cracky.

Victoria   *(more quietly)* What did we put for Richard?

Sheila   I've put 'very gentlemanly; interested in fine china and eighteenth-century English furniture. Likes visiting cathedrals, classical music; semi-retired business consultant looking for quiet, refined companion.'

Victoria   Well, you're quiet.

Sheila   Yes, but I'm not refined. I wouldn't know a Hepplewhite wotnot from a quarter of wine gums.[204]

Victoria   It doesn't matter. Just be yourself.

Sheila   And we weren't a classical music family. If Joe 'Piano' Henderson couldn't play it we didn't hear it.[205]

---

204 George Hepplewhite, eighteenth-century cabinetmaker.

205 Pianist and composer whose heyday was in the 1950s. Sheila may know his work, but in 1989 few viewers would have done.

Victoria	What you want to do – is meet him for a drink and take someone really vulgar and thick with you – then you come out looking erudite and tasteful, he's bowled over and whisks you away in his Rover. What do you say?
Sheila	Well I can see the reasoning[206] behind it – but I don't know anybody vulgar. Mother wouldn't even have our scissors sharpened because the woman had pierced ears.
Victoria	Well – meet him at the wine bar . . .

John comes in.

John	Is it working OK now?
Sheila	Yes, it wasn't irretrievably jammed, thank you, John. I had in on *pause*.
John	*(moving away)* That's good. Now, Ted, come on – no eating your sandwiches here – it's not really fair on the other readers.

Ted pretends to put them away. John leaves.

Victoria	What we'll do – you meet him at the wine bar . . .
Madge	*(coming in from nowhere)* When will you people appreciate this is an area set aside for silent study – it is not an annexe of the Millwomen and Fishwives' Debating Society.
Victoria	Sorry.
Madge	*(as she sniffs and wheels round)* You – put those sandwiches away at once. I will not have chutney on my periodicals.

Inside a quiet emptyish wine bar. Richard, a grey-haired, distinguished man in a quiet suit, sits sharing a bottle of wine with Sheila.

Richard	Well, here's to a pleasant evening.

---

206 Changed to 'seasoning'.

Sheila	Yes, 'heres'.

She drinks.

Richard	I was having a quiet chuckle to myself this morning.
Sheila	Oh yes?
Richard	Radio 3 – Alicia de Larrocha[207] with the Granados[208], *Quejas a la maja y el ruisenor* – very amusing interpretation. Did you catch any of it?
Sheila	No, I would probably have had on the Ken Bruce programme.
Richard	Really? *(Pause.)* I'm pleasantly surprised by the acceptability of this bouquet – are you?
Sheila	*(struggling to keep up)* Mm, I'm astounded.
Richard	Are you, as they say, 'into' wine?
Sheila	We used to make it at one time.
Richard	Really – you had a vineyard?
Sheila	We had a scullery.
Richard	*(recovering)* I should think with homemade wine one would have to be extremely patient – is that so?
Sheila	Oh yes – that's the bugbear with it – keeping your hands off the dustbin till the full ten days. *(Pause.)* Van Gogh's a very nice painter, isn't he?
Richard	I assume you're using the work in its incorrect sense – interesting.
Sheila	I love the Great Painters.
Richard	And they are . . . ?
Sheila	They're a set of table mats.[209]

Pause.

---

207 Spanish pianist.
208 Enrique Granados, Spanish composer.
209 This exchange evokes a sketch about a blind date in the *W&W* pilot.
    Man: Do you like Manet?
    Woman: I spend it when I've got it obviously.

Richard	You say a friend of yours is joining us?
Sheila	Just breezing through. Here she is now actually.

Victoria comes in, a vision in skin-tight dress, tormented hair, jewellery, stilettos, the lot.

Victoria	Ooh, give us a swig of your vino, crumb-bum; I've been banging like a navvie's drill all affy.
Sheila	This is –
Victoria	Sapphire. Ciao.
Richard	Very pleased to meet you, Sapphire – I'm Richard Casey.
Victoria	He looks a bit of a Richard, dunt he, Sheila? Hey, hutch up, I'm sweating cobs. *(She sniffs her armpits.)*
Richard	May I pour you a glass, Sapphire?
Victoria	Pour us a bin bag – I'm gasping. I tell you, that window cleaner, what a snogger! I've never had such clean tonsils. And never mind a chammy – he certainly buffed up *my* corners.
Richard	And what do you do, Sapphire?
Victoria	Eh? A bit of this, bit of that, loads of the other! No, to be serious, Richard – I'm an artiste in the entertainment business. *(She fishes in her cleavage.)* Where's my card? *(She gets it out and wipes it.)* 'Miss Sapphire – Poses with a Python'. Now don't get the wrong idea – it's right artistic. Costume-wise, I never wear less than the full three tassels, and between shows I am at that python with the Dettox and a damp cloth even if he haven't been nowhere. *(She slurps her wine.)* God, I needed that – my guts! I don't care what they say on t' adverts – Malibu does not go with piccalilli. The wind I've had, Rick – I won't beat about the bungalow – I've been flatulating – and, boy, have I stunk! I mean, I don't mind for t' punters but it's not pleasant for the python. Hey – top us up, Dicky – I've got a big job on tonight. Do you ever get days, Dick when you think, 'I just do not want to thrust my groin in people's faces – I want to go home

	and have a go at my corns with a potato peeler.' Do you?
Richard	Well, I can't say I –
Victoria	So what do you think to our Sheila then? Eh? I mean talk about tasteful. She isn't like me; she wouldn't know a rubberised posing pouch from a sink plunger. Still – if it's a good party, who cares? *(She laughs.)*
Richard	Shall I order some more wine?
Victoria	No, I'd better push off, Rick – I've got to glue a little novelty toilet into my navel and it takes forever to dry.
Richard	Oh, no, have a little champagne before you leave. Waiter!
Victoria	All right, just a quick bottle. Now, Sheila – have you told Richard about how you're really into classical music?
Sheila	Oh yes. Ravel's 'Bolero', what a pulsing rhythm. Superb for tackling the ironing.
Richard	*(patronisingly)* And Sapphire? Any views on Ravel?
Victoria	What were he, a juggler?
Richard	*(amused)* No, a rather famous composer.
Victoria	Oh. Cos jugglers often wear boleros.
Richard	You probably know it as the Torville and Dean music.[210]
Victoria	Weren't they a lovely couple? And they never did it. Mind you, she spent so much time lying face down on the ice, I'm not surprised.
Richard	You're not keen on the classics, then, I take it?
Victoria	Never heard of them – what are they?
Richard	Beethoven's Fifth.
Victoria	No.
Richard	Moonlight Sonata.
Victoria	Sounds like a hatchback. No.
Richard	1812 Overture.
Victoria	That rings a bell.
Richard	Daddle addle daddly dat dat dah.
Victoria	Oh yeah – my friend Suleema used to do an act to that.

---

210 Torvill was misspelt in the original edition. The gag involving Britain's greatest ice dancers, neither VW's first nor her last, was written at speed in rehearsal when the script was found to come up short.

Richard   What sort of an act?

Victoria   Sort of a contortionist. I won't go into details, but Christmas round her house they never needed a bottle opener, a nut cracker, or somewhere to keep the satsumas.

Richard   *(snuggling up)* This is fascinating.

Victoria   Sheila, tell Richard about your Elaine Paige records.

Richard   Elaine Paige?

Victoria   You know – blonde, titchy, goes 'Bleuh!' What a Hobsons. How they passed her over for the Royal Wedding beats me. I know she's small, but they could have stood her up on a bucket. Still, that's the Establishment for you.

Richard   You're bloody right: we're too damn stuffy about these things. God – you're refreshing.

Victoria   *(drinking, pulling a face at Sheila)* Bottoms up.

Sheila   *(leaving)* I'll just go and powder my nose.

Victoria   Don't forget to flush it!

Richard   Crikey – you're funny. So, er, what do you wear on stage exactly? Black leather boots or stilettos? Let's have the full gen.

Victoria   Er –

The library, a couple of days later; Victoria is hanging around Fiction as before.

Victoria   Sheila's given up on this video dating. She says the next time she goes out with a man, she'll be lying down with her eyes shut and he'll be carrying the coffin. What a night with Richard. I mean when a man's on the lookout for quiet refined companionship you don't expect him to try eating pork scratchings out of your cleavage. He was dreadful in the taxi – I haven't been groped so inefficiently since I was fifteen. Once he saw me he never took another look at Sheila – good job – she finished off the champagne and was last seen in the gent's toilets flicking Quiche Lorraine over the cubicle doors.

Madge	*(looming round a unit)* Are you looking for anything in particular?
Victoria	I'm browsing.
Madge	Well don't finger the bindings. *(She heads for the counter.)* John! What on earth are you doing with your sleeves rolled up? This isn't a massage parlour!

Sheila comes round the shelves, holding a book.

Victoria	Got one?

They walk to the counter where John is being torn off a strip by Madge.

Sheila	It's very difficult to find a book with no alcohol, no sex and no reference to men whatsoever.
Victoria	What did you get?
Sheila	*The Wincey Willis*[211] *Book of Wholemeal Pasta.*

They wait to have the book stamped; Madge is still in full flow.

Madge	And it isn't just your clothing, John – though heaven knows, training shoes are hardly compatible with a love of literature. It's your wishy-washy liberal attitude – video machines and Asian novels here, taped reminiscences there – mark my words, John, make people welcome in the library and it's the thin end of the bookmark; before you can say 'Monica Dickens' they'll be drying their underwear on the radiators and doing boil-in-the-bag noodles behind the photocopier. Kindly digest. If anybody wants me I shall be in the stacks with a Jackie Collins and a felt-tip pen.

---

211 *TV-am* weather girl. She sportingly played herself in an unused spoof of *Treasure Hunt* in the second series of *ASOTV* and was among the celebrity guests in *An Audience with Victoria Wood.*

She leaves.

John   Just the one book, Sheila? Er – sorry about that –

Sheila   Oh, she doesn't bamboozle me. I remember her when
              she first came – never seen so many kirbys in a French
              pleat.

John   Cookery book, eh? Now that's my absolute blind spot,
              I'm afraid. I really am clueless.

Sheila   Oh I'm nuts on cuisine.[212] I really miss having somebody
              to cook for. There's a lovely thing in here with courgettes
              but it's not worth doing for one.

John   Well, if you ever need an extra mouth . . .

Sheila   Well I was thinking of doing a little meal this evening if
              you've no plans afoot?

John   No, I haven't but –

Victoria Sheila!

Sheila   I'm not being forward, Victoria. I like to think of myself
              as liberated – I could have burnt my bra but it was long-
              line and I didn't have the time. So would you care to
              accept my invitation to dinner?

John   Certainly – and I very much appreciate it.

Sheila   Eight o'clock then. Bye.

They leave.

Victoria You didn't give him your address.

Sheila   He's a librarian. He'd find it sharp enough if I owed 8p
              on a Georgette Heyer.

*Victoria and Sheila are walking along a quiet street of
semis.*

Victoria Just have somebody in the house with you – that's all I'm
              saying. Haven't you got an Auntie Lill or a Cousin Ida?

---

212 Changed to 'fizzine'.

Sheila	I've got an Auntie Lill *and* a Cousin Ida. One's in Toronto and the other's body-building in Hendon.

They stop outside the house.

Victoria	Well, shall I do it?
Sheila	Oh no, we've had the last twice.
Victoria	I'll hide in the garden – keep an eye through the window.
Sheila	You can't, we've got vigilantes. Mr Brewer's forever up and down the avenue with a beret and a ping-pong bat.
Victoria	*(striding up the path)* I know! Come on!
Sheila	Hang on – my Yale's under my Wincey Willis.

Sheila's house. The hall, stairs, and bathroom door at the top of the stairs. All is clean and neat and ten years out of date. Sheila stands anxiously outside the bathroom door.

Sheila	Are you nearly ready?
Victoria	*(Voice Over)* Yeah, I won't be a sec. Now, you know the plan?
Sheila	I take him in the kitchen, introduce you, explain you won't be joining us for dinner then take him through into the dining room.
Victoria	*(Voice Over)* And I'll be in the kitchen the whole time so just give us a shout if he gets frisky.
Sheila	If he gets what?
Victoria	*(Voice Over)* Frisky!
Sheila	*(pattering down the stairs)* Will do! I thought you said frisky!

Victoria's puzzled face appears round the door.

Sheila's hall. She opens the front door to a nervous John.

Sheila	Oh, come in.

He trips.

	Mind the mat. It's from the Philippines – and I'm not sure they always take quite the trouble.
John	Well it's rather a corrupt society.
Sheila	Oh I know. Take your coat off. I saw a documentary. It looked to be quite an uprising, even with the sound off.
John	*(standing by the coat stand)* Shall I? *(He hangs coat on a knob.)*
Sheila	Yes do. *(All the coats fall down.)* Oh, that coatstand. I arranged to have it renovated but they lost interest when they heard it was just a knob.
John	I could probably glue it back on for you.
Sheila	Oh could you?
John	If you have any glue, perhaps after dinner –
Sheila	I may have some UHU left over from the Nativity. Anyway – come through to the kitchen . . .

Inside Sheila's kitchen. It is clean but dreary; lots of pots and pans are bubbling away. Victoria is at the kitchen table in old lady dress and woolly hat. Sheila and John come in.

Sheila	This is my auntie *(she casts around the room)* Marjoram – Marjorie.
John	I'm very pleased to meet you.
Victoria	'Appen as mebbe. But you'll know what they say?
John	No, what's that?
Victoria	Pleased to meet is sorry to greet come Michaelmas.
John	Now, I've never heard that; isn't that fascinating!
Victoria	Now you don't want to waste your time with an old out-house like misen – get the knees under t' table and set to supping.
John	You're not joining us for dinner then, Mrs – ?
Victoria	Witherstrop. Nay – I topped up long since. Nice plate of brains and a ginger nut. Tek him through, Sheila – I shall be all right here.

Sheila	Right – John – ?
John	*(sitting down)* I'm sure there's time for a little chat, Sheila?
Victoria	Oh, no, you get about your dining arrangements. Them as chat shall never grow fat.
John	That's another lovely saying I've never come across.
Sheila	*(at the stove)* I'll just finish off if you're all right, John?
John	Certainly. Gosh, it's warm in here. Can I take your hat, Mrs Withersdrop?
Victoria	I can't tek it off, lad. I lost every hair on my head the day they bombed Eccles.
John	Blast.
Victoria	That's what I said.
Sheila	I'm sure John doesn't want to hear about that, Marjorie.
John	No, I'd love to.
Victoria	February the eleventh, 1941. I was clocking off from work – aye, from munitions – they had to convert when war broke out – they had been making liquorice torpedoes so it weren't too much of an upheaval. Vera Lynn were coming over the Gannex –
John	I beg your pardon?
Victoria	The tannoy. Big Ellen Mottershead turned to me – her crossover pinnie was wet with tears. 'It's a bomber's moon, Marjorie,' she said, 'It's a bomber's moon.'
John	Look – I'm sorry to interrupt – this is absolutely fascinating and just what I need.
Victoria	Eh?
John	My taped reminiscence programme – it's been very hard to get it off the ground – a lot of opposition from Madge. These stories of yours are just what I need to get the ball rolling. Sheila – would you mind if I just fetched my tape recorder?
Sheila	No.
John	I won't be one sec.

He dashes out of the back door.

Sheila	I thought you said no one could possibly have an interest in an old woman. What a marvellous evening I'm going to have.
Victoria	Well, I'll keep it short.
Sheila	How? He wants your life story.
Victoria	I'll tell him I was killed in an air raid.

John reappears with a tape recorder.

John	Actually, Mrs Withersdrop, I've been thinking – it's awfully rude to suddenly conduct an interview with you when Sheila has this lovely meal already prepared.
Victoria	Aye, well.
John	So what I thought was, rather than me bombarding you with questions, if Sheila doesn't mind, my uncle's in the car outside – if he could perhaps come in, I'll set the machine going and you could both chat together, I should think you're pretty much of an age.
Sheila	Bring him in, by all means.
John	*(shouting from the doorway)* Uncle Ted! Come in then!
Sheila	But what's he doing in the car? I don't follow.
John	Well I'm sure you'll think I'm a bit of a weed – but you read such terrible things in the papers; men kidnapped by fanatical women, used as sex slaves – I brought Ted as a safety precaution.
Sheila	I wouldn't kidnap a man for sex – I'm not saying I couldn't use someone to oil the mower.

Ted comes in.

Ted	Hey up, fans!
John	This is Mrs Withersdrop, Ted. She's going to tape her memories of the raid on Eccles.
Ted	*(sitting down)* There never were a ruddy raid on Eccles – there were nowt worth bombing, bar two tarts at the bus station.

Victoria	Aye, well – my memory's not what it was.
John	Well I'll just leave the tape running – you two settle down and have a really good chat about the old days and Sheila and I can get stuck into our dinner.
Sheila	Lovely. If you'll just push the trolley, John.

John goes out with the laden trolley.

Offer Ted a beer, Marjorie – you may be in for a long evening.

Sheila leaves with a bottle of wine. Victoria snaps open a beer for Ted. He slurps and belches.

Ted	Pardon.
Victoria	Right, well, let's get it over with. I was born in a one up one down. My mother washed everything by hand, and I didn't set eyes on a sprout till I was seventeen.

Ted switches off the tape.

Ted	Never mind John's old rubbish. *(He hutches his chair up and lays a heavy hand on her leg.)* By! That's a leg and a half. I tell you what – I may be seventy-eight but I've still plenty of snap in my celery. You know what they say?
Victoria	What?
Ted	There's many a new piston under an old bonnet.

WE'D QUITE LIKE TO APOLOGISE

A motorway with a long shot of non-moving traffic.

Radio Jingle Travel News.

David Jacobs *(Voice Over)* And because of that earlier incident, traffic is still tailing back from the airport turn-off for several miles. Police advise motorists to keep calm and on no account to erect sun loungers on the hard shoulder . . .

Inside Victoria's car. There is a banana skin on the passenger seat.

David Jacobs *(Voice Over)* Well if you are stuck in that jam, and I hope to goodness you're not . . .

Victoria I am, thank you, David.

David Jacobs *(Voice Over)* Why not sit back and relax to the velvety tones of Jack Jones as he tries to find the way, not to the airport but to Amarillo.

Victoria snaps the button to Radio One.

Gary Davies *(Voice Over)* Good good. So you play golf?

Young male contestant *(Voice Over)* Pardon, Gary?

Gary Davies *(Voice Over)* You play a bit of golf, Paul?

Paul	*(Voice Over)* What's that, sorry?
Gary	*(Voice Over)* The game with the clubs.
Paul	*(Voice Over)* Yeah, I go to the clubs, Gary.
Gary	*(Voice Over)* But you don't actually play golf?
Paul	*(Voice Over)* Not with you, Gary.

Victoria changes to Radio Four and the sound effect of a car not starting.

Nigel   *(Voice Over)* It's no use, Shulie – that organic yoghurt is marvellous stuff but I don't think putting it in the petrol tank was a terribly good idea.

Shula   *(Voice Over)* Oh, Nigel – what are we going to do? It was bad enough being caught half naked in Felpersham Cathedral, but if I'm not on the Borchester By-Pass in fifteen minutes I'm jolly well going to miss that plane!

Archers' theme.

Victoria switches off radio, looks at watch and sighs.

Inside the airport multi-storey short stay car park. Two queues of cars are going in to park, one moving reasonably quickly, the other, with Victoria's as the third car, stationary. Inside Victoria's car there are now five banana skins on the passenger seat. She is peering agonisedly out of window at old buffer at head of queue gazing out of his car window at the ticket machine.

Victoria   Press the button and take the ticket, you dithering old pillock.

He does so and the car moves forward.

And stop being so BALD!

The woman in the heading car looks at the ticket machine.
She turns to her passenger.

Victoria   Hurry up!

The woman peers at the machine again.

It's a ticket machine – get a blinking ticket out of it!

The woman gets out of her car. She puts on glasses, which are
on a chain round her neck, and peers even closer.

Victoria   Stop looking at it. It's not a Henry Moore.

She gets out of the car and approaches the woman.

Victoria   What's happening? This is a ticket machine. Are you
                 looking for a sell-by-date?
Woman   I was just trying to see what –
Victoria   What this says? It says 'manufactured 1987 by Denby
                 Ticket Machines Ltd, Ticket Machine House, Dids-
                 bury'. This says 'Press for Ticket'. Press for Ticket. Take
                 Ticket. Get in car. Find Space. Park. Get on plane. Go
                 on holiday. Sunbathe. Drink.

She leads the woman back into her car and slams the door.

Have sexual intercourse with Portuguese Timeshare
salesman. But first get in the car and move!

The woman moves off and Victoria goes back to her car. A
hoot from car behind.

Hello!

Victoria's car winds quickly and none too accurately up and up and up to the only space. Victoria gets out of her car, locks it, and runs in the direction of the lift.

Inside the lift. Victoria dashes in. Another woman is holding the doors open.

Victoria   Thanks.

*The woman continues to hold the doors open.
Victoria looks at her.*

Woman   My husband's just coming.
Victoria   *(Pause.)* Where from – Bangladesh?

She looks at her watch and dashes out of the lift, side-stepping a man with trolley piled high. She runs along a corridor, then pounds along the travelator. She stops for breath, checks her watch, relaxes slightly. She smiles at a second man surrounded by cases.

Second man Don't suppose I'll need half this luggage.
Victoria   Luggage –

She suddenly turns round and dashes madly the wrong way up the travelator.

Victoria   Hold the lift!

Inside the airport is a main hall with check-in desks. Victoria appears at the far end with baggage and makes one last dash to the 'Sunflight' desk furthest away. She leans against the desk, shattered.

Victoria   Alicante – am I in time?
Girl   Well, we do like people to check in two hours in advance of flying.

Victoria	I know – I'm sorry. It was the traffic.
Girl	To be explanatory – you have ample minutage because your flight is carrying a small delay.
Victoria	Oh that's great *(She puts her bags on the scale.)*
Girl	You're just on your kilo limit – so if you're bringing back souvenirs you will have to leave something else behind. Current rate of exchange is one ashtray to three bikini briefs – that's for a normal smoker and a twelve to fourteen hip.
Victoria	How long's the delay?
Girl	Not too distressing. Just the four or five hours.
Victoria	Oh great – sorry – hours?
Girl	Four or five – we're pending on a definite there. Or six. They're fairly confident it won't balloon to seven. Talking or non-talking?
Victoria	Talking.
Girl	Any particular seat? *(She turns to a plan.)* This one has toilet access. This one has apricot jam on the armrest and this has restricted view of the movie.
Victoria	What is the movie?
Girl	*Police Academy Nine.*
Victoria	I'll sit there. And I asked for a vegetarian meal.
Girl	That's right.
Victoria	So will I be getting that?
Girl	No.
Victoria	Oh.
Girl	To be almost direct – there have been inadequacies re in-flight cuisine. Our Clipper Club Business Members have been particularly vocal over the breakfasts. As they say – how can they shuttle on a bran muffin? They're very dissatisfied cum hygiene.
Victoria	Are they?
Girl	In fact, one particular gentleman was so dissatisfied he died. The problem is, so many journalists have infiltrated the catering side to expose airport security, your lunch is probably being cobbled together by two feature writers

from the *Independent*. Enjoy your flight – should there be one.

Victoria Thanks.

Inside the airport's main concourse café. Victoria is seated at a table.

Victoria *(to us)* Three hours I've been here now. There's nothing to do. I've been in the Sock Shop seventeen times. I've bought something in the Body Shop, the Tie Rack and Knickerbox. I'm so brainwashed I went in the Ladies and said how much are your soap dispensers? I've read *Woman*, *Woman's Own*, *Woman's Realm*, *Woman's Weekly* and *Boxer Shorts Bulletin*. My free gifts have included a bronzy pink lipgloss, a muesli bar and a macaroni effect toast enhancer.

I've done three quizzes to put me in touch with myself, and now realise I'm too agoraphobic to leave the country; I should be working with my hands and wearing navy. I've just spent £16.52 on a glass of water and a salad sandwich that took me twenty minutes to open because it was double shrink wrapped to avoid tampering. When I did get it open it was so boring I took it back to the counter and asked if someone could tamper with it.

I've eaten so much chocolate: I've had the chocolates that melt in your mouth and not in your hand. I've had the chocolates that don't melt in your mouth and get stuck in your fillings. And I particularly enjoyed the chocolates that melt in your handbag without ruining your appetite. Do you think I've missed an announcement? Do you think while I'm sitting here everyone else is doing the Birdy Song up and down Alicante high street?

Do you think my luggage is being picked over by Spanish lavatory attendants? 'Don't think much to her sponge bag do you, Concepcion?' *(She taps her fingers, and looks at her watch.)* I've only come away to relax. Everything's getting on top of me. I can't switch off. I've got a self-cleaning oven – I have to get up in the night to see if it's doing it.

I worry about the ice caps melting. Some tropical islands are going to be submerged altogether. As it is, where we live we stand to lose a bit of privet and a bird table. People tell me worry beads are good. Suppose they break and somebody trips on them? *(She gets up.)* Somebody must know something.

The 'SunSeaKing' information desk; just a little counter and chair, unattended. Victoria is hanging around it. Una comes up, a small worried woman in her fifties.

Una	Oh dear – is there nobody here?
Victoria	No.
Una	I don't know what's happened to SunSeaKing. Last year they couldn't have been more helpful. We were only delayed ten minutes and they were in there handing out colouring books. Are you 603 for Alicante?
Victoria	Yes.
Una	Isn't it terrible? I feel like going home, I really do. I'd leave now but I've promised to deliver a walking frame.
Victoria	Have you?
Una	You can't obtain them there. Well they're such a proud peoples – I think they prefer to limp. I thought you were on my flight. I spotted your labels in the Sky Shop. I was seeing if they had anything fizzy for malaria. Are you staying at the Casa D'Oro?
Victoria	Yes.
Una	I go every year. Marvellous. The only hotel on the Costa Blanca to serve Bengers.
Victoria	It's not all English food is it?
Una	Oh no – I've very happy memories of their Scotch

pancakes. They do have a Spanish menu but I have to think twice, having only half a colon.

Victoria   A semi-colon.

Una   I wouldn't normally toss my bowels into the conversation this early but I'm travelling alone and it pays to be open. I did advertise for a holiday companion – capable widow, no sense of humour, some knowledge of haemorrhoids preferred – not a reply.

Victoria   Really?

Una   That's Eastbourne for you. I mean, it's cheaper with two isn't it? Somebody to go halves on the verucca tablets. Perhaps we could chum up.

Victoria   Mm.

Una   Stick with me and you may never have to speak to a Spaniard the whole fortnight. I do think somebody ought to come and tell us what's happening. Is there nothing behind there – a message or –

Victoria   *(going behind the desk)* There's a half-eaten packet of Cheese Murmurs – would you like one?

Una   Not when I'm tense. That sort of savoury niblet sets my ulcer hopping like a ping-pong ball.

John and Barbara come in. She is downtrodden and carrying all the hand luggage. He is fuming, middle-aged. He approaches the desk and addresses Victoria.

John   Now look – we have been here since 10.15 this morning. We had a heck of a drive from Knutsford – the windscreen washers packed up and my wife spent the last fifty miles hanging out of the sunroof, picking flies off as and when they landed. We've been here for eight hours with nothing to do but buy socks and, quite frankly, it's not adequate enough. There's been no apologies, no information. Good Golly – the delays with Summerbird last year were marvellous: Bingo, Community Singing – we were sorry to leave and go on our holidays. What's

going on, is my question quite simply – don't fob me off
with flannel. I'm in contract carpeting and in contract
carpeting, we carpet first, flannel later. So – and my wife
is witnessing this – what is your name, what position do
you hold in this company, and why do you not have the
common courtesy to be wearing a uniform? Well?

Victoria   OK – my name's Victoria, the position I hold is holiday-
maker, I do have a uniform; it is very small, very brown
and if I was wearing it I would do this and dance round
a toadstool.

John   Point taken. No offence. I laid my carpet there without
preparing my floorboards. John Appleby.

Victoria sits down.

Una   We're waiting for news as well. Isn't it dreadful? I wish
I'd given Spain a miss this year – I nearly plumped for
a crochet week in Rhyl. I was going to have a stab at a
batwing blouson.

Barbara   I'll ring this bell, shall I?

John   You'll be lucky. Good griffin, they can put a man on the
moon, microwave ovens . . .

Una   Oh, not the hard floor. That's how mine started. Haven't
had peace in the powder room since.

John   *(half to himself)* It beats me – we've got silicon chips,
videos . . .

Barbara   I think someone's coming now.

*In comes Joyanne, tanned, in her thirties, lots of jewellery,
and denim jacket with diamante; a professional girlfriend.*

Joyanne   Are you flying to Alicante?

John   Trying to. Good goblins – we've got non-stick pans,
weathermen . . .

Joyanne   Have they said how much longer it's going to be?

Victoria   There's nobody here.

Barbara We've rung the bell.

Una And that was what – half a minute ago?

Joyanne Tuh. The first two or three hours I didn't mind, because I was choosing stockings but this – honestly – *(She looks at a tiny watch)* talk about retarded!

Una I don't mind waiting for myself, but it's my intestines –

Kathy comes in, a friendly, pleasant girl in her mid-twenties.

Kathy Is this the SunSeaKing desk?

John Supposed to be, Good Gordon!

Una We're waiting for someone to come.

Barbara I've rung the bell.

Una And that was what – just over a minute ago?

Kathy And nobody's come?

John Need you ask? I don't know, we've got Thermos flasks, air fresheners . . .

Kathy *(calling)* Alan! Over here! Everyone's over here!

Alan comes in, a nice young man. They kiss.

Kathy Missed you.

Alan Missed *you*. So – what's happening?

Kathy They're waiting for someone to come.

Barbara I've pressed the bell.

Una That's about a minute and a quarter ago now, I should think.

Joyanne Well you'd rung it before I got here, hadn't you?

Una That's right.

Alan And has nobody come?

Kathy That's what I said – telepathic!

Alan Love you.

Kathy Ditto.

Victoria is getting more and more fed up as this goes on.

Una	Nobody's come so far.
Joyanne	Three hours.
Barbara	It's getting ridiculous.
Joyanne	Well it's more than ridiculous really, it's silly.
John	When you think we've got satellites, vitamins, shower curtains . . .
Una	I mean, no one minds waiting for a limited period.
Joyanne	Or even a bit longer than that.
Kathy	We bought a pair of socks, didn't we, Alan?
Barbara	I must say this airport is very good for socks.
John	Button it, Barbara, for heaven's sake.
Alan	So, sorry, can I just recap on the situation?
Kathy	I love the way you say 'situation'.
Alan	The bell's been pressed?
Una	Yes, this lady pressed it – I would say over two minutes ago.
Alan	But nobody's come?
Una	To be fair, nobody's come 'as yet'.
John	Talk about Waiting for Godot.
Joyanne	At least Godot turned up. *(She thinks.)* Or was that Hamlet? One of those books anyway.

Guy, a sprightly young man in airline uniform (not Sun-SeaKing) crosses behind the desk.

Victoria	Excuse me?
Guy	*(rather offhand)* Yes?
Victoria	Do you know anything about the delay on the Alicante flight?
Guy	No – is it very exciting?
Alan	Perhaps we should start at the beginning.
Barbara	I saw the bell and I thought I should press it.
Una	We'd seen it previously but hadn't gone as far as to ring it.
Joyanne	When I got here – that had already happened.
Kathy	And we arrived bang in the middle – didn't we, Alan?
Guy	*(to Victoria)* Where do you fit in?

Victoria	I'm the understudy. If anybody drops out I'll be right in there – I know all the lines.
Guy	Well I'm sorry, you'll just have to carry on waiting.
Barbara	Carry on waiting – sounds like a 'Carry On' film.
Una	*(to Barbara)* Like *Carry on Camping*.
Joyanne	*(to Una) Carry on Nurse*.
Alan	*(to Kathy) Carry on Doctor*.
Kathy	*(to Alan) Doctor in the House*.
Victoria	Could you maybe find out what's happening? We've been here ages.
Joyanne	Two or three hours you don't mind –
Victoria	*(through gritted teeth)* Thank you, would you mind?

Guy sits down at the desk and picks up the phone.

Guy	Mm – Cheese Murmurs – aren't they more-ish? Si? It's Guy. Hi. *(Pulling his eyelid back and rolling his eye up)* Beg pard? No, I'm just fiddling with my contact lens. Oh I'm glad you enjoyed it – it wasn't a bad moussaka for a first attempt, was it? *(He laughs.)* No, I put Daz on it – it came out no trouble. *(He laughs, then stops.)* Anyway, Si, SunSeaKing 603 Alicante – any joy? Yeah, yeah, OK, all right – I'll see you there – and don't forget the dry ginger – take it easy!

He puts the phone down, and reverts to his off-handedness.

	You were right.
Victoria	What?
Guy	It's delayed.
Victoria	What shall we do?
Guy	We usually advise people in this situation to mill aimlessly about.
Una	Is that all?
Guy	You could always buy socks. I should check with your SunSeaKing representative.

Una	She's not here.
Guy	*(looking blankly around)* Oh. *(He strolls away.)* Ring the bell, I would. Take it easy.
Una	Well at least we know where we stand – we're not just late – it is a delay.
John	Well I'm going to find the head honcho. This is an abomination. To put it in carpeting terms, we've been here five hours and we haven't even got our gripper-rods down.
Kathy	If we don't get there tonight I'm going to have a sun top left over.
Alan	Oh darling, which one?
Kathy	The little white strappy one with the anchor.
Alan	How rotten, darling.
Joyanne	Perhaps we should ring the bell again.
Una	Well it has been rung twice.
Barbara	Yes, because I pressed it originally.
Una	And we're going back about four minutes now.
Victoria	Look!

Flying towards them, bright and breezy, is the 'SunSeaKing' girl, Carol. General relief all round. She is very cheerful, fluffs her hair, and plonks clipboard down on desk.

Carol	Hi! I'm Carol, your SunSeaKing representative. I'm flying out to replace Donna – she's still in hospital, she had an accident, she fell off an architect. Are you all for Alicante?

General murmurs of 'Yes, if we ever get there' etc.

Una	*(out of the general chat)* Hope we don't have to wait another five hours.
Carol	*(blankly)* Five hours?
John	We were supposed to leave at two.
Carol	Were we? *(She checks her clipboard.)* I could have sworn that was a seven! *(She laughs.)* Good job it was delayed

– I'd have missed it altogether. *(She laughs again.)* Oh – so – how long is it delayed for?

Alan   We thought you would know.

Carol   Me? I've been at the hairdressers.

Victoria Well, anyway, what do we do now?

Carol   I'm not really sure – have you tried ringing this bell?

At the departure gate. There are seats, tables, and a small snack bar. All the company met so far plus a few extras are sitting down, waiting. Victoria is next to Kathy; Alan brings over teas.

Alan   I missed that – what was it?

Victoria Thanks.

Kathy   I was telling Victoria how we adopted Keith last year on holiday.

Alan   That's right. We don't like to see anybody lonely.

Kathy   He said he was a loner. He said he was quite happy on his own. I said, 'Keith – you're coming with us.'

Alan   And we never let him out of our sight the whole fort-night, did we?

Kathy   No; wherever he went, we found him. He could be all on his own sunbathing or having a quiet drink –

Alan   And we'd pop up – go 'Boo!'

Kathy   Drop a few ice cubes down his swimming trunks – do a bit of a prank on him . . .

Alan   Sometimes he'd say, 'Kathy and Alan will you please leave me alone,' and he'd even get quite irritated.

Kathy   But he wasn't – he needed us. Funny – the last night of the holidays – we'd been with him all day helping him windsurf – come the Fancy Dress Barbecue, we couldn't find him anywhere.

Alan   Room was empty –

Kathy   They found his clothes in a little pile on the beach, but of Keith – no sign. Funny . . . but it makes our holiday having someone to look after.

Alan	Course you're here on your own, Victoria, aren't you?
Victoria	Yes.

Carol rushes in.

Carol	My fault everybody! When I said, 'Please proceed to the gate the plane is on the tarmac,' apparently it was on the tarmac, but not our tarmac, it was on some other tarmac – in Belgium. But it is on the way now. Please help yourself to drinks and refreshments – it's all courtesy of SunSeaKing holidays – thank you.

Later in the day. Everyone is more dishevelled; all have changed around; there is more litter on the tables. Joyanne and Victoria are now together, Kathy and Alan nearby, whispering sweet nothings.

Joyanne	What are you reading?
Victoria	Evelyn Waugh.
Joyanne	Is she good? *(Pause.)* I wouldn't have thought she'd have time with her problem page. I've brought a book – oh what's it called? It's got a little penguin on the cover – it's just one big word.
Victoria	*Lace – Scruples?*
Joyanne	*Groin!* Have you read it?
Victoria	No is it good?
Joyanne	Yes it is, actually, because it's not just sex, there's quite a lot of literature in it as well.

She thrusts her wrist in Victoria's face.

	Gorgeous, isn't it? It's nothing in the bottle, but on the nipple it's fabulous. *(Pause.)* Is someone paying for this holiday for you?
Victoria	No I'm paying for it.
Joyanne	Now that's silly, Victoria – and I'll tell you for why. The

more you get them to pay for, the more they respect you. I have three serious boyfriends, OK – Malcolm pays my mortgage; Mustapha's furnished my maisonette right through to the fixtures and Tony – well, you name it with Tony – rebounder, sheepskin jacket, dogfood – he's very much the gentleman is Tony.

Victoria Doesn't Malcolm mind about Tony – or –

Joyanne My motto is very much, you don't have to be ugly to be a woman's libber. I don't go along with everything they wear, don't get me mistaken, but if I want three boyfriends and perhaps a couple of carnal relationships ditto to that – well, *vive la France*. And the good thing about the Casa D'Oro is it's next to the Hotel Golf and that's where you find a lot of trousers with nothing to spend their money on. Do you like Scotch?

Victoria No.

Joyanne I came back with a bottle *that* big, three silk blouses and a pair of court shoes and I was only there five days. So what say I pick you up tomorrow evening, nine-ish? *(She starts looking through her handbag.)*

Victoria Sorry?

Joyanne All right, nine-thirty. Nice and glam though, yes? *(She laughs.)* I can see you're like me, Vicki, when you're travelling, any old rags will do!

She gets a photo out of her bag. Carol comes in.

Carol Well, it's good news and bad news I'm afraid. *(Groans.)* The bad news is our plane has lost its place in the queue and the pilot's having to circle for half an hour or so before he can land. *(More groans.)*

Victoria What's the good news?

Carol It's my birthday tomorrow.

She escapes amidst boos and paper cups being thrown etc.

Joyanne   These are my curtains, Victoria. This is my wallpaper.
Real leather. Mustapha's family are *in* leather . . . And
these are my banisters . . .

*The same, later. Chairs have been pushed into a circle – all
are entertaining each other. Una has a joke book.*

Una   I'll just read one more and then somebody else can have
a go. Right. Victoria – why did the chicken cross the
road?

Victoria   It saw two Mormons coming out of Woolworths?

Una   *(seriously)* Hang on. *(Drops book.)* What page were we
on? Elephant jokes – we've had all those.

Victoria   All those.

Barbara   *(having had far too much wine)* Well, it's my turn to en-
tertain everybody.

John   Pipe down, Ba.

Barbara   No I will not pipe down, John! He thinks I can't do anything. When he was in ceiling tiles he used to look up to
me, but now he's in contract carpeting he treats me like
underlay.

John   My wife's a little bit tired I think.

Barbara   Yes; I'm a little bit tired of you!

John   When did this all start?

Barbara   The second night of our honeymoon if you must twig.
I was upstairs in a slit-sided *peignoir* – he was in the TV
lounge glued to 'Sunday at the London Palladium'.

John   Only till 'Beat the Clock'.

Barbara   Twenty-seven years I've suffered in silence – matches in
every fireplace – never a lavatory seat down when you
want one –

Victoria   Shame.

John   Don't you assist.

Barbara   She understands. Not everyone's an unthinking barbar-
ian like you. The things I could tell you, Victoria. His
underwear habits alone would baffle a psychiatrist –

Carol comes in.

Carol   All right everybody – we're ready for take-off.

Cheers and general packing up.

So if you'd like to get on the bus . . .

Moans and grumbling.

And to really get us into the SunSeaKing holiday atmo-sphere – all together *(singing)* 'One man went to mow, went to mow a meadow . . .'

She carries on singing and gradually everyone joins in as they shuffle to the door.

Inside a small airport bus, Victoria is jammed into a man's armpit. Standing. The song continues – 'Seventeen, sixteen, fifteen' etc.

Carol   *(Voice Over)* We think we've located the correct runway, folks, so not long now.

Victoria   *(to us)* I don't mind the man that goes to mow and I'm not too fussed about the meadow – but the thing that really gets on my wick is the dog. *(Voices – 'And his dog, Spot'.)* In this case – Spot. I can't believe he's any help mowing the meadow can you? Spot – doesn't sound very reliable to me. I can just see him panicking and getting caught up in the combine harvester. And it would give the whole song a lift – cos God knows the suspense factor is nil – if it went 'five men four men three men' – I may not have the lyrics quite right – 'three men, two men, one man and his dog – oops – fell into the mower', like ten green bottles, wouldn't that be improved if the wall fell down and the bottles stayed up there?

The bus lurches Victoria up against armpit.

Now if I'd travelled as a VIP it wouldn't be like this. I wouldn't have my nose up an armpit from start to finish – well, only from choice. I'd have been in the celebrity lounge at Heathrow now, sipping herb tea and reaching past Anne Diamond for the Twiglets. Don't tell me Jason Donovan and Kylie Minogue sit there singing 'One Man Went to Mow' – it's a little bit of a profound concept for one of their songs. I shouldn't have come on a package – I should have been adventurous, struck out, pushed mind and body to the limit: freezing water, primitive people, strange food – but Butlins isn't like that anymore apparently. Even my next-door neighbours went to Brazil, brought back some lovely souvenirs; woodcarvings, wallhangings – twins. I don't know what they'll do when they get too big for the bay window. The only good thing is, I'm not at the Casa D'Oro itself – I'm in the annexe. Self-catering, so with any luck I won't have to see any of those upsetting misfits ever again.

The bus jerks to a halt and Victoria is crushed up against armpit.

Doing his bit for the ozone layer.

Inside the plane. Victoria sits next to Una, Joyanne and Barbara across the aisle. Behind Victoria are Kathy and Alan. They all have their hand luggage on their knees.

Una   I've left my joke book behind.
Victoria Never mind.
Una   *(anxiously)* Yes, but I keep thinking – why *did* that chicken cross the road? What was on its mind?
Pilot   *(Voice Over)* I'd like to take this opportunity to welcome you all aboard flight 603 to Alicante. We hope to take

off as soon as possible – just a couple of procedures to be gone through first. I'm waiting for clearance and I also have a couple of egg sandwiches to finish.

Carol stops by Victoria with a clipboard.

Carol May as well save time at the other end by running through room allocations, excursion and so on and *et cetera*. Now I'll give you all your vouchers now – this is for tonight on arrival – in reception, 'Punch and Pudding Party'.

Victoria Pudding?

Carol Yorkshire pudding. So one for you, Joyanne, Una and here's yours –

Victoria I don't need one: I'm not in the hotel – I'm self-catering in the annexe.

Una Oh that looked lovely in the brochure – artist's impression.

Carol *(laughing)* It's like that terrible Spanish holiday joke: looked good in the brochure, hasn't been built yet.

Victoria How do you mean?

Carol It hasn't been built yet. You're in the hotel, block seven, segment W.

Una That's my segment!

Carol Well we thought rather than pay the supplement you could share a room with Una – you've got Kathy and Alan on one side, Barbara and John on the other, and Joyanne just across the way, so you'll be able to join in all the fun.

Una Is there a donkey excursion this year?

Carol I believe so. *(She reads.)* Yes, 'Leisurely ramble through the geranium-filled winding lanes ending up at Miguel's Mini Mart and Paella Parlour'. A burger and bun comes *with* that.

Victoria I think I'll give that one a miss.

Kathy Put her name down, Carol! Alan and I will get her on that donkey or our name's not Warburton.

Victoria	Is their name Warburton?
Una	Yes.
Victoria	Oh.
Carol	I'll leave you the list, shall I?

Victoria reads, each one is greeted by enthusiastic cries.

Victoria	Raffia Demonstration. Tour of castanet factory. Wicker donkey weaving and charcoal grill. Poolside limbo and sombrero parade. Winetasting and Flamenco night.
Una	Does a burger and bun come with that too?
Victoria	No, just a bucket and a damp cloth.

Bing Bong from P.A.

Pilot	*(Voice Over)* Captain Lewis speaking again, I'm afraid. You'll be glad to hear I've finished my sandwiches – I'll have the apple and the wafer biscuit once we get going. Now there's nothing to worry about, but a little warning light has appeared on the dashboard here –
Victoria	*(to camera)* Dashboard?
Pilot	*(Voice Over)* Probably means nothing at all, but it's prudent not to leave until we've located the source of the problem. I'm afraid we can't offer you any drinks while we're waiting, but the flight attendants will be circulating with a tray of objects which you're welcome to memorise.
Una	I'm so thrilled we're sharing a room – someone to give a hand with all those little female procedures. I've got the most marvellous device I adapted from shampoo spray . . .
Barbara	Victoria! I'll be knocking on your door tonight I expect – twenty-seven years of marital grievances – I shall enjoy sharing them with you.
Joyanne	*(passing photo over)* These are the men we're having dinner with tomorrow, Victoria. He on the left, Nobby

	– you'll like him – he's very witty. I bet you've never seen a medallion hung round that before.[213]
Victoria	*(handing it back)* No.
Kathy	*(hanging over her seat)* I hope you're an early bird!
Victoria	Eh?
Kathy	We want you on that diving board at 6.30, don't we, Alan?
Alan	Yes we do!
Kathy	And don't think you can just lock the door and go back to sleep, because we're very persistent.
Alan	And we're only one balcony aw– ay . . .
Victoria	Mm.

Bing Bong from P.A.

Pilot	*(Voice Over)* Captain Lewis again, I'm afraid. Well, we've located the source of the trouble. *(Cheers.)* We've checked with the engineers what the warning light mentioned actually indicates. Apparently it means there's a dry roasted peanut somewhere in the fuel line. *(Interested murmurs.)* So until that's pinpointed and removed, it's back to the terminal building, I'm afraid, with our apologies. *(Groans.)*

Carol bustles past, calling back to an unseen stewardess.

Carol	What do we do, Kim, wait for the bus?

On the runway. One very small bus is followed by Victoria, Joyanne and extras on top of a luggage wagon. They are singing 'One Man Went to Mow'. Joyanne is showing Victoria photos.

---

213 Nobby was the nickname for an old boyfriend of VW's who worked in TV. In *ASOTV* the continuity announcer glares off camera when an item she's cued up isn't available and says, 'Thanks very much, Nobby.' History does not relate whether (or where) he wore a medallion.

A café with tables outside, in bright sunshine. Victoria sits in different clothes drinking lemon tea. A Spanish waiter arrives at the table.

Waiter   Enjoy your drink, yes?
Victoria   Yes thanks.
Waiter   Beautiful weather, ehy? Nice tan for ladies.
Victoria   Yeah. How much was that?
Waiter   *(in Spanish)* One cheese sandwich, one tea with lemon. Altogether, one pound fifty *(in English)*.
Victoria   *(putting down money)* Cheers. Bye.

(She walks to her car. The café is part of a Little Chef, or another motorway services, somewhere very British and unattractive.)

Well of course I didn't go. I may be mad but I'm not stupid.

She drives away.

OVER TO PAM

Daytime. Victoria's car is pulling up outside a little town house on a smart new estate. Victoria gets out, goes to the front door and rings the bell. Lorraine shouts through an upstairs window.

Lorraine   I'm just drying my nails!

Victoria   OK. *(To us.)* You know daytime television? You know what it's supposed to be for? It's to keep unemployed people happy. It's supposed to stop them running to the social security demanding mad luxuries like cookers and windows. I don't see how, though, do you? I suppose the idea is you sit there and say, 'Well I may be out of a job but at least I'm not standing next to a library assistant called Meredith shouting out eight words to do with toast.' Of course quiz programmes do help the unemployed – because they're all hosted by people who could never be given a job anywhere else. I won't name names, I shall just say perm and V-neck sweater. That's six of them for a start. I don't mind the quizzes so much as the discussion programmes. The ones where they go, 'Yes, you – the lady with the blotchy neck – do you think they should bring back capital punishment for parking offences?'

'Well I don't really think so because you might hang

someone for double parking then find out it was a *bone fide* delivery, Eric.'

You see, Lorraine – this is my friend Lorraine that I'm waiting for – she's being interviewed on television this afternoon, and I'm taking her because she's my friend, and because I'm *au fait*. I'm *au fait* with television – I am. I know them all – Katie Boyle,[214] Sooty.[215] I worked with Judith Chalmers before she was brown.

This programme Lorraine's doing is called 'Live with Pam'. It's a women's programme. I don't really like women's programmes. I always think they're going to whip up their pinnies and say, 'Well the incision was from here to here, Miriam.' But this 'Live with Pam' this afternoon, it's all about success; because Lorraine is like the classic success story – started as a Saturday girl at the hairdressers and now you can't have your hair washed in this county without it being one of Lorraine's girls soaking your polo neck and saying, 'Is the water all right for you?'[216]

Lorraine comes out of the front door, slams it and runs down the path.

Lorraine   I'm sorry I'm sorry I'm sorry I'm sorry I'm sorry . . .

Inside Victoria's car. Victoria is reversing up the street.

Victoria   What's that perfume?
Lorraine   Isn't it vile. It's called 'Take Me'! I got it at a tupperware party. They should have called it 'Put Me Back and Shoot Me'. God, this bra.

---

214 Actress and television personality.

215 From VW's 1990 live show: 'They'd actually come to see one of those sexy bedroom farces. You know, starring somebody off the television. It's got explicit nude scenes in it apparently. It doesn't bother most of the cast but the man who works Sooty is panicking.'

216 In 1984, VW wrote a song about a nervy hairdresser's assistant called 'I Work in a Salon' and delivered it in precisely the same voice used in the recording here.

Victoria	What's up with it?
Lorraine	I ordered it out the back of the *Daily Mirror.* I'd feel better wearing a potting shed and two dozen fast-growing conifers.[217]
Victoria	I've never seen 'Live with Pam'.
Lorraine	Me either, but the girls at work say Pam is like really, really warm and understanding and sympathetic.
Victoria	*(to perfectly innocent pedestrian at side of road)* Oh stop dithering about, you chronic old trout!
Lorraine	Very much like yourself.

Inside the reception area at Console Television. The main feature is the desk, with seating area nearby, various doors off, a lift, and blow-up photos of the station's personalities. A glamorous and unattractive fiftyish receptionist – Saundra – is taking calls, parcels, and waving at everyone who passes by. Victoria approaches Saundra who is in full flow on the phone.

Saundra	Well I can try the gallery, Petra, but I don't think they'll go till the bike gets here with his toupee. I know – we're all saying it – yes, she did – I said I agree with you, Dame Judi – he's actually more attractive without it. No I won't, Petra, I'm having a yoghurt thanks. Ciao. *(She turns to Victoria and says nastily)* Yes? *(She recognises her.)* Oh I didn't recognise you. What do you want – fifth floor?
Victoria	No – we –
Saundra	*(Taking a call)* 'Scuse I. A terrapin, Nigel? Not at the desk, no. Oh it is – I thought it was an indoor plant thing. All right, Nigel – ciao.

217 Cut from 'God, this bra' to here and replaced with:
Lorraine: I only bought it because I pitied the woman. She had those puffy ankles. You know, elephants.
Victoria: Elephants what?
Lorraine: Elephant's ankles.

A girl comes in from outside with a dry cleaning bag.

Is this Pam's? Isn't it gorgeous? Those little pleats are dinky, aren't they? Mm, it's to die for.

She takes the dress, and the girl goes out.

OK, Marilyn, take care. Now who did you say you . . . *(She takes a call.)* Console Television, how may I help you? Ringing for you now, Tony. When are you going to do some more lovely plays for us? No they were superb. Well that was it, Tony – they were popular and yet they didn't seem to catch on with the public. Oh you're through – ciao, Tony. *(To Victoria.)* Your last series – really super – just what we need in this miserable old environment of ours. Jennifer not with you?

Victoria   I'm Victoria Wood. I've got Lorraine Spence – 'Live with Pam'.

Saundra   Well I'll try 739 but with this flu . . . *(She dials.)* I should have been off at ten to – and it's not a nice flu – it's quite intestinal. *(She calls across to Marge.)* Marge! *(Into phone)* Yes, Miss Spence is in reception for you. Marge! They'll be down in a moment.

Marge crosses over to the desk. Victoria sits down.

You're looking marvellous – you've lost weight.

Marge   Oh I haven't.

Saundra   Oh you have. You really have. Because you were quite hippy at one point, weren't you? What's your secret – I won't tell anybody!

Marge   My father died, and . . .

Saundra   Did he? And you lost weight? Isn't that so funny? When my mother passed on I really picked. I really did. Talk about Pig Avenue. Ciao, Marge – take care.

Marge leaves.

Lorraine   *(nodding at wallmounted photo)* That's Geoffrey Paige. He's my heart-throb. I wish I was doing his programme. Look at his hair – the root-lift on that is fantastic.

Saundra   *(to Victoria)* I say, Victoria, I've got my yoghurt here.

Victoria   Ha.

Saundra   I have! In a polythene bag just under here.

Victoria   Ha.

Saundra   Tropical fruit!

Victoria   Ha.

A biker comes in with toupé, hands it to Saundra and leaves.

Saundra   Well I hope it doesn't smell of Hamlets this time, Alan.

Caroline, a researcher, extremely trendy, in her late twenties, enters and looks vaguely around.

Caroline   Dr Najitwar, Saundra?

Saundra   *(less smarmily)* She's been taken to Make Up, Caroline, and 774 know she's been taken to Make Up so why they've sent you here for her I do not figure. I don't know why I bother dialling. Might as well be the Pope for all the benefit I do on this switchboard. Except I can't speak Italian.

Caroline   Oh I know, Saundra, I'm sorry. Charlotte's got the flu now so . . . *(She checks her list.)* Lorraine Spence?

Lorraine   Hiya.

Caroline   'Hiya'. Sorry to keep you – it's a bit chaotic today – everyone's got this terrible flu – I really wouldn't get it if I were you. *(She leads the way to the lift.)* It's really awful; people have just been throwing up like nine pins.

Sue   *(on her way to the desk)* Hiya, Caroline.

Caroline   Hi, Sue.

Sue	You know I have to have a whole new sidelight – twenty-seven pounds.
Caroline	Really? How chronic. God this lift – it's really really slow – the times they've promised to mend it. I mean, they just haven't mended it – well they're a union, I suppose they don't have to. Sorry – I'm Caroline. Charlotte, you spoke to her, yeah? Well she's off so I'll be just running through it with you, OK?
Lorraine	Yeah, OK, whatever.
Caroline	God, what an amazing accent! Is it Brummie?
Victoria	No, it's Liverpool.
Caroline	Oh hi – I didn't recognise you, I love that thing you do, God, you know, the fifties er dancing – so funny, with the handbags.
Victoria	That was French and Saunders.
Caroline	Oh right. They're really funny, aren't they? We wanted them for 'Take My Pet' but I think one of them was having a baby or something. Oh lift, brilliant.

They step into the lift. Caroline presses buttons ineptly.

Caroline	God, these doors, You could be here all day trying to get them to shut; they're really gloomy news. There's some sort of a delay I think – so if there's a fire . . .
Victoria	What?
Caroline	What?
Victoria	If there's a fire, what?
Caroline	That's right.
Lorraine	Carpet up the walls.
Victoria	Laura Ashley's Broadmoor collection.

The doors begin to close.

Caroline	See, they're closing now.
Victoria	Oh yeah.

Pam, Joan Collins' age, in Carmens and casuals, strides across the lobby with an armful of papers and a tiny tape recorder.

Pam   Hold the doors! *(She steps into the lift. They all shuffle round to make room.)* Five! *(Caroline presses the button. Pam switches on tape recorder, checking a memo.)* To Michael Soper, executive producer, 'Live with Pam'; very disturbed by your memo[218] re proposed plan to reduce my slot from two hours to twelve and a half minutes. *(Doors begin to close.)* Darn. *(To Caroline.)* Er – get my dress. It's at the desk. Straight to my dressing room, please. Padded hanger.

Caroline   Oh sure, Pam.

Caroline starts to leave and stands wedging the door open.

Pam   *(into tape)* You describe my interviewing technique as synthetic, which, by the way, is spelt with a 'y'. *(To Caroline)* Yes!

Caroline   Oh yes – sorry – *(To Lorraine and Victoria.)* Could you sort of make your way to Make Up?

Victoria   Where is it?

Caroline   First floor – sort of just outside the lift doors and it says 'Make Up' on it in writing. Is that OK? I'll catch you later.

She slithers away; the lift doors close.

Pam   You can underline this next sentence –

Lorraine   *(whispering)* If we stay in here much longer my hair'll go out of fashion.

Pam   Please – I am dictating – a most crucial memo . . . I have never in twenty-two years broadcasting . . .

---

218 Pronounced as 'meemo' on both occasions Pam says it.

A small make up room. At the far end are an over-excited old couple, Jim and Alma, being made up for 'Chuck a Sausage', and Dr Rani Najitwar. Victoria and Lorraine enter, to be met by Sue their very nice make up lady. By Sue's place is a very elaborate blonde wig on a stand.

Sue   Lorraine? 'Live with Pam'?

Lorraine   Yeah.

Sue   Just pop yourself down, Lorraine, get yourself comfy, I'll just get my little sheet . . . *(She wanders away.)*

Lorraine   What shall I have done?

Victoria   Nothing, you look great.

Sue   *(as she comes back in)* OK. Right, Lorraine – here's Caroline's memo – 'nice and tarty really slap it on' – that sounds fun. I'll pop this robe on. Teresa?[219] Have you got that new palette, 'Nauseating Neons'? It's all right, they're in my fishing bag, going blind here.

Victoria   Why is she supposed to look tarty?

Sue   I think I'll just lard it over whatever you're wearing, Lorraine.

Lorraine   All right.

Victoria   Well actually . . .

Sue   Sorry – is this wrong? This is what I was told.

Neil, a busy boy assistant floor manager, rushes in.

Neil   Chuck a Sausage? Alma? Will she be long?

Sue   Teresa's on 'Chuck a Sausage', Neil. You know it was twenty-seven pounds just for that sidelight.

Neil   God, was it? Cheers. I'm doing everybody this morning. Paula's got flu. She's lying on the props room floor like a draught excluder. *(He runs over to Teresa.)*

Sue   Well my lady'll be half an hour! She's Live with Pam. Now – *(She looks around.)*

---

219 Changed to 'Sven'.

Lorraine	Do you have to look like what they say then?
Victoria	No.
Sue	Peach finesse, where are you?
Lorraine	You tell her.
Victoria	I think Lorraine wants to look like, well, more like she looks, more or less . . . *(To audience)* Golly, I'm forthright and incisive, aren't I?
Sue	I only go by what's on my sheet. I only honestly came in two minutes ago, because someone dented my wing mirror, you see, So . . . *(Caroline comes in.)* Oh Caroline – can you sort this out? I've got 'tarty really slap it on' and apparently the lady's not too happy about it.
Caroline	Oh right. Well, fine. It's just that our other two interviewees – one's very sort of country tweedy and our lady doctor, she's quite Asian – so we thought if you could be more, sort of, well not exactly common, but a bit *tacky*, we thought that would be sort of like a contrast, and you know, quite funny.
Victoria	Well she *is* here as a top businesswoman.
Caroline	Oh God, absolutely. No obviously we're not trying to say 'and now here's a sort of total sleaze-bag', it's just you know, we thought, because you've got that marvellous name . . .
Lorraine	What, Spence?
Caroline	No, Lorraine. It's brilliant isn't it?
Sue	Would you like a few Carmens in there, Lorraine?
Lorraine	Maybe a few small ones.

Sue and Lorraine busy themselves at the Carmen trolley.

Caroline	*(to Victoria)* I mean 'Lorraine', it's sort of like 'Wyne' and 'Trycey', it's really sort of, I don't know *(in useless London accent)* 'Lorrine', it's really, dunno . . . *(She laughs.)*

Neil hustles Jim and Alma to the door.

Neil	Now, it's right at the top of the stairs – have anything you like – put your badges on and they won't charge you.
Jim	You know what I haven't had in a long while?
Alma	Go on.
Jim	Brains.
Alma	You haven't had brains since Violet Wythenshawe moved in two doors up.
Neil	Only you do need to be back in your dressing room by five to.
Alma	You're never that punctilious with our privet.
Neil	*(suddenly remembering)* Terrapin! *(He rushes out.)*
Caroline	Oh, Neil – this is Lorraine – 'Live with Pam'.
Neil	*(Voice Over)* Back in a tick!
Victoria	Hey, Lorraine, do you want a bun or something?
Lorraine	Oh yeah, great.
Caroline	*(imitating Victoria's accent)* A boon!
Victoria	Yah. *(to Lorraine)* What do you want?
Lorraine	I'll have coffee and a croissant, thanks.
Caroline	I have to go and look at some pop sox now, OK? But I'll return back and we'll go through the questions, yeah?
Lorraine	OK, fine.
Victoria	Do you want anything from the canteen, Caroline?
Caroline	No I'm on a diet thanks; I'll probably have something on Wednesday.

Victoria leaves.

Lorraine	This is creased, isn't it?
Caroline	I could get it pressed really easily actually.
Lorraine	Oh great, thanks!

She rips off her jacket to reveal a respectable T-shirt underneath.

Ta.

Caroline	God, you're really physically uninhibited, aren't you? Is that from living in a terrace?

Lorraine thinks about that one.

In the canteen. Jim and Alma are at the counter scrutinising the hot and cold dishes carefully. They are both wearing large sausage badges with their names on. Saundra is just making her way back past them with a lemon tea. Victoria joins Alma and Jim.

Saundra	*(to Victoria)* Lemon tea! Aren't I good?
Victoria	Aha.
Alma	Hutch in, Jim. Come past, we're only dithering.
Victoria	No, you're all right.
Alma	We had pasties on the minibus but we're rumbling to beat the band now.
Jim	I say – my belly thinks my –
Alma	Jim! Bring him to a television programme, he starts naming parts of the body. Show me up.
Victoria	Which programme are you doing?
Alma	'Chuck a Sausage'.
Jim	'Chuck a Sausage' with Geoffrey Paige.
Alma	With Geoffrey Paige. Ooh, and he's friendly. If he's said hello once – well he's said hello once. Yes that's right. Now what are you having, Dad? Think on, we haven't got long.
Jim	*(reading)* Macaroni Cheese. Do I like Macaroni cheese, Alma?
Alma	Yes.
Jim	Am I having that, then?
Alma	No! He would if I let him. He'd wolf it down most successfully if I let him. Then the next thing you know he'd be sat bolt upright in bed shouting about Goering! Have the haddock.
Jim	Haddock Mornay – that sounds appetising.

Alma   *(to server)* Two of the haddocks please, and er cauli- with one and er –

Pam whizzes in, still in rollers.

Pam   Scusi, folks – it's rather important I'm served.

Alma   Oh no – you push ahead – we don't –

Victoria   Excuse me, there's a queue, these people haven't been served yet.

Pam   Very possibly, but I am making a television programme, and I rather think that ranks a little higher in importance than the sustenance of pensioners. You – any croissants?

Victoria   They're making a television programme too. And I'm after them anyway.

Server   There's two croissants left.

Victoria   Yes – I'll have those, thank you.

Pam   Now look. I am no ordinary well-preserved early middle-aged woman with a keen brain and an overwhelming sexual magnetism. I am Pam! Yes, Pam, of 'Live with Pam', and it is essential that I leave this cafeteria replete with the requisite number of calories in under eight and a half minutes or the most innovative and enthralling women's daytime discussion programme on network television will be off the air!

Victoria   The croissants, a coffee and a tea please.

Pam   I need those croissants. I am a borderline hypoglycaemic, diagnosed pastry-dependent and if you persist in defying me I have a simple choice: either I sink immediately into a dangerously deep coma, or I am forced to commandeer those croissants for the sake of liberty, freedom of speech and daytime television.

Victoria licks each croissant.

Victoria   You look. You only want these croissants because I've got them. If you really needed pastry at least two of these *(pointing to Carmens)* would be sausage rolls so you could pick them off in an emergency. Just because you're on television is no reason to go barging to the head of the queue like a heat-seeking missile in sling backs. And if you did drop comatose to the floor and 'Live with Pam' had to be replaced by soothing music and an illustration from *The People's Friend*,[220] half your audience wouldn't even notice and the other thirty-seven would find the new version unbearably stimulating and have to lie down.

Pam   I see. Well now you have jeopardised the health of day-time television's most caring presenter, perhaps I could be permitted to reach by you for a Wagon Wheel. Could I?

In the dressing room corridor. Victoria comes in with the tray. Sue follows with make up bucket.

Sue   I think I'm getting my period. Tuh! *(She leaves.)*

Neil skids round the corner.

Victoria   Excuse me – do you know which dressing room Lorraine Spence is in?
Neil   *(checking his clipboard)* Is she 'Chuck a Sausage'?
Victoria   No, 'Live with Pam'.
Neil   'Live with Pam'. I'm just about to flip my boko with this lot – I'm doing 'Chuck a Sausage', 'Live with Pam' and 'Take my Pet'. Lorraine Spence – thirty-two. I'll walk you down. Everyone's off with flu but me – I said, ooh I'll have it when everyone else has finished with it. I've got eight contestants, three interviewees, an alcoholic weatherman and a giant terrapin to keep track of. It's like trying to do the ironing on the *Titanic*.

220 Magazine founded in 1869, aimed at older women.

Victoria	Do you know where they all are?
Neil	They're in the studio, they're in the canteen, he's in the gents with a vodka and tonic.
Victoria	And where's the giant terrapin?
Neil	It *was* on a car rug. It's probably in a rissole by now. *(He stops by the door.)* Thirty-two. Please keep Lorraine here till I come to take her to the studio – one false move with Pam and she'll have my underpant enhancers for a table decoration. Oh cripes, Jim and Alma!

He rushes off the way they've just come.

Inside Lorraine's dressing room. It is the usual cell; washbasin, mirror, hard tweedy bed etc. Lorraine is now nicely made up but not dressed. Victoria comes in with tray.

Lorraine	Oh great – chuck us a croissant.
Victoria	Guess which old biddy I had to fight to get it?
Lorraine	Who?

Caroline comes in with Lorraine's jacket, another top and a filofax.

Caroline	Everything OK?
Lorraine	Yeah – have you got my jacket?
Caroline	*(hanging them both on the rails)* Well what I've done, basically, I've brought the jacket, but actually this – Pam thought *(holding up a skimpy, low cut lurex top)* would look better on camera –
Lorraine	I don't normally wear that kind of thing.
Caroline	Oh sure, but Pam thought it would sort of fit in with the whole ethos type thing, perhaps.

Lorraine holds it up against her chest.

Anyway – before Neil takes you into the studio, I'll just

run through the interview, because it is live . . . *(She opens filofax. Lorraine pulls a face at Victoria.)*

Victoria   You don't want to wear that, Lorraine.
Caroline   I think Pam is pretty keen –

Neil comes in.

Neil   You haven't seen a stupid old man wearing a sausage, have you?
Caroline   Sorry, clueless.

Neil goes out.

Neil   *(Voice Over)* Try wardrobe, Jackie!
Caroline   *(finding her place in filofax)* So – the interview – it's pretty much as you discussed over the phone. Early days.
Lorraine   I was a Saturday girl – yeah.
Caroline   And didn't your boss use to pinch your bum or something?
Lorraine   *(slightly taken aback)* Yeah, once, but –
Caroline   That's sexual harassment, OK, which is nice for us, so any dirt there – erm – you got married at seventeen, had a baby, lived in a council flat, very depressing obviously.
Lorraine   It was quite nice actually.
Caroline   So any vandalism stories – people peeing in the lifts?
Lorraine   They didn't.
Victoria   Not without putting a pedestal mat down first.
Caroline   Well, anything scuzzy; Pam really wants to hear about it – Valium?
Lorraine   I thought I was going to talk about building my hairdressing business from nothing.
Caroline   Oh sure. And how the pressure led to solvent abuse.
Lorraine   Eh?
Caroline   Didn't you say something here about sniffing hair lacquer?

Victoria	She's a hairdresser! Of course she sniffs lacquer. That's like accusing Fatima Whitbread of sniffing javelins.[221]
Caroline	Well any mental problems, incest, baby battering, trot it all out – that *is* Pam's bag.
Lorraine	*(bemused)* OK. Is there a loo?
Caroline	Yeah – there's quite a bizarre situation about it actually; it's on the second floor, so you have to like go up two flights of stairs – creepy!
Lorraine	See you. *(Lorraine goes out.)*
Caroline	She's amazing, isn't she? I mean if I'd had to live in a council flat I think I'd probably, you know, just give up breathing.
Victoria	Why? Lots of people live in them.
Caroline	That's right. My really good friends have one in Stepney but they're barristers; it's more of a statement.
Victoria	I was wondering if you'd ever had a tweed sofa inserted quite a long way into your mouth?
Caroline	Mm, at a party, in Brighton.
Victoria	Lorraine! Wait for me!

In another bit of corridor leading to stairs.

| Victoria | Lorraine! |

She passes Saundra, who is on her way downstairs carrying a small tupperware.

| Saundra | None of your skits – this is a Ryvita! |
| Victoria | Ha. |

She catches Lorraine up, they walk together.

---

221 Javelin thrower and, no doubt partly because of the rhythm of her name, a favourite of VW's. 'I'm not Fatima Whitbread,' says the continuity announcer in *ASOTV* when asked to make Wally Wallaby do more hops on her desk for younger viewers. 'I'm really upset,' says Anita in *DL*. 'I look like Fatima Whitbread.'

	Are you sure you want to do this thing with Pam?
Lorraine	Eh?
Victoria	Television does funny things to people. Look at Angela Rippon.[222]

Neil rushes by.

Neil	If you find any marbles – they're mine.
Lorraine	I'm only chatting with Pam. She's supposed to be genuinely sympathetic.
Victoria	She's not. She's the woman in the lift with the tape recorder. The day she's genuinely sympathetic is the day a piranha genuinely prefers an omelette.

They stop outside the ladies loo.

Lorraine	*(torn)* Yeah, but I want to be on television. It's been my life's ambition. I mean, you know my family; none of us have ever been on telly – except my dad's brother – and that was a photo-fit; the eyebrows were rubbish.

Ladies loo. Victoria is attempting to work the roller towel.

Victoria	Look – there's millions of ways to get on television. You can hang around a shopping centre and see if Esther Rantzen offers you a tray of peculiarly shaped vegetables.[223] You can go on *Songs of Praise* and just open and shut your mouth with a hat on; I'll get you on *Blankety Blank* – they'll have anybody – bring your own magic marker, you can host the next series. What do you say?

222 The BBC newsreader famously stunned viewers by doing a dance routine on *The Morecambe and Wise Christmas Show* in 1976.
223 Having worked on Rantzen's consumer affairs show *That's Life* in 1976 never stopped VW from making jokes about her.

Dr Rani comes out of a cubicle, and rinses her hands.

Dr Rani   Quite an interesting idea but I think I'll stick with med-
                 icine.

She pulls the roller towel; it works perfectly.

*A studio corridor, outside the gents. The door is flanked by
two others marked 'Studio One' and 'Studio Two'. Neil is in
agitated conversation with Alma. Victoria enters.*

Alma   I said he should have stuck to the cauli, they're not even
                 his dentures you see.[224]
Neil   Have you seen your Lorraine?
Victoria   No, she's not in the dressing room – isn't she in the
                 studio?
Neil   *(looking at watch)* I thought things couldn't get any
                 worse today. I've got a terrapin that won't come out of its
                 shell, a contestant with food poisoning and an inebriated
                 weatherman who's just insulted everyone in Wiltshire,
                 Avon and the cloudier parts of Somerset.
Victoria   Who's got food poisoning?
Alma   It's Jim. We were going great guns to the semi-final – I
                 was answering and he was chucking the sausages – then
                 he keels over shouting, 'Loosen my braces, Alma, it's the
                 haddock mornay!' He's never been right since Bispham.
Neil   Look – I can't stay, Alma, I'm needed on Pam; you go in
                 and sit with him.
Alma   You shut your palate – I've gone seventy-three years
                 without nudging up against a urinal and I'm not coming
                 to it now. I'll take a seat down the end. If anybody wants
                 me I'll be on that buffet under Pearl Carr and Teddy
                 Johnson.[225]

---

224 The first half of this speech was cut.
225 Husband-and-wife entertainers, popular in the 1950s.

Alma moves off.

Neil   Silly old tea-towel – look, your friend Lorraine is due in that studio in two minutes on a live programme – it's my job to get her there and I've looked everywhere except the boilerman's left armpit. Don't tell me you think she's done a runner?

Victoria   I think she's done a runner.

Neil   Well that's it. I've had it. 'Chuck a Sausage' they can muddle through – anyway I live with the producer – but Pam . . . if she says, 'Please welcome Lorraine Spence,' and Lorraine Spence isn't there to be please welcomed I'm out. I won't work in this business again. I shan't be able to buff up the carafes on *Newsnight*. And we've got a mortgage. And we're halfway through erecting an outdoor dining ambience – I feel like putting a wig on and going on myself, I do. *(They stare at each other blankly.)*

'Live with Pam' studio. There is a ripple of applause from the small female audience as Pam turns to 'her' camera.

Pam   A success story from Dr Rani Najitwar there. But you don't need to be an immigrant to experience all the difficulties life can throw up. One of life's battlers, ladies – please welcome Lorraine Spence.

Victoria appears in the top rejected by Lorraine and blonde wig seen earlier, and hasty lip gloss. She sits down.

Pam   Lorraine – life hasn't been easy for you, has it?

Victoria   No, it's been rubbish.

Pam   Tell me about it. What sort of childhood did you have?

Victoria   In care . . . truanting . . . shoplifting.

Pam   You were a deprived child.

Victoria   Never had hotpants, never had a gonk.

Pam	Those hurts run deep, don't they, Lorraine. Did you turn to pregnancy as a way out?
Victoria	I had seven children before I were eighteen. But I couldn't cope. I were too stupid to cope. I kept leaving them in skips. Then I got to the housing list and the council give me my own skip – it were super, Pam!
Pam	And then you got married, didn't you, Lorraine?
Victoria	Yeah, but I were just as miserable, only with less room. He drunk, he scratched hisself, he kept pork niblets in his Y-fronts. I were a battered wife, Pam – I were in Casualty so often I had my own cubicle. But I loved him. I loved him, Pam!
Pam	You were a working mother, weren't you, Lorraine? Was it a good job?
Victoria	Oh yeah. Pickwick's Biscuits. They reckoned I had a flair for bourbons but I got a cross foreman and he put me back on dodgers.
Pam	What happened with the foreman, Lorraine?
Victoria	It were just sexual harassment,[226] Pam – it don't matter. I don't want to disclose about it.
Pam	It's distressing I know, Lorraine – but it may help to bring it out and tell the viewers.
Victoria	Oh it's just that every so often they stripped me naked and pushed me round the boardroom on an orthopaedic sun lounger.
Pam	That's appalling, Lorraine – how often did this happen?
Victoria	Every tea break.
Pam	Really, yes, yes . . . Did you turn to any means of escape? Tranquillisers?
Victoria	Valium, Mogadon – I were living in a dream world, Pam; I were in a daze. I were even watching daytime television! Then when I got hooked on booze as well as tranks that's when it got really difficult –
Pam	Why, Lorraine?

---

226 Mispronounced by VW as 'rahassment'.

Victoria	I were sleeping so many hours a day I couldn't get any drinking done.
Pam	We've heard from Rani how education helped her out of her very poor background to the position she now holds in the World Health Organisation: do you think it would have helped you?
Victoria	Not really, Pam.
Pam	Don't you think it might have made you more aware of your situation as a – and I mean this so kindly, Lorraine – as a rather feeble and inadequate member of the proletariat?
Victoria	You've lost me, Pam. You're bamboozling me with long syllables.
Pam	So you don't think CSEs as they then were, or a St John's Ambulance qualification, would have shone a little light into your murky darkness?
Victoria	Not really, no, Pam. I come clean, Pam. CSEs passed me by, Pam. You come knocking to me for a CSE, Pam – I can't give you one – cupboard's bare, like.
Pam	I thought so, Lorraine.
Victoria	Cos to be frank, Pam . . .
Pam	Oh please do be . . .
Victoria	I couldn't be frigged to get any, Pam.
Pam	That's very undstandable when you're a little bit stupid.
Victoria	I couldn't be frigged to get any, Pam – because I've got ten 'O' levels, five 'A' levels, a BA, an MA, a PhD, Grade 8 cor anglais, a wig *(taking it off)* and an insatiable desire to expose hypocrisy, amateurism and plain economy-sized rudeness on land, sea or television studio. You are the most patronising old cow to hit the airwaves since Mrs Bridges caught Ruby with her corsets on back to front, and I for one will not cease from mental fight till 'Live with Pam' is off the air.[227]

---

227 A reference to *Upstairs, Downstairs*, which ran on ITV from 1971 to 1975.

Applause from the audience.

Pam   *(fanning herself)* My handbag! I need pastry!

She faints.

In reception. Saundra is on duty; Lorraine and Victoria are standing by a pile of prizes.

Lorraine Well I was thinking about what you said about Pam and that – and I popped into the other studio to have a look at 'Chuck a Sausage', cos you know I'm nuts on Geoffrey Paige. Then this old bloke conked out in the semi-final and they asked for a volunteer so I rushed up; brilliant – and as well as all these I'm getting a fridge-freezer, a dining table and a weekend for two in Hamburg.

Sue approaches the desk. Neil ushers Jim and Alma out.

Neil   I think everyone else is on the minibus so –
Alma   *(looking at the prizes)* They could have been our table mats, James Mottershead. I may forget but I'll never forgive.

They leave.

Victoria Where's your terrapin?
Neil   *(shrieks)* Great balls of fluff, I left it in the blinking urinal, licking the disinfectant! They're bringing your things round now, OK? See you!

Madge enters. Sue leaves the desk.

Saundra   Sue! Sue! What happened about your sidelight?
Sue   Twenty-seven pounds!
Saundra   And they still won't bring back hanging.

Sue	*(leaving)* I know! *(To Madge.)* Have you lost weight, Madge?
Madge	No!

She runs off. Pam, a coat draped over her shoulders, is being escorted by Caroline to a nearby seat.

Caroline	I'll just check with Saundra about the cab, OK?
Pam	When you've checked and only when it has arrived and you have placed me very carefully in the back seat, you may remove your possessions from the 'Live with Pam' production office. From tomorrow morning you will be third assistant animal researcher on 'Take My Pet' and that is absolutely final and I will brook no ripostes.
Caroline	Right. *(She crosses to Saundra.)*
Saundra	Pam's cab's on the way, Caroline. Pam – Pam – that was superb today. What a finish to a series. My goodness.
Pam	There are seventy-seven more to be transmitted.
Saundra	No, Pam – not so – I took Michael's memo while you were on air – from M. Soper, Exec Producer 'Live with Pam', blah blah, shall I read it, save you popping over? 'Further to my memo of this morning, tuned into to-day's transmission to witness most appalling shambles (bit cheeky!). As from now 'Live with Pam' is cancelled and your contract with Console Television (it actually says "helevision") is terminated.' Shall I put it in your pigeon hole? Oh your cab's here! Ciao, Pam.

Pam and Caroline move slowly to the door.

Caroline	Is it on the account, Saundra?
Saundra	Well no, not if Pam's been fired, you see. Have to be cash. Take care, lots of it.
Victoria	*(to Lorraine, who's been packing the prizes into 'Chuck a Sausage' tote bags)* Who are you taking to Hamburg? Geoffrey Paige?

Lorraine   No; what a let down *he* was – he wears a whacking great
                toupé. No, I'll take you.

Victoria   All right. *(To Saundra who's eating a biscuit.)* Bye!

Saundra   It's only a small one!

Victoria   Ha.

Lorraine   What do they eat in Hamburg?

Victoria   What do you think?

Lorraine   What?

Victoria   Pizzas, silly!

They leave.

VAL DE REE[228]

The Yorkshire Moors; the Dales; the Peak District; any large expanse of walking country. In the distance are two figures striding along merrily, both with backpacks, tents, dangling mugs etc; Victoria and friend Jackie. Both are singing 'The Happy Wanderer'.[229]

Victoria   Val de ree . . .
Jackie   Ha ha ha ha ha . . .
Victoria   Val de rah . . .
Jackie   Ha ha ha ha ha . . .
Both   My knapsack on my back!
Victoria   This is the life, eh? The air, the landscape, the exercise – I could go on forever. How long have we been walking now?
Jackie   Ten minutes!
Victoria   Shall we have a sit down?

They sit down. Jackie starts fiddling in her rucksack.

---

228 While *Chunky* went with the shorter title, on television the episode was billed as *Val de Ree (Ha Ha Ha Ha Ha)*.
229 Popular hit in 1954 whose lyrics, originally in German, were written in the nineteenth century.

Victoria	This is our heritage, this landscape you know, Jackie. It's timeless. You feel any minute now Christopher Timothy[230] could come round that corner in a baby Austin, fresh from ramming his hand up the parts of a cow other actors cannot reach. What are you doing?
Jackie	Looking for the orange juice.
Victoria	No, save that. Come on. *(They get up.)* What we'll do, we'll stop at a farm and get milk. *(They start walking.)*
Jackie	Can you do that?
Victoria	Course. Have you never read *Swallows and Amazons*? They couldn't set foot outside their tents without loveable old farmers' wives thrusting half a pint of gold top down their necks. We might even get a bun.
Jackie	What sort of a bun?
Victoria	A bun! A glass of milk and a bun type bun. Haven't you read any of those books!
Jackie	Well you know I'm a slow reader. I'm still only half way through *The Secret Diary of Adrian Mole Aged 12¾* . . .
Victoria	I wouldn't bother. He's twenty-seven now, he works in a bank in Melton Mowbray. Look – there's one. *(Points out a white-washed farmhouse.)* I bet you there's some apple-cheeked old biddy round the back there in a gingham apron doling out the speckly eggs and the cottage cheese.
Jackie	Brilliant – let's go and get some milk then, all lovely and frothy and fresh from the udder. *(She sets off.)*
Victoria	Do you have to bring udders into it?

A very done-up farmyard, all clean white paint and hanging baskets. Victoria and Jackie are in conversation in the porch with very dim, posh girl.

Girl	Milk?
Jackie	We're on a walking weekend and we passed your farm

---

230 Played James Herriot in the BBC vet drama *All Creatures Great and Small* from 1978 to 1990.

and we thought, how lovely, fresh milk straight from the udder.

Victoria Jackie!

Girl You thought you wanted some milk?

Victoria Yes, but it doesn't matter, honestly.

Girl The thing in the carton, yeah?

Jackie It's OK, really.

Girl What, sort of to drink, did you mean?

Jackie Yes – we thought this was a farmhouse.

Girl Oh, it is a farmhouse – it's called Dendale Farmhouse.

Jackie So we thought there might be cows.

Girl Cows!

Victoria The things with the four legs and the big brown eyes – go moo.

Girl Oh, got you. I saw a documentary about them – it was amazing – Christopher Timothy was in it. It's on every week . . .

Jackie So we thought we'd just stop and get a drink of milk.

Girl Right. I'm on it. We don't have milk, I'm sorry.

Victoria It's OK.

Girl I could maybe find some Perrier –

Jackie No, honestly, it doesn't matter – really.

Jamie appears in the doorway in shorts.

Jamie Is there a problem, sweetie?

Jackie No, it's all right.

Girl These people really wanted some milk, Jamie.

Jamie *(incisively)* The stuff in the carton, yeah?

Girl Yeah.

Jamie *(on the case)* Do we have any?

Girl Not really.

Jamie Can we get some faxed?

Back in open country, Victoria and Jackie are marching along.

Victoria	This is good, isn't it?
Jackie	It's brilliant! Wonderful idea of yours, to come camping. The air! *(She breathes in.)* Mm – pure hormone.
Victoria	Ozone.
Jackie	Well, what's hormone then?
Victoria	Hormones – you know what they are.
Jackie	What are they?
Victoria	They're women's things. You don't notice you've got them till you run out of them.
Jackie	Like split peas.
Victoria	Yeah – but if you run out of split peas you don't go red and grow a moustache.
Jackie	I might if I had time.[231]
Victoria	Have you heard of Hormone Replacement Therapy?
Jackie	No?
Victoria	Neither have I. You know what I fancy now?
Jackie	What?
Victoria	That chocolate.
Jackie	What chocolate?
Victoria	That huge great bar in your rucksack. *(Silence.)* Have you got it?
Jackie	I haven't exactly got all of it.
Victoria	Have you been eating it? How much is there left?
Jackie	Well, just the paper.

They stop walking.

Victoria	You've eaten that huge bar of very expensive chocolate that I bought – when did you eat it? I never saw you put anything in your mouth. How did you have it, as a suppository?
Jackie	I was behind a hedge.
Victoria	You said you were having a wee. I thought you were a suspiciously long time. I imagined some latent bladder

---

231 Changed to 'I wouldn't bank on it.'

problem brought on by the unaccustomed exercise – it never crossed my mind you were crouched in the grass with your shorts round your ankles frantically gobbling Fruit and Nut.

Jackie   I only meant to have one square.

Victoria   One square foot?

Jackie   I have a problem with chocolate.

Victoria   So do I now. I want some and I can't have any.

They walk on in silence.

Jackie   Do you want to sing 'The Happy Wanderer'?

Victoria   No. I want to sing How Much Is That Piggy with the Rucksack?

Pause.

Jackie   Why are you limping?

Victoria   Am I limping? Muscle fatigue brought on by sugar deficiency, I would imagine.

Jackie   Pity there's no such thing as Sugar Replacement Therapy.

Victoria   There is. It's called chocolate. If you must know, I think I'm getting a blister.

Jackie   It's a shame you didn't soak your feet in a bowl of surgical spirit as I think I suggested earlier.

Victoria   Have you tried buying enough surgical spirit to fill a bowl? The woman in Boots thought I was a wino having a cocktail party. I had to buy a toilet-roll holder just to prove I wasn't homeless.

Jackie   Well, I'm having another wee if you'll excuse me.

Victoria   *(grabbing the rucksack)* A-ah. I'll mind this. Don't want you licking the dehydrated pasta whirls.

Jackie   I need something out of it.

Victoria   Use a dock leaf.

Jackie   I want to blow my nose.

Victoria   Use two – one for each nostril.

*Further on, it is a little bleaker and windier. They are poring
over the map which is in a plastic pocket on Jackie's chest.*

Victoria	Well I think we're here.
Jackie	But where are the three little trees?
Victoria	No, they're not real trees – they're symbolic.
Jackie	Like Pinter?
Victoria	Look – we came up a little track like that, didn't we, and the river was there, and the little hilly thing – so we're here.
Jackie	But which way are we facing?[232]
Victoria	Well, we want to go north.
Jackie	Which way's north?
Victoria	Towards the top of the map.
Jackie	But we've had it the other way round, to read it.
Victoria	North's always in the same place.
Jackie	Is it? Even in summer?
Victoria	Yeah.
Jackie	Right. And they didn't change it for the farmers or anything?
Victoria	No.
Jackie	*(efficiently)* OK. So north's to the top of the paper. Which way do we actually want to set off?
Victoria	This way.
Jackie	This way's north, is it?
Victoria	*(not so sure)* Yeah . . .
Jackie	How do you know?
Victoria	Well the sun goes from east to west, right?
Jackie	OK. I didn't know that.
Victoria	Well of course it does – how do you think you get sunsets?
Jackie	I thought that was the sea tipping up.
Victoria	It starts in the east –
Jackie	What, like Ceylon?

---

232 Cut.

Victoria	Yeah. Then it crosses over –
Jackie	*(intelligently)* Yes, that's right – that's the equinox.
Victoria	No, this is every day.
Jackie	Right.
Victoria	So all we have to do is[233] look at the sun.
Jackie	Yes.
Victoria	Look at the time.
Jackie	Yes.
Victoria	Then you work out where north is.
Jackie	I see.
Victoria	So what's the time?
Jackie	*(agreeing)* Yes.
Victoria	What *is* the time?
Jackie	The time now?
Victoria	No. The time Jesus first made a fitted wardrobe. What time is it?
Jackie	I don't know.
Victoria	I told you my watch was broken. I phoned you up. I said have you got a watch, you said yes I have. Didn't you?
Jackie	Yes.
Victoria	Where is it?
Jackie	In my cardigan pocket.
Victoria	Where's your cardigan?
Jackie	In my car.
Victoria	Well, if we can't find this campsite, Jackie, and I die of exposure trying to fetch help, you will have to write to Mrs Margaret Thatcher explaining how it was the country came to lose a much loved and irreplaceable entertainer.[234] I hope you understand that.
Jackie	Yes I do.
Victoria	Right. Come on. I think this is north.

---

233 A large section from 'Towards the top of the map' to here was cut and replaced with 'I'll tell you. You look at the sun.'

234 Changed to 'well loved', though this could have simply been VW forgetting her own line.

They set off.

Jackie   I'm sure you're right. In fact it feels a little bit colder
                already, don't you think so?

                Moorland; nothing is to be seen for miles except a track, a
                stream, maybe a few sheep. Victoria and Jackie are unpack-
                ing the tent.

Victoria   Course, we probably wouldn't have liked the campsite if
                we had found it.
Jackie   Oh no, this is much more of an adventure. Just like your
                book, what was it – *Seagulls and Cannibals*?
Victoria   *Swallows and Amazons.* Swallows and Amazons for ever!
Jackie   What's it about?
Victoria   Well, they all go off in a boat, right – Susan and John
                and Roger and Titty.
Jackie   Roger and who?
Victoria   Roger and Titty.
Jackie   And this is a children's book?
Victoria   Yes. Shut up. Now – is that all the bits?
Jackie   Yep.
Victoria   You put the tent up – I'll get the water. Where's that
                folding buckety thing?
Jackie   I don't know how it goes up.
Victoria   No, but they're all basically the same, aren't they? You've
                been camping enough times.
Jackie   I've never been camping. That's why this is such a
                thrill.
Victoria   What do you mean you've never been camping?
Jackie   Haven't ever been; sorry.
Victoria   Jacqueline Thomson – when I met your mother did she
                or did she not say that as an adolescent you were always
                in tents?
Jackie   Intense! I was always intense! I haven't a clue about
                camping.

Victoria	Well your mother wants elocution lessons. I'm going to phone her up.
Jackie	She's not on the phone.
Victoria	Then I shall send her an offensive bouquet.
Jackie	Well I thought *you* knew all about it; you know all the words to 'The Happy Wanderer'.
Victoria	I know all the words to 'Climb Every Mountain' but I'm not a Mother Superior.
Jackie	Well, it can't be that difficult to put up. I'll read out the instructions and you join the bits together. Right. Take Tube A and apply to Bracket D, with flange channel outermost.
Victoria	Tube A . . . Tube A . . .

The same, later. Bits are scattered in odd groupings; Victoria and Jackie look slightly harassed.

Jackie	Right. Start again. Take Tube A and apply to Bracket D with flange channel outermost.
Victoria	Outermost. I've done that.
Jackie	*(mumbling)* Figure three . . . repeat with tubes B, F and J.
Victoria	Yes
Jackie	Figure four – then *quasi* tighten Socket Cap E until semi-protruding Locking Hinge K is engaged.
Victoria	Yes, I've done all that.
Jackie	Yes, but I think this is where we went wrong before. Is your Socket Cap *quasi* tightened?
Victoria	Yes!
Jackie	And is your semi-protruding Locking Hinge engaged?
Victoria	I think so.
Jackie	*(earnestly)* Well, check that it is engaged, Vic, because –
Victoria	What do you want me to do, ask to see its engagement ring? It clicked, didn't it?
Jackie	OK. Gather up Canvas Panel M, taking care that stitched gully faces Braided Thongings C, H and W, otherwise

Waxed Proofing Flap O will be rendered inoperable.
OK?

Victoria   What do you mean 'OK?'?

Jackie   Gather up Canvas Panel M –

Victoria   Which is it?

Jackie   Which what?

Victoria   Which is Canvas Panel M?

Jackie   The one with the stitched gully, obviously.

Victoria   They've all got a stitched gully, you pinhead. That's what you stick the rods up. How do you think the sides stay together – hormones?

Jackie   Gather up Canvas Panel M.

Victoria   I don't know which one it is. Stupid thing! I don't think these are bits of tent anyway. I think there's been some hideous mix-up at the factory, and these are actually the individual sections of some compulsive eater's pinafore dress. There's probably some poor woman in a back bed-room in Henley-in-Arden sobbing, and trying to squeeze her buttocks into a waxed proofing flap. It doesn't make sense.

Jackie   Oh come on. This is ridiculous. We're both intelligent people – a little bit of serious thought and we should have the problem solved in no time.

Victoria   That's what Neville Chamberlain said to Hitler.

Jackie   I keep telling you – I haven't read *Swallows and Amazons*. *(She pauses.)* Right, take Tube A and apply to Bracket D . . .

The same, later. Bits are scattered everywhere. They're on their knees, facing each other. Jackie is trying not to shout.

Jackie   *(very slowly)* Take Tube A and apply to Bracket D.

Victoria   Reading it slower does not make it any easier to do.

Jackie   I'm sorry – you read it out then.

Victoria   It doesn't matter who reads it out. You could re-write it as a duet for Cyndi Lauper and Placido Domingo, we

	wouldn't be any nearer putting up the stupid thing.
Jackie	Well I can't believe you've dragged me all the way out here without a smidgeon of technical expertise.
Victoria	What about you? Keen as mustard in the car – now it turns out you've never done anything more adventurous than step on an escalator in soft-soled shoes. What did you DO in your summer holidays for heaven's sake? Why weren't you a guide? Why *didn't* you go camping?
Jackie	I was in the Youth Orchestra. On the oboe.
Victoria	Well that fits together, doesn't it? Good God[235], what is a tent when you think about it – it's only four big oboes and an evening dress.

She stares at the bits of tent.

Jackie	There's somebody coming! A man!
Victoria	Does he look like he knows about tents?
Jackie	He's got shorts on.
Victoria	That's good. Have they got a semi-protruding locking hinge on them?
Jackie	Hello!

Mim and Daddy move into view; she is small, sprightly and jaunty, sixty-nine. Daddy is sixty-nine. They are both dressed for a nice day's fell-walking, in shorts and with little rucksacks.

Mim	*(breathing in)* Isn't it glorious? You can practically smell those hormones!
Jackie	*(under her breath)* You see?
Mim	Are you drinking it in? The scenery? Are you? We are. Aren't we? Daddy! Aren't we? Drinking it in. The scenery.
Daddy	There's plenty of it.
Mim	He's joking. He is. Aren't you? Daddy. Joking. He is. He's

---

235 Changed, presumably for blasphemy-sensitive ears, to 'Good heavens'.

	dry, is Daddy. Aren't you? He's like a dry white wine. Dry.
Victoria	We're having a bit of trouble with our tent, actually.
Mim	Hear that, Daddy? Trouble. Trouble is meat and drink to Dad. Isn't it Dad? Meat and drink. Well, not meat – we've given up due to the cruelty. Daddy has the odd Cumberland sausage but he was at Dunkirk so it's understandable. Two days on a lilo in full battle dress, it's not humorous.
Daddy	What's the problem?
Mim	See – straight to the heart of the topic. This is the man who terrorised the cardboard box industry for forty years. *(She pauses.)* Go on.
Jackie	I'm sure it's all perfectly obvious – we're probably being terribly dim . . .
Victoria	No we're not.
Jackie	We just cannot seem to fit the silly thing together.
Mim	Fret not. *Finito de fretto.* Leave it to Dad. He'll be at those instructions like an SAS man through an embassy window.[236] You set to, Dad, and I'll break out the beverages.

The same, later. A little way from the tent and Daddy, who are out of sight behind a rise, Mim, and Victoria and Jackie sit relaxed, enjoying the view, drinking tea from Mim's Thermos. Victoria and Jackie are sharing a cup.

Mim	What a lovely weekend you're going to have – what did you call it?
Victoria	Backpacking.
Mim	Backpacking. What a phrase or saying that is! I'd walk for miles but we're tied to the Honda with Daddy's groin; and really now, he's not up to humping the equipment.

---

236 In 1980 the SAS conducted a daring raid on the Iranian Embassy in central London after six gunmen took 26 people hostage.

Nor am I, to be brutal. I mean, I'm whippy for my size but I couldn't shoulder a toilet tent, come what might.

Jackie *(finishing the tea)* That was lovely – thank you.

Mim What do they say of tea? The cup that cleans but doth not inebri-ise.

Jackie I hope we've left enough for your husband.

Mim His tea drinking's pretty much censored since his operation. Excess liquid puts too much pressure on his tubular grommets apparently. *(She calls.)* Are you nearly done, Dad?

Dad *(Voice Over)* I'm just adjacent to finishing.[237]

Mim Course he's lucky in one way with his groin – you can't see it. I mean, if it was in a sling he'd be forever fending off queries.

She packs up the Thermos.

They're marvellous, aren't they, thermice? I won this in a competition – had to put eight lightweight trusses in order of comfort and adaptability; we chuckled home with that one.

Daddy appears over the rise.

Mim All done, Dad?

Daddy More or less.

Mim Isn't he marvellous? *(She straps him into his backpack. Victoria and Jackie stand by gratefully.)* And he's not just red hot in the handiwork area[238] – he sings opera.

Victoria He doesn't!

Mim He does. Don't you, Daddy? Sing opera. He's always running himself down re the professionals but I say

---

237 'Mim' was added to the end of the speech, otherwise viewers would never have known the character who calls her husband Daddy had her own name.

238 Changed to 'a handyman'.

where would José Carreras be with a Rawlplug? We're all trotting up different snickets, aren't we?

Victoria   That's right.

Jackie   Well, thank you very much, that really was kind of you.

Dad   Pleasure.

Jackie   No really – thank you ever so much.

Mim   Come on, Dad, off we go, heading for the wild blue Honda. Bye!

Victoria and Jackie wave them off and rush over the rise to inspect the tent. They stare at it. It is up, but only half of the rods have been used so it is only about two foot high and very droopy. The unused rods are in a neat pile on the grass.

Jackie   It's not too bad.

Victoria   It is too bad. It's like a starter home for guinea pigs.

Jackie   At least it's up – I mean we can manage.

Victoria   Of course we can manage. Jesus managed.

Jackie   When?

Victoria   In the wilderness. I mean he managed for forty days and forty nights, but did he have a good time? Did he send a postcard home saying, 'Wish you were here, the weather is fabulous'? No. He was miserable. If he'd had a fortnight in a stationary caravan at Cleethorpes there'd be no such thing as Lent.[239]

Jackie   Well I think it's very nice – I'm going to get the stove out and make some supper. We don't need all that space above our heads anyway – we'll only be lying down.

Victoria   That's true. And if you sleep chest down we can drop it another foot.

After supper. Victoria and Jackie are sitting in front of the tent.

---

239 Cut from 'At least it's up' to here.

Victoria	That was good, wasn't it? *(She looks at the empty packet.)* I never knew that.
Jackie	What?
Victoria	If you dehydrate pasta whirls with cheese sauce and vegetables, put it in a packet, take it out of the packet, add back the water and cook it –
Jackie	Yeah?
Victoria	You get grout.
Jackie	Do you? I thought you got that from drinking port.
Victoria	Shall we get sorted before it gets dark? Have you got the bedrolls?
Jackie	*(rooting in the rucksack)* Yep. White or granary.
Victoria	Bedrolls.
Jackie	No, I haven't got them.
Victoria	I told you to get them out of the back of the car.
Jackie	Sorry. What are they?
Victoria	They go under the sleeping bags. If you haven't got them it's very painful going to sleep.
Jackie	Why?
Victoria	Because A, the ground is very hard, and B, the person who forgot them is going to get kicked all night.
Jackie	I bet they didn't have bedrolls in Whatsits and Amazons.
Victoria	They had palliasses. *(They look at each other.)* Don't ask.

The next morning. It is raining hard, and Victoria and Jackie are sitting in the tent opening, looking out at the weather.

Jackie	Do you think it's going to stop?
Victoria	No.
Jackie	Is there enough blue to make a sailor a pair of trousers?
Victoria	There isn't enough to make him a pair of popsox. If he wants grey trousers we could manage it.
Jackie	This is really depressing.
Victoria	Oh don't moan. We'll wait ten minutes, right?

Jackie	What then?
Victoria	Then we'll moan. Oh let's pack up and get going, shall we?
Jackie	All right. Let's just finish the crossword, shall we? *(She picks up yesterday's* Mirror. *Victoria groans.)* Nine across – where Stanley found Livingstone.
Victoria	The chippy? The lost property office? Freeman Hardy and Willis by the laces?
Jackie	Don't know. I'll leave that. Eight down: Grace Darling's father kept one.
Victoria	Scrapbook.
Jackie	Doesn't fit.
Victoria	Lighthouse.
Jackie	That's right! How did you know?
Victoria	Have you never heard of Grace Darling?
Jackie	She was in *High Society* with Bing Crosby.[240] Twelve down: location of football's 'Accies'.
Victoria	Partick Thistle.
Jackie	Why?
Victoria	Because it's always Partick Thistle in crosswords. Put it in.
Jackie	Shall I?
Victoria	Yes, come on, I want to go. *(She starts to undo the tent.)*
Jackie	There's too many letters.
Victoria	Well write small.

Later on. Victoria and Jackie are trudging along a deserted road. They are very wet.

Victoria	Jackie – even if we get to the campsite we don't know how to put the tent up.
Jackie	We'll ask some boys – it'll be good fun.

---

240 Cut from 'Nine across' to here.

Victoria	Boys? I'm thirty-six. Who do you think I am? Mrs Robinson?[241]
Jackie	No.
Victoria	You don't know who I'm talking about, do you?
Jackie	Yes I do. Mrs Robinson.
Victoria	Who is she then?
Jackie	Margaret Thatcher's mother – so squash!
Victoria	We've got nothing to sleep on, Jackie – I'm not spending another night like last night; I've got to sleep in a bed. We could use your cash and go to a hotel.
Jackie	You said just bring enough for two days' chocolate.
Victoria	I thought that would be at least 150 quid.[242]
Jackie	Well let's hitch back to the car and go home.
Victoria	Home? Jackie – we're backpacking – we're on the road. Good golly, have a bit of British grit, woman. We've got to see this thing through. Look at Sherpa Tensing and Hillary.
Jackie	Who are they?
Victoria	A magic act.
Jackie	Well if we're not going home, and we can't afford a hotel, we'll have to go to that youth hostel.
Victoria	Jackie – I have been in a youth hostel. I know what they're like. You are put in a kitchen with seventeen venture scouts with behavioural difficulties and made to wash swedes. You are locked out in all weathers from ten o'clock in the morning till eight o'clock[243] at night and only admitted if you know all the harmony to 'Row Row Row Your Boat Gently Down the Stream'; the toast is made three days in advance and if anybody finds a raisin in their muesli they get a round of applause. And

---

241 The older woman, played by Anne Bancroft, with whom Dustin Hoffman's character has an affair in *The Graduate*.

242 Cut from 'We could use your cash' to here.

243 Changed to 'ten o'clock'.

	no matter where you are in the building somebody somewhere is singing 'The Happy Wanderer'.
Jackie	Well it's that or trying to put the tent up.
Victoria	*(singing)* Val de ree . . .
Jackie	Ha ha ha ha ha . . .
Victoria	Val de rah . . .
Jackie	Ha ha ha ha ha . . .
Victoria	Val de ree . . .
Jackie	Ha ha ha ha ha . . .
Victoria	Val de rah ha ha ha . . .

The approach to the youth hostel. Victoria and Jackie are limping up to the front door. It's wet.[244]

Victoria	Course, they've probably changed a lot since I stayed in one. I should think they're probably run more like hotels now.
Jackie	Oh yes. Everything very simple and plain.
Victoria	*(pressing the bell)* But very hospitable and welcoming.

The door is flung open by upper-class woman, Susan, dressed in hiking boots, floral summer dress, and quilted body warmer, with wild greying hair. Years of running a youth hostel have driven her slightly mad.

Susan	Can't you read? Are you quite blind? We're not not not open until six o'clock. This is not a hotel – I'm getting increasingly peeved by this persistent inability to grasp the roles of the establishment. Now shoo away with you. You may not loiter by the porch or verandah; if the weather worsens you may stand behind the gazebo and

---

244 Added:
   Jackie: How long do you have to wait for a hip operation?
   Victoria: My knickers are doing it again now.
   Jackie: Are they?

in cases of epilepsy or appendicitis you may oscillate the kitchen doorbell and request the telephone number of the nearest dental surgeon. Never, never ring this bell again, and cease leaning against the architrave; your mug is scratching the paintwork.

She slams the door.

Jackie   Are you going to let her speak to you like that?
Victoria   Yes.
Jackie   *(catching sight of Susan through a nearby window and dashing to it)* Quick – let's try again!

Jackie taps on the window. Susan looks at her.

Could we just come in for a moment?
Susan   *(whipping the window open)* Say again?
Jackie   If we could just come in for a minute –
Susan   Do I have to elucidate yet further? I am not the Statue of Liberty and as printed quite clearly in the handbook this establishment is closed closed closed from ten o'clock in the morning until six o'clock at night.[245] I am driven to near-madness by this unceasing insubordination and relentless stupidity on the part of people who are quite quite quite old enough to know better and who persist in treating these premises as if they were an hotel of the deluxe class. If I have any more examples of this contin-ual harassment I shall telephone the National Trust. Is that clear?

She bangs the window shut and moves away.

Victoria   Come on! Round the back! Head her off! Quick.

---

245 Cut from 'as printed quite clearly' to here.

They run round the side of the house to the kitchen door at the back of the hostel. Victoria and Jackie see Susan in the huge empty kitchen. They wave.

Victoria   Hey!

Susan   *(flinging open the door)* And?

Victoria   If we could just have a word with you?

Susan   This is not the Oxford Debating Society and I am not Dame Sybil Thorndike[246] – there will be no indoor conversation out of hours stated, and any emergency chatter must be conducted through the drying room hatchway without boots. Has that clocked or have I to drawing-pin another memo? *(She pronounces it 'meemo'.[247])*

Jackie   Well, can we book a bed for tonight or something?

Susan   The dormitories are at top chock capacity – as it is I have had to place two inflatable mattresses in the Ping-Pong Lounge. There may possibly be a top bunk going a-begging at the Greywalls Hostel thirteen miles across the valley.[248] Now please go hither and yon – we have a lecture this evening and I am up to my shoulder bag with stress and confusion.

Victoria   We've come for the lecture.

Susan   I crave your pardon?

Jackie   Yes – we're here for the lecture.

Susan   You're here to give the lecture?

Jackie   Yes.

Susan   You're Miss Gough and Miss Calthwaite?

Jackie   Yes.

Susan   *(standing back welcomingly)* Come in, my dear girls – I didn't expect you so early. *(They take off their rucksacks.)* Come along – this is marvellous – I insist you have a

---

246 Pillar of the English stage for whom George Bernard Shaw wrote *Saint Joan*.

247 As in *Over to Pam*.

248 Cut from 'as it is' to here.

hot cup of tea straightaway. Yes, a hot cup of tea and a Bakewell Segment! Connie!

They go in.

Inside, Susan's private drawing room, faded chintz etc, Jackie and Victoria are relaxing with a tray of tea.

Victoria	Yes, but what are we going to do when the real people turn up!
Jackie	She's not going to turn us away now – we'll just say it was a mistake.
Victoria	Aren't there any more chocolate biscuits?
Jackie	*(surprised)* Oh no, they're all gone. Funny, mmm, anyway, she's not going to throw us out into the night even if she's cross, is she?
Victoria	Course she is – she's barmy. Tuh. There's only fruit cake left now.
Jackie	It's very nice fruit cake.
Victoria	It's not very nice. It's the sort you have to buy on the train when they've run out of sandwiches.

The phone rings.

Jackie	Where's she gone; did she say?
Victoria	She's upper-class – she could be anywhere. Probably out machine-gunning pheasants.
Jackie	Peasants?
Victoria	More than likely.[249] Oh answer it, Jackie.
Jackie	*(picking the phone up)* Hello? Could you just hold on a moment? It's Elizabeth Gough! They're just about to catch their train!
Victoria	Tell her it's cancelled.
Jackie	The train?

---

249 This and the preceding line were cut.

Victoria	The lecture. Then they won't come and we won't get found out.
Jackie	Hello, Miss Gough – I'm afraid the lecture has had to be cancelled . . . yes, it's this terrible weather. The roads are practically blocked, practically . . . oh I'm sure we will, as soon as the floods die down, yes we'll be in touch – well I'm speaking from the roof, so . . . thanks very much for phoning, so sorry – bye!
Victoria	Brilliant, Jackie. We can relax, have a nice evening. Bit of ping-pong – whip-whap.
Jackie	What about the lecture?
Victoria	Well it's been cancelled, hasn't it? They're not coming.
Jackie	They're already here: we're them.
Victoria	Oh blimey. You'll have to give a lecture.
Jackie	Me?
Victoria	Yep.
Jackie	I can't do it.
Victoria	Why not?
Jackie	I'm tired – I haven't the strength.
Victoria	Tired? You've just had seventeen chocolate biscuits, you should be tossing the Telecom tower from hand to hand.
Jackie	What is it anyway? The lecture. What's it on?
Victoria	Oh cripes, Jackie. Come on – we'll go and find a poster. *(They dash out.)*

At the youth hostel's main entrance: a large space with a closed shop, reception desk etc. Victoria and Jackie are scrutinising a large noticeboard covered in info.

Victoria	Got it! Sunday lectures.
Jackie	What's tonight's?
Victoria	They're all written in a circle, it hasn't got any dates on. 'Tales of the Hebrides' – did she sound Scottish?
Jackie	No. 'Nursing for Men': it's probably not that either.
Victoria	'Travels with a Harp' – lecture and recital: can't be that or she would have said, 'Where's your harp?' wouldn't she?

Jackie	What does that leave? 'Survival', exclamation mark.
Victoria	'The Russ Conway Years'[250].
Jackie	And 'Herbs for Health and Beauty'.
Victoria	What did she sound like on the phone? Camomile tea-ish, or as if she'd just come down the Eiger on a tea-tray, or what?
Jackie	She just sounds ordinary.
Victoria	Was she humming 'Sidesaddle'?
Jackie	No. *(They stare at each other hopelessly.)*

Susan bustles in.

Susan	Ah, there you are!
Victoria	We were just admiring your noticeboard.
Susan	We're very thrilled. Plywood. Now I'm off to supervise supper, but do feel free to dally in the environs.
Victoria	Have the lectures been going well?
Susan	Very. 'Nursing for Men' and the harp recital[251] were particularly enjoyable – but I feel tonight's will be very special. But then it is, as you know, a mini-obsession of mine. Do call for more tea if you would like any.
Jackie	Do you have herb tea?
Susan	Oh yes – are you interested in herbs?
Victoria	Erm –
Susan	I've a lecture in October on herbs.
Victoria	Ah! *(She whistles a bit of 'Sidesaddle'.)*
Susan	Is that dear old Eddie Elgar? *(She checks her watch.)* Ah – I must fly fly fly, I'm afraid I have no ear for music whatsoever – *(running off)* 7.30 in the Activity Bay! Connie!
Jackie	It must be 'Survival', exclamation mark – she just said she's practically tone deaf.
Victoria	Since when has that stopped anyone enjoying Russ Conway?

---

250 Pianist whose most popular composition was 'Side Saddle'.
251 Changed to 'travels with the harp'.

Inside the hostel TV room. There is a small stage at one end with Jackie and Victoria sitting on it. Susan is in mid-address to a small group of hearty hikers.

Susan   So if washers-up could please please please remember the kitchen segment must be vacated, cloths aired, by 9.10 at the latest. And in case anyone failed to get a slip in their packed lunch today, cocoa privileges have been withdrawn indefinitely. When we can trust hostellers not to write offensive remarks in the skin, they may possibly be reinstated. *(Cheering up)* Now – it is a very great thrill for me to introduce tonight's lecturers: Miss Gough and Miss Calthwaite are no strangers to youth hostelling, but they really hit the outward-bound headlines when they undertook to live for sixteen weeks on the remote island of Och na Peig in the Outer Hebrides off Miss Calthwaite's native Scotland.

Victoria   *(mouthing to Jackie)* That's you.

Susan   Armed only with the bare minimum of provisions, Miss Gough and Miss Calthwaite's story of that testing time is at once plucky *(they pull appropriate faces)* heartwarming, amusing and yet very, very serious. Miss Gough and Miss Calthwaite!

Leading the applause, she steps down and sits eagerly nearby. Victoria stands.

Victoria   Thank you. Well, I don't know about Morag here, but I think my worst moment came three weeks into the experiment: we hadn't eaten for six days, we were cold, damp and morale was decidedly low. Then I happened upon quite a sizeable red squirrel native to Och na Peig. Killing it was no problem – I used the hypnosis and rubber band garotte technique – Morag'll be explaining that in full a little bit later – but the most almighty row blew up. I wanted to grill it with pine cones and Morag insisted on slipping it into her kagool to keep the chill off her kidneys. But perhaps we should start at the beginning. Morag!

Victoria sits. Jackie stands.

Jackie   *(in a Scottish accent)* It was a cold wet February morning when Elizabeth Gough and I stepped out of the dinghy and looked at the bare rock that was to be our home for the next 112 days . . .

Later on, hikers are milling about eagerly discussing the lecture. Victoria and Jackie are talking to Susan.[252]

Susan   So inspiring! Really. When you fended off the rabid seal with the rubber glove.
Victoria   It had to be done.
Susan   And I certainly never realised bladderwrack could be so appetising, Morag . . .
Jackie   Och yes!

Susan claps her hands.

Susan   Lights out in half an hour, people!
Victoria   Yes, we'll be glad to get to bed, won't we?
Jackie   Actually, Elizabeth and I almost prefer the bare rock to a mattress these days!
Susan   Yes, I thought that: I'd already decided not to insult you by offering you bed and board here.
Victoria   No it's all right –
Susan   I wouldn't be so insensitive. But do please please pitch your tent anywhere in the grounds. I can't promise you your particular favourite seagull, but we have limitless

---

252 Added:
   Victoria: Very glad you enjoyed it.

nettles and I daresay you'll happen upon the odd nutritious little vole! Now where is your tackle? Connie?

That night on the hostel lawn. The tent is in bits as before. Victoria and Jackie are staring at it.

Victoria   Right, Jackie. Take Tube A and apply to Bracket D with flange channel outermost . . .

STAYING IN

Inside Victoria's living room. It is night and the room is lit by television set only, so only thing to be seen is a sofa with Victoria on it, watching TV. A brief shot of a TV picture shows a blonde woman opening a door; then back to Victoria.

TV soundtrack
male voice I came to return your coffee
Female voice So I see. Do you always carry jars of coffee stark naked?
Male voice When it's Café Blend, who needs underpants?[253]

The phone rings. Victoria presses the remote control to cut off TV sound and answers it.

Victoria Hello? Hello, Jane![254] *(To us)* Bossy friend! I'm watching television. It's a film with James Robertson Justice, Joan Sims, Hattie Jacques and Norman Wisdom.[255] Who directed it? Ingmar Bergman. *(To us)* She's an intellectual – it's a shame.

---

253 A celebrated series of ads for Gold Blend had been running for two years when VW wrote this. She would return to spoofing coffee commercials in *ADB* with a brand called Romany Roast. She also fronted a genuine ad for Maxwell House.

254 Jane was based on a university friend of VW's.

255 This film starring the cream of popular actors from the 1950s doesn't actually exist.

What sort of party? A cocktail party. Of course I don't want to go to a cocktail party; it's number two on my list of things I never want to do. Eh? Sharing a jacuzzi with Mrs Thatcher, and number one is plumbing it in . . . I don't want to go, Jane. Because if I wanted to stand around with a load of people I don't know eating bits of cold toast I can get caught shoplifting and go to Holloway . . . I know I never go out – that's because I have a nice time staying in. There isn't a cocktail party in the world that can compete with a baked potato and the *Antiques Roadshow* . . . Well you may not find it stimulating, but the expression on the face of some avaricious old bat who's just been told her Rubens is from the British Home Stores gets my pulse up till at least Tuesday. Yes, yes, yes. *(To audience)* Now she's saying it's about time I mixed with people of a higher mental calibre like the ones at this party.

Yes I know. I know I've got a degree. Why does that mean I have to spend my time with intellectuals? I've got a life-saving certificate but I don't spend my evenings diving for a rubber brick with my pyjamas on . . . I haven't got anything to wear . . . It's got baked potato down it . . . Well I haven't . . . I don't know when I last went to one, but I remember when people danced, the breeze from their loon pants kept blowing the joss sticks out . . . A party dress? I haven't worn a party dress since they gave you a bit of cake to take home in a serviette. Anyway, I'm not going, Jane, thank you . . . Will you take no for an answer . . . ? Well, will you take *(raspberry)* for an answer . . . ? It's the same answer but not so easy to spell. *(To audience)* Now she's saying she's got nobody else to go with . . .

You've got millions of friends. They can't all be skiing, the Alps would tip over. All right, well it better be good. I've got to go. Norman Wisdom's standing on the edge of a swimming pool and I can't imagine what's going to happen next. Bye. *(She puts the phone down.)* Bum! *(She turns TV sound back up.)*

TV soundtrack Aaaargh! *(Splosh!)*

A street of grand detached houses at night. Inside Jane's car, Jane is doing last minute make-up adjustments. Victoria is sitting in the front passenger seat. Jane is elegant and bespectacled and rather brisk.

Jane I honestly don't see why you're so apprehensive. It's only a party.

Victoria I don't know anybody. I'm shy. I know you consider it a wasted week if you haven't shared cheese straws with at least twenty-three total strangers but I like to be with people I know.

Jane Like Norman Wisdom.

Victoria If Jimmy Edwards is busy, then yes.

Jane Anybody would think you'd never been to a party.

Victoria I've been to them. I've been to many a teenage party where the boys would be sick in the garden and the girls would dig it into the herbaceous border with a spaghetti spoon.

Jane I hope that won't happen tonight.

Victoria Well I've brought one just in case. But the best one was when I actually ended up in the spare room under the coats with an apprentice fitter called Martin.

Jane That was good?

Victoria Except they were maxi coats. After twenty minutes we had to be lifted clear by the fire brigade.

Jane Well; Moira is famous for her Christmas parties.

Victoria Moira?[256]

Jane Yes, Moira! Anything wrong?

Victoria No. *(She pulls a face. Jane doesn't see.)*

---

256 Pronounced 'Mwahra'.

Jane	This is my first invitation – I'm very honoured. She's very intelligent, cultured, musical and I would say an inspired and very creative hostess.
Victoria	So we won't be doing the hokey-cokey.
Jane	You go and ring the bell – I'm not entirely happy with my lip-line. Shan't be a moment.
Victoria	OK.

She gets out of the car and goes towards a grand Georgian house with a Christmas wreath on the front door. She rings the door bell. Moira, an extremely well preserved fifty, flings the door open welcomingly. Her face drops when it's nobody she recognises.

Moira	Carols?
Victoria	Sorry?
Moira	Well one verse only, please. *(She pauses.)* Come on, 'Once in Royal David's City', chip chop.
Victoria	*(singing)* Once in Royal David's city
	Stood a lowly cattle shed
	Where a mother laid her baby
	In a manger for his bed.
	Mary was –
Moira	Thank you so much. Do drop by another time and give me the dénouement. *(She makes to shut the door, then stops as Jane joins Victoria.)* Jane! How lovely! *(They kiss.)*
Jane	Moira. This is the friend I told you about.
Moira	Oh is it. The comedienne! I see. *(She decides not to pursue it.)* Well, come in – let the merrymaking commence. Ha ha. *(She stands back to let them in.)* Ailsa will take your coats. She used to live in a cardboard box, you know!

The entrance hall, leading through to a large drawing room: very House and Garden. *Victoria and Jane are handing over their coats to Ailsa, the young Scottish housekeeper.*

Victoria	Thanks.
Jane	Now just go in and be yourself.
Victoria	I wasn't going to go in as Al Jolson.[257]
Jane	No, but throw yourself into the party, really let yourself go; jokes, routines – people will love it.

A small Philippino waitress proffers a tray of drinks. They each take one.

Victoria	Thanks.
Jane	(*speaking as if the waitress were senile and deaf*) Thank you. Is this champagne?
Waitress	(*thinking*) Merry Christmas. (*She leaves.*)
Jane	Now I'm going to seek out Moira – there's a little career move I think she may be able to help me with. Why don't you start with that group over there? Go and introduce yourself.

She pushes Victoria into a group of two men and two women in the doorway. She hovers by them; they smile but continue with their conversation.

First man	Of course, the marvellous thing about investing in sheltered housing is that you're never going to run out of old people.
Second man	Renewable resource, ah ha.
First woman	I don't think people are as old these days, do you?
Second woman	Do you know, I'd never thought of that.
Second man	Oh I think people are living longer, Dulcie, don't you?
Second woman	Well you say that, Gerald, but you look in the *Daily Telegraph*; you'll still see an awful lot of deaths.
First woman	Even quite poor old people go to Spain for weeks and weeks in the winter now.

---

257 Vaudevillean star of *The Jazz Singer*, the first talking picture.

First man   I believe so.

Second woman Now I never knew that, Hilary.

First woman   Oh yes. Months and months for threepence a week practically.

Second woman Nice places, or . . . ?

First woman   Oh no. Nowhere one would want to go oneself . . . It was on the television. I was only half attending, I was waiting for the wildlife programme.

First man   Yes, we don't view a tremendous amount, but David Attenborough I do not like to miss.

First woman   Yes, he communicates so well.

Second man   He's a first-rate communicator, no doubt about it.

First woman   Apparently he's related to Richard Attenborough.

Second woman Now, I never knew that Hilary.

First woman   Oh yes. I think they were at school together.

Moira whizzes in.

Moira   Everybody hunkydory?

First man   Super show, Moira.

Second woman Lovely party.

First woman   Gorgeous tree. Did you dress it?

Moira   No, I simply ordered fistfuls of tartan ribbon and set the Philippinos on to it.

Second woman It's very effective.

First woman   Yes, because it's Christmas and yet Scottish.

Moira   Well that was a little gesture for Ailsa, she's from 'overr therr borrderr' as they say up there. She used to live in a cardboard box you know.

Second woman How marvellous.

Moira   Have you all met? Gerald, Hilary, Dulcie, Charles, this is Victoria. She's a comedienne! Yes! On telly. Now you must excuse me. I must just check . . . there's the most marvellous man – I shall bring him over in two ticks – his name's Jim and he's a miner! Yes!

Second woman I don't know where you find them, Moira.

Moira	I know! I surprise myself sometimes! Excuse me.

She bustles off. There is a slight pause.

First woman	So you're a comedian?
Victoria	Yes.
First woman	*(as she turns)* I don't think I've ever met a comedian, have I, Gerald?
Second man	Who was that chap in Barbados, then?
First woman	He was a plasterer.
Second man	So he was.
Second woman	How extraordinary!
First man	On television, eh?
Victoria	Yes.
First man	One thing I've always wanted to know . . .
Victoria	Yes?
First man	I've never met anybody who could tell me this . . .
Victoria	Yes.
First man	What happens to the prizes they *don't* win? What do they do – send them back?
Second man	And are those David Attenborough's own safari jackets?

A deserted part of the entrance hall. Victoria is skulking about. Alan, a huge, bull-necked, aggressive Yorkshireman, detaches himself from the crowd and joins her.[258]

Alan	Sickening, bloody sickening.
Victoria	I beg your pardon?
Alan	Southern parasites. Licking the fat of the land while the north lies dying. Close the conservatory door, lad, there's bones inside.

---

258 'This is Colin Welland,' VW wrote on a note attached to Jim Broadbent's script. An actor and writer best known for the Oscar-winning screenplay for *Chariots of Fire*, Welland was instrumental in founding a rugby league club in Fulham, which is very close to Chiswick.

Victoria	Nice tree.
Alan	Are you from the north?
Victoria	Yes.
Alan	I can tell. There's a pain behind the eyes, a sob in the voice. I never marched from Jarrow but those men's feet ache in my heart.
Victoria	What are you getting for Christmas?
Alan	What's any Northerner getting? Misery, hopelessness, an empty selection box and a rotten orange.
Victoria	I'm getting stabilisers for my bike!
Alan	*(coming out of his reverie)* Alan Hammond! Yorkshire-man, writer, surgeon. My pen's my scalpel. I'm excising the cancer of complacency and I don't give a toss about post-operative complications.
Victoria	You write plays, don't you?
Alan	I write the truth. I write the misery, the hopelessness, the empty selection box.
Victoria	Mm.
Alan	OK – I write plays. But do you know what I write them for?
Victoria	The money?
Alan	The people. The dockers, the railwaymen – the north. I love it. I love it! I feel passionately about it. They're choking it to death and I'm saying, 'Rage, rage against the dying of the light,' because they're killing it. They're letting it die – my north.
Victoria	Whereabouts do you live?
Alan	Chiswick.

Moira swoops down on them.

Moira	Now this is very mischievous of you, skulking away out here like a sculpture – now follow me. *(She leads them away.)* Everyone's dying to meet you both. I've been telling everyone about your new play, Alan – what was it called again?

Alan	*Buttocks.*
Moira	So t'was. *(She stops and drops Victoria off at a chaise longue with Judith and Julia on it.)* Now this is Victoria – she's a comedienne! On telly! Yes! Julia and Judith, by the way. Now have you had Jim, the miner?
Julia	Yes – he was sweet.
Moira	Yes, isn't he? And surprisingly clean, I thought. Now I have a rock star somewhere for you to meet later and I shall bring Alan back in a moment. He wrote that marvellous play with the slag heap.
Judith	That does sound fun.
Moira	Come along, Alan. *(She has a sudden thought.)* You've had Jim the miner?
Julia	We've had the miner, but not the rock star.
Moira	I shall bring him forthwith. Pip pip.

Judith and Julia make a space between them for Victoria. She sits.

Judith	So you're in showbusiness? Gosh!
Victoria	Yes.
Julia	I should think it's jolly hard work, isn't it?
Victoria	Yes.
Judith	But fun?
Victoria	Yes.
Julia	Yes, jolly hard work but lots of fun.
Victoria	Yes.
Julia	Marvellous. *(Pause.)* Did you ever meet Dickie Henderson?[259]
Victoria	No.
Julia	He always seemed very nice, I thought.
Victoria	Yes.
Judith	Was he the one with the handbag?

---

259 Popular performer who started out in music hall and, from 1958, starred in ITV's *The Dickie Henderson Show*.

Julia	No, that was Eric Morecambe.
Judith	Eric Morecambe?
Julia	Of 'The Two Ronnies'.
Judith	Ah yes.
Julia	Did I hear Moira say you were a comedienne?
Victoria	Yes.
Judith	But you don't actually tell jokes?
Victoria	Yes.
Judith	Good heavens!

A pause.

Julia   Now I saw something that was supposed to be funny – what was it? – there was a very tall man, and a little foreign waiter in some sort of hotel.

Victoria 'Fawlty Towers.'

Julia   That's right. My cousin said, you must watch it, it's set in Torquay; but I saw about twenty minutes and quite frankly it could have been set anywhere. What a shambles!

A pause.

We really only have television for the news and the wild-life programmes.

Judith   And the nanny!

Julia   *(in her idea of a northern accent)* Nanny couldn't do without t'telly!

Judith   I do think David Attenborough's the most marvellous communicator.

Julia   Yes, he radiates enthusiasm.

Victoria leaves the sofa; they don't notice.

Judith	And I would imagine he's a tremendously nice man.[260]

A staircase rising from the hall. Victoria is sitting alone by some potted palms. Jane runs up.

Jane	There you are!
Victoria	Hello.
Jane	You're supposed to be mingling.
Victoria	I've mingled.
Jane	Well mingle some more.
Victoria	I'm no good at it.
Jane	What would you do if everybody came out and sat on the stairs?
Victoria	I'd hutch up.
Jane	I bring you to this beautiful house, the cream of café society; I do think the least you could do is make an effort to sparkle and not lurk in the greenery like a wallaby. Now I must find Moira; her husband could be rather useful to me. But I shall be checking up on you, so get back in there and effervesce!
Victoria	Mer mer mer.
Jane	What did you say?
Victoria	Nothing.

She plods downstairs under Jane's watchful eye to rejoin the party.

A busy part of the drawing room. A group comprising Dulcie, Hilary, Charles, Gerald and others is in full cry. It is some drinks later. Victoria hoves in, madly smiling.

Victoria	*(in a voice similar to theirs)* Hello! Marvellous party!
Dulcie	Yes, isn't it?

---

260 Added:
   Julia: You can always tell.

Victoria	I was admiring the tree earlier.
Hilary	Apparently one of Moira's little Philippinos did it.
Victoria	How marvellous!
Dulcie	I was just saying, I wish we could run to a Philippino. Moira says they work all the hours God sends and all on little bits of leftovers!
Victoria	Good heavens.
Hilary	I'm sure we met earlier but I haven't a clue what you do – isn't that awful?
Charles	Hilary's supped bloody well and not very wisely!
Hilary	Rotter.
Dulcie	We were just discussing kitchens. Are you into kitchens?
Victoria	Yes, I've just had a new one put in.
Dulcie	Oh, who did it? Crummets of Winchester?
Victoria	No, I met the man from Crummets of Winchester but I thought he had flimsy knobs so I plumped for Withy's of Totnes.

A general chorus of 'Withy's of Totnes, they're the best, how marvellous' etc.

Gerald	Withy's are not cheap.
Victoria	No, they're not cheap but they do do the whole thing for you and really I think sixty-five thousand pounds is worth it because you never have to meet the labourers.
Charles	What is it, pine?
Victoria	We pondered over distressed teak, but we wanted a farm-housey feel so we edged back to pine. And where we live is very rural so . . .
Hilary	Oh, where's that?
Victoria	It's a little village just off the Kingston by-pass.
Dulcie	Oh lovely! And Withy's of Totnes use genuine old pine don't they?
Victoria	Oh yes. All from old buildings. You flick through the brochure, see a church or chapel you particularly like, and they demolish it for you.

Gerald   Yes, that's very good, isn't it?

Moira comes in with Kevin, a young, Phil Collins type rock star.

Moira   Now this is Kevin. He's a rock star! Yes! Three number one records in America.

Kevin   *(shyly)* Hello.

Charles   We've had Kevin, actually.

Moira   Oh, you've had Kevin. In that case I shall take Kevin away pronto? Have you had Jim the miner.

Dulcie   Oh no, we haven't had a miner.

Moira   Well, I shall deliver Kevin elsewhere and bring you Jim the miner. He paints welders! Everyone all right for *hors d'oeuvres?*

There are cries of 'delicious'.

Moira   My housekeeper made them. Ailsa. She used to live in a cardboard box, you know. Right – come on, Kevin, I'll swop you with Jim . . . and I did have a comedienne somewhere . . .

Dulcie   That sounds fun.

Moira   Yes, doesn't it. She'll be telling jokes later and Kevin will be singing! *(She drags him away.)*

Kevin   Well that's a bit difficult actually . . .

Charles   Well, call me old-fashioned but I don't like to see a woman telling jokes.

Hilary   Charles thinks women aren't funny.

Gerald   Well, I'm sorry; I agree.

Hilary   But there are hundreds of funny women. There's the woman who does the column in the *Sunday Telegraph* for a kick-off.

Charles   Well you name me a funny woman who's attractive with it.

Dulcie   Attractive narrows it down.

Charles   You see.

Hilary   Got it!

Charles   A funny woman you wouldn't kick out of bed?

Hilary   Felicity Kendal!

Dulcie   Oh, Felicity Kendal.

Hilary   She's so sweet, isn't she?

Gerald   She makes *me* laugh.

Dulcie   So funny in that thing with the man from the other thing.

Hilary   And I always imagine that she's a tremendously nice person.

Victoria   Oh yes.

Dulcie   Do you know her?

Victoria   Yes I do – and do you know, she makes all David Attenborough's safari jackets.

Moira comes back in with Jim, a fiftyish small, sweet little man.

Hilary   How lovely.

Moira   Are you the people who hadn't had Jim?

Gerald   Yes – we'd had Kevin –

Moira   The rock star – but you hadn't had Jim. And have you had Alan?

Charles   Alan?

Moira   The playwright. He's having the most tremendous success with his clever *Buttocks*.[261]

Charles   No, he hasn't reached us yet.

Moira   Well, he's edging through the throng your way, and he's very kindly offered to give us all an extract from his *Buttocks* a little later on. So this is Jim – he's a miner and he also paints pictures of welders – isn't that cunning? Do excuse me.

---

261 Changed to 'his very clever *Buttocks*'.

Moira goes out. Jim stands sheepishly.

Hilary	So how's life down t'pit?
Jim	My old pit's closed down actually. I pretty much paint for a living now.
Dulcie	I suppose a lot of pits have closed down, have they?
Jim	A fair few.
Dulcie	I suppose there's not the demand for coal that there was.
Jim	No, maybe not.
Dulcie	I suppose what has happened is we don't really need coal now we've got electricity.
Jim	Mm.
Jane	*(coming in)* Hilary!
Hilary	Jane! *(They kiss.)* What do you think of the party?
Jane	I'm having a splendid time. Are you?
Hilary	We were thinking of moving on, actually. Eleanor Spencer's starts at nine and she supposedly has Morris dancers and at least one Dimbleby.
Jane	Oh but you must stay for our alternative comedienne – *(She looks at Victoria.)*
Victoria	Oh, who is that, Jane? I hope she's not one of those terrible feminists holding the government up to ridicule.
Jane	Could I have a word with you?
Victoria	Yes, do excuse me. *(Being dragged away)* So thrilled to meet you, Jim – you must show me your Davey lamp . . .²⁶²

In the plush cloakroom, Jane faces Victoria angrily.

Jane	What on earth were you doing?
Victoria	I was mingling and effervescing. I was doing jolly well, I thought.
Jane	And did you tell them you were a comedienne?

---

262 Added:

Dulcie: We were just discussing Felicity Kendal.

Victoria	No. It doesn't work. Either the conversation grinds to a halt or they tell you some long story about a dog being run over and say, 'Now that would make a jolly good sketch!' So I decided to just fit in with everybody else.
Jane	You're not supposed to be fitting in.
Victoria	Why not? I got in enough trouble for clutching the banisters.
Jane	Because you are supposed to be a novelty.
Victoria	What do you mean?
Jane	I needed an invitation to this party because I'm trying to deal with Moira's husband; I was invited on the understanding that I brought with me a raunchy, anarchic, foul-mouthed, alternative comedienne.
Victoria	Why?
Jane	Because the one Moira had found had dropped out to play Dick Whittington in Windsor.
Victoria	Right.
Jane	Which is why I thought of you.
Victoria	Right.
Jane	And if you don't get out there and launch into the old men's willies and Thatcher routine you're going to put me in an impossible position.
Victoria	Right.
Jane	If I let Moira down, I haven't a hope of pulling off this deal with her husband.
Victoria	They're getting divorced.
Jane	How do you know?
Victoria	One of the Philippinos told me.
Jane	You don't talk to Philippinos – you hand them your used cutlery. Oh. So Moira's not a blind bit of use to me anyway.
Victoria	Isn't she?
Jane	*(looking at her watch)* Well I may as well slip straight round to Eleanor Spencer's. I shan't be driving you home, all right? Bye. *(She leaves.)*

Victoria	*(thinking)* Bye. She wasn't very nice was she, boys and girls?

In the drawing room Alan is holding forth to a bemused group; Judith, Julia and others. The party is thinning out. In a corner is Kevin showing Victoria and Jim photos of his baby. In the background Moira is calling despairingly to leaving guests.

Moira	Must you go? It's barely nine. We're having a play-reading and rock singing and raunchy comedy . . . Oh well, Merry Christmas anyway.
Alan	Writing's not an art with me. It's a job. A craft. I graft at it. They call me a writer, but I'm really a grafter; I'm a lathe operative, turning words. I'm a panel beater, hammering sentences into shape . . . I'm a master baker –
Julia	That's fascinating. And have you ever worked with Felicity Kendal?
Moira	*(directing Philippinos)* Yes, chairs round the piano, Doris, please. Chip chop, Phoebe. Everybody! *(She claps.)* Now you all know Alan Hammond's *Buttocks*. Yes? Well, he's very kindly offered to perform one half for you this evening, so gather round; then we'll have some very alternative comedy, followed by lovely, lovely rock singing and then Jim our little miner will be doing instant portraits in the orangery. So get a drink and settle down.

A general kerfuffle.

Victoria	Did you offer to do portraits, Jim?
Jim	Did I heck! Anyway, I can't do noses. That's why I paint welders.
Kevin	He's twelve weeks old here. You can see he's completely different to what he was at eleven weeks.
Victoria	Ah, he's sweet.
Moira	Lights down, Doris please. *(The lights dim. Alan takes*

up a position in front of the seated guests.) Mr Alan Hammond and his *Buttocks.*

Moira stands to one side attentively.

Alan The stage is in darkness. The silence is broken by the noise of an eighteen-stone riveter retching into a rusty bucket. *(Murmurs of distaste.)* Lights up to reveal Spud, a mentally defective window cleaner, naked except for a bobble hat and fingerless gloves. He speaks. (I want my mam! Mam! Why did they put you in that box, Mam? Why were you so cold, Mam? Mam! I don't like it on my own. They're giving me funny looks, Mam. And I can't find my underpants . . .)

Jim I can't stand much more of this.

Victoria Nor me.

Kevin It's you next.

Victoria I'm not doing it, are you?

Kevin Well – I don't know how to say no.

Victoria Let's hide.

Kevin Where?

Victoria I know. Follow me.

They creep out behind floorlength curtains. Rustles and uncomfortable coughs from audience.

Alan Enter Lana, a one-legged prostitute from Tiger Bay. *(In Cardiff accent)* All right, lovey?

In the kitchen. Kevin, Jim, Victoria and Ailsa are sitting round the table with a pot of tea, playing cards. A very jolly atmosphere. Radio Two is playing organ music.

Kevin *(obviously for the seventeenth time)* Er – what's trumps?

Other three Spades!

Kevin Bother!

He puts a card down, the others follow suit, and Ailsa takes the trick.

Ailsa	Thank you.
Jim	You've played this before, Ailsa.
Ailsa	When we were sleeping rough there wasn't a lot else to do.
Victoria	What was it like, living in a cardboard box?
Ailsa	It wasn't too bad. At least mine had all its flaps. More tea anybody?
Victoria	Please.
Jim	Is there any more shepherd's pie?
Ailsa	Help yourself. Doris made it. She's from the Philippines but she's really got to grips with mince.
Kevin	*(pushing the photos over)* That's my baby, Ailsa.
Ailsa	Oh yeah – I read you'd had a baby. What's the stuff in the bowl?
Kevin	That's the placenta.
Ailsa	It's nice.
Kevin	Yeah, I never thought much of placentas before but I really like that one.

Moira enters rather agitated.

Moira	Oh there you are! I couldn't begin to think where you'd gone. I think Alan is approaching an interval, or what one might describe as a cleft in his *Buttocks* and I rather fear if we don't nip in quick and plug the gap he will carry on with the entire second half. *(She waits, then gestures.)* Coming along, yes? *(Jim and Kevin look down at the floor, Ailsa busies herself at the sink and turns the radio off.)*
Victoria	No.
Moira	I beg your pardon?
Victoria	We don't want to.
Moira	I'm not with you.

Victoria	Jim doesn't want to do any portraits, Kevin doesn't want to sing and I don't want to tell any jokes.
Moira	Well I'm sorry – we all have to do things we don't want to do. I don't particularly want to be the most successful hostess in London society but that is the furrow I have been given to plough, and plough it I will.
Victoria	But we're your guests.
Moira	So I see. You're quite happy to yomp your way through a quarter of Darjeeling and sit down here while that dreadful Yorkshireman brings my entire party to a shuddering halt. *(She pauses.)* Have I read the situation aright?
Victoria	Yes.
Moira	I see. In that case there's nothing more to be said but BAARGH! *(She bursts into tears and runs out.)*
Victoria	Someone'll have to go after her.
Ailsa	Well I can't.
Kevin	I can't, I can't bear people crying.
Jim	I'd be useless. It's not even as if she was a welder.

Victoria sighs and goes out.

In the cloakroom Moira is mopping up her make-up.

Victoria	It's not anything against you – it's just that we want to relax and enjoy ourselves like everybody else. You do see.
Moira	Oh yes. *(She sniffs.)* What do I look like? Barbara Cartland without the vitamins comes pretty darn near. It's just one has been rather known for one's parties and it's harder and harder to keep going, with Eleanor Spencer coming up on the rails with her Morris dancers – and then there's this stupid divorce; not a very nice way to end a marriage. I shall be lucky to come out of the settlement with a five-bedroomed cottage in Wiltshire and one Philippino.
Victoria	Which one will you keep, Doris or Phoebe?

Moira Oh Doris, undoubtedly. Phoebe's sex mad, which I don't mind *per se*, but it affects her ironing. So this was somewhat in the nature of a last bash, but it seems to have turned into something rather less festive than the three-day week.[263] Any bright thoughts?

In the drawing room. Victoria is playing the piano and all the guests, including Moira, Alan and Kevin are playing musical chairs. The music stops. They scramble madly for chairs, and all sit down. The music begins again. Jim is by the piano drawing a donkey to pin the tail on. Ailsa is making up a package for 'pass the parcel'. The music stops and they scramble again.

Ailsa There's something wrong with this game.
Victoria What?
Ailsa They've all got a chair. We've never taken one away.
Victoria Oh yeah. I thought it was taking a long time.

At the front door. Moira is seeing guests out. Each one is handed a piece of cake in a serviette, and most are holding balloons. Gerald, Charles, Dulcie and Hilary are leaving. There is a general chorus of goodbyes, Merry Christmasses, lovely party, etc.

Moira Merry Christmas! Do mind your balloon.
Alan *(storming out)* Bourgeois pillocks.
Moira Well I'm sorry, Alan – the music stopped and your leg was wobbling.

Kevin, Victoria and Jim leave.

Your chauffeur is just outside, Kevin.

---

263 Owing to industrial action, in early 1974 the Conservative government limited commercial use of electricity to three days in the working week.

Kevin	Cheers. Night night.
Jim	Bye. Thanks for the shepherds pie.
Victoria	Bye.
Moira	It really was marvellous – thank you so much.
Victoria	I enjoyed it.
Moira	I'm having a little dinner party soon – just eighteen or nineteen people – I'll phone you.
Victoria	OK. Night.

Victoria's living room, as before. Victoria is watching TV on the sofa, as before.

TV soundtrack
voice of George
Formby	Well I've never played my ukelele in a bunker before.
Female voice	Oh George, you are marvellous. And did you notice – even Hitler joined in!
George	
Formby	Turned out nice again.

Music from the TV. The phone rings. Victoria thinks about answering it. She doesn't and it stops. A shot of the TV screen – blonde girl is on once more.

TV soundtrack
female voice[264]	I believe I owe you a cup of coffee.
Male voice	Café blend?
Female voice	No, it's too expensive. This is from the VG shop.[265]

---

264 Played by VW.
265 Franchised chain of small supermarkets offering cheap own-brand products.

CAST LISTS

UP TO YOU, PORKY

Skin Care	*Girl*	Victoria Wood	WW
	Assistant	Julie Walters	
Brontëburgers	*Guide*	Victoria Wood	LB
The Woman with	*Woman*	Victoria Wood	WW
740 Children	*Reporter*	Julie Walters	
Girls Talking	*Jeanette*	Julie Walters	WW
	Marie	Victoria Wood	
	Interviewer	Russell Dixon	
Young Love	*Gail*	Victoria Wood	VWASOT
	Carl	Andrew Livingston	WW
This Week's Film	*Jean*	Julie Walters	WW
	Smithy	Richard Longden	
In the Office	*Beattie*	Victoria Wood	VWASOT
	Connie	Julie Walters	
Dotty on Women's Lib	*Dotty*	Julie Walters	WW

Cosmetic Surgery	*Girl*	Victoria Wood	VWASOT
	Customer	Celia Imrie	
The Reporter	*Widow*	Victoria Wood	VWASOT
	Reporter	Julie Walters	
	Butch	Jim Broadbent	
On Campus	*Selina*	Tilly Vosburgh	VWASOT
	Mummy	Barbara Graley	
	Daddy	Peter Bland	
	Maggie	Suzanne Sinclair	
	Hilary	Victoria Wood	
Shoe Shop	*Customer*	Victoria Wood	VWASOT
	Assistant	Julie Walters	
	Janine	Celia Imrie	
Dandruff Commercial	*Actress*	Julie Walters	VWASOT
Toddlers	*Toddlers*	Victoria Wood	WW
		Julie Walters	
The Practice Room	*Pianist*	Victoria Wood	WW
	Cleaner	Julie Walters	
Supermarket Checkout	*Till girl*	Victoria Wood	VWASOT
	Customer	Celia Imrie	
Kitty	*Kitty*	Patricia Routledge	VWASOT
This House Believes	*Schoolgirl*	Victoria Wood	LB
Groupies	*Bella*	Victoria Wood	WW
	Enid	Julie Walters	
	Star	Alan Lake	
Margery and Joan	*Joan*	Victoria Wood	VWASOT
	Margery	Julie Walters	
Film Classic	*Barry*	Pete Postlethwaite	VWASOT
	Freda	Kay Adshead	
Service Wash	*Old Bag*	Victoria Wood	VWASOT

The Boutique	*Customer*	Victoria Wood	VWASOT
	Assistant	Julie Walters	
Giving Notes	*Alma*	Julie Walters	VWASOT
Cleaning	*Ursula*	Victoria Wood	VWASOT
	Kent	David Foxxe	
Just an Ordinary	*Anthea*	Felicity Montagu	VWASOT
School	*Babs*	Tracy Childs	
	Ceal	Georgia Allen	
	Dinner Lady	Barbara Miller	
	Headmistress	Zara Nutley	
Turkish Bath	*Pat*	Victoria Wood	VWASOT
	Thelm	Julie Walters	
Whither the Arts?	*Bessie*	Victoria Wood	VWASOT
	Presenter	Duncan Preston	
	Deb Kershaw	Celia Imrie	
	Carla	Deborah Grant	
	Sir Dave Dixon	Patrick Barlow	
	Dennis (pianist)	David Firman	
Madwoman	*Woman*	Julie Walters	VWASOT

LB = *Lucky Bag,* first performed at the King's Head Theatre, Islington, in October 1983.

WW = *Wood and Walters,* shown on Granada TV in January 1982.

VWASOT = *Victoria Wood As Seen on TV,* shown on BBC2 in January 1985.

BARMY

All the sketches in this volume were first performed in *Victoria Wood As Seen on TV* (second series), shown on BBC2 in November, 1986, with the exception of the first six episodes of 'Acorn Antiques', which were performed in the first series, shown on BBC2 in January, 1985, and those marked with a *, first performed in a special programme on BBC television in autumn 1987.

Nora	*Nora*	Victoria Wood
No Gossip	*1st Lady*	Victoria Wood
	2nd Lady	Julie Walters
Margery and Joan	*Margery*	Julie Walters
	Joan	Victoria Wood
Men Talking	*1st Man*	Michael Nightingale
	2nd Man	Eric Richards
	3rd Man	Graham Seed
Today in Hospital	*Corin*	Duncan Preston
	Cleaner	Peter Martin
	Receptionist	Heather Baskerville
	Elaine	Victoria Wood
	Conrad	Andrew Livingston
	Doctor	Benjamin Whitrow
	Mrs Jones	Myrtle Devonish

	1st Student	Nicholas Barnes
	2nd Student	Ravindar Valia
	3rd Student	Richard Brenner
	Noreen	Kathryn Apanowicz
	Della	Beverly Martin
	Kevin	Philip Lowrie
	Drunken Man	Clive Panto
Kitty	*Kitty*	Patricia Routledge
Salesman	*Man*	Duncan Preston
	Woman	Celia Imrie
Reports Local	*Man*	Duncan Preston
	Woman	Celia Imrie
Dr Who*	*Doctor*	Jim Broadbent
	Fiona	Georgia Allen
	Crayola	Duncan Preston
	Guard	Johnny Worthy
Craft Shop	*Owner*	Rosalind March
	Girl	Celia Imrie
Wine Bar	*Man*	Ronnie Letham
	Girl	Carolyn Pickles
Acorn Antiques	*Babs*	Celia Imrie
	Mrs Overall	Julie Walters
	Clifford	Duncan Preston
	Bertha	Victoria Wood
	Trixie	Rosie Collins
	Derek	Kenny Ireland
	Jerez	Peter Ellis
	Extras	Albert & Michaela Welch
The Making of Acorn Antiques*	*Marion Clune*	Maggie Steed
	Simon	Sam Kelly
	Roberts	Nicholas Barnes

	Mickey	Bryan Burdon
	Make-up Girl	Jane Hardy
	PA	Deborah Grant
	Assistant Floor Manager	Colin Simmonds
Spaghetti	*Philippa*	Julie Walters
	Faith	Victoria Wood
	Waiter	Gerard Kelly
Medical School	*1st Man*	Terence Longdon
	2nd Man	Duncan Preston
	Sarah	Victoria Wood
	Woman	Celia Imrie
He Didn't	*Kelly*	Victoria Wood
	Pal	Mary Jo Randle
Tattoo Parlour	*Woman*	Victoria Wood
	Eric	Michael Gunn
	Paul	Gerard Kelly
Partly Political Broadcast	*Barbara*	Julie Walters
	Jean	Victoria Wood
Susie (Continuity)*	*Susie*	Susie Blake
Mr Right	*Pam*	Anne Reid
	Corin	Duncan Preston
	Mother	Dora Bryan
	Poll	Meg Johnson
	Girl	Victoria Wood
	Donald	Michael Nightingale
	Waiter	David Adams
	Doctor	John Nettleton
We're Half Asleep	*Girl*	Celia Imrie
	Louise	Nadine Wilson
The Trolley	*Alan*	Graham Seed
	Tim	Duncan Preston

	Waitress	Victoria Wood
	Head Waiter	Chris Sanders
Lady Police Serial	*Juliet*	Victoria Wood
	Wilberforce	Duncan Preston
	Voice	Stephen Hancock
Self-service[*]	*Enid*	Julie Walters
	Wyn	Victoria Wood
	1st Girl	Sue Wallace
	Woman	Celia Imrie
	2nd Girl	Lill Roughley

RIGHT DOWN THE MIDDLE

These three sketches, each starring Victoria Wood, were first performed in the series *Victoria Wood: Live in Your Own Home*, shown on BBC2 in 1995.

MENS SANA IN THINGUMMY DOODAH

The plays in this volume were first performed in the series *Victoria Wood* on BBCTV, in the autumn of 1989.

Mens Sana in Thingummy Doodah

Victoria	Victoria Wood	**Nicola**	Julie Waters
Lill	Lill Roughley	**Judy**	Selina Cadell
Dana	Liza Tarbuck	**Maintenance**	
Connie	Meg Johnson	**Man**	Brian Burdon
Enid	Anne Reid	**Girl on Video**	Rosalind March
Sallyanne	Georgia Allen	**Man in café**	Peter Martin

The Library

Victoria	Victoria Wood	**John**	Richard Kane
Sheila	Anne Reid	**Keith**	Philip Lowrie
Ted	Danny O'Dea	**Richard**	David Henry
Madge	Carol MacReady		

We'd Quite Like to Apologise

Victoria	Victoria Wood	**Guy**	Tristram Wymark
Una	Una Stubbs	**Woman in car**	Rosalind March
John	Philip Lowrie	**Woman in lift**	Valerie Minifie
Barbara	Lill Roughley	**Man on trave-**	
Joyanne	Julie Walters	**lator**	Peter Martin
Kathy	Jane Horrocks	**Girl at check-in**	
Alan	Richard Hope	**desk**	Susie Blake
Carol	Celia Imrie	**Spanish waiter**	Joe Fraser

Over to Pam

Victoria	Victoria Wood	**Jim**	Hugh Lloyd
Lorraine	Kay Adshead	**Alma**	Margery Mason
Saundra	Meg Johnson	**Dr Rani**	Charu Bala Chokshi
Madge	Shirley Cain	**Sue**	Lill Roughley
Caroline	Julia St John	**Neil**	William Osborne
Pam	Julie Walters	**Server**	Alison King

Val de Ree

Victoria	Victoria Wood	**Jamie**	Michael Lumsden
Jackie	Celia Imrie	**Mim**	Avril Angers
Girl on farm	Siân Thomas	**Daddy**	Michael Nightingale
		Susan	Joan Sims

Staying in

Victoria	Victoria Wood	**Hilary**	Phyllis Calvert
Woman on TV	Celia Imrie	**Dulcie**	Lill Roughley
Jane	Deborah Grant	**Judith**	Susie Blake
Moira	Patricia Hodge	**Julia**	Celia Imrie
Ailsa	Dawn Archibald	**Alan**	Jim Broadbent
Waitress	Susan Leong	**Kevin**	Richard Lintern
Charles	John Nettleton	**Jim**	Brian Burdon
Gerald	Roger Brierley		

'Mens Sana in Thingummy Doodah', 'We'd Quite Like to Apologise', 'Over to Pam' and 'Val de Ree' directed by Keith Bishop and produced by Geoff Posner.

'The Library' and 'Staying in' directed and produced by Geoff Posner.

IMAGE CREDITS